Library of
Davidson College

AFROCOMMUNISM

AFROCOMMUNISM

David and Marina Ottaway

AFRICANA PUBLISHING COMPANY
A division of Holmes & Meier Publishers, Inc.
NEW YORK • LONDON

First published in the United States of America 1981 by
Holmes & Meier Publishers, Inc.
30 Irving Place
New York, N.Y. 10003

Great Britain:
Holmes & Meier Publishers, Ltd.
131 Trafalgar Road
Greenwich, London SE10 9TX

Copyright © 1981 by Holmes & Meier Publishers, Inc.
All rights reserved

Library of Congress Cataloging in Publication Data

Ottaway, David.
    Afrocommunism.

    (New library of African affairs; 1)
    Includes bibliographical references and index.
    1. Communism—Africa. 2. Socialism in Africa.
I. Ottaway, Marina, joint author. II. Title.
III. Series.

HX438.5.O87   1980   335.43'096   80-24289

ISBN 0-8419-0664-5
ISBN 0-8419-0699-8 pbk

   This publication was prepared under a grant from the
Woodrow Wilson International Center for Scholars,
Washington, D.C. The statements and views expressed
are those of the authors and are not necessarily those of
the Wilson Center.

Manufactured in the United States of America

Contents

Foreword	vii
I The New Tide of Radicalism	1
II From African Socialism to Marxism-Leninism	13
III African Socialism Revisited	36
IV Mozambique	68
V Angola	99
VI Ethiopia	128
VII Nationalism and World Revolution	157
VIII The Case for Afrocommunism	193
Notes	215
Index	233

Foreword

This book is the culmination of 18 years of observing and studying African socialist regimes, eight of which were spent in Africa. Our direct experience with Algerian socialism, pre- and post-Ahmed Ben Bella, with Ethiopian Marxism-Leninism in the crucial years of the revolution there, and with Zambian "humanism" at a time of severe crisis in that country provided much food for thought. This work is an attempt to systematize and synthesize our own experiences, putting some order into our thinking about the varieties of African socialism and the apparent new commitment to Marxism-Leninism.

We owe a debt of gratitude to many, but we can only mention some of those who helped us to clarify our thoughts in the final writing stage. David Albright provided us with many insights into the Soviet's own perception of the African Marxist countries. Gerald Bender and Allen Isaacman were of invaluable help concerning Angola and Mozambique respectively. Ann Reid and her associates were kind enough to offer critical comments on our case for Afrocommunism. Our research assistant, Douglas Lofland, was of great help in following up on some of our initial hunches and transforming them into concrete information. Finally, we wish to thank our friends and associates at the Woodrow Wilson International Center for Scholars in Washington D.C. for providing a pleasant and relaxed atmosphere in which to work for ten months.

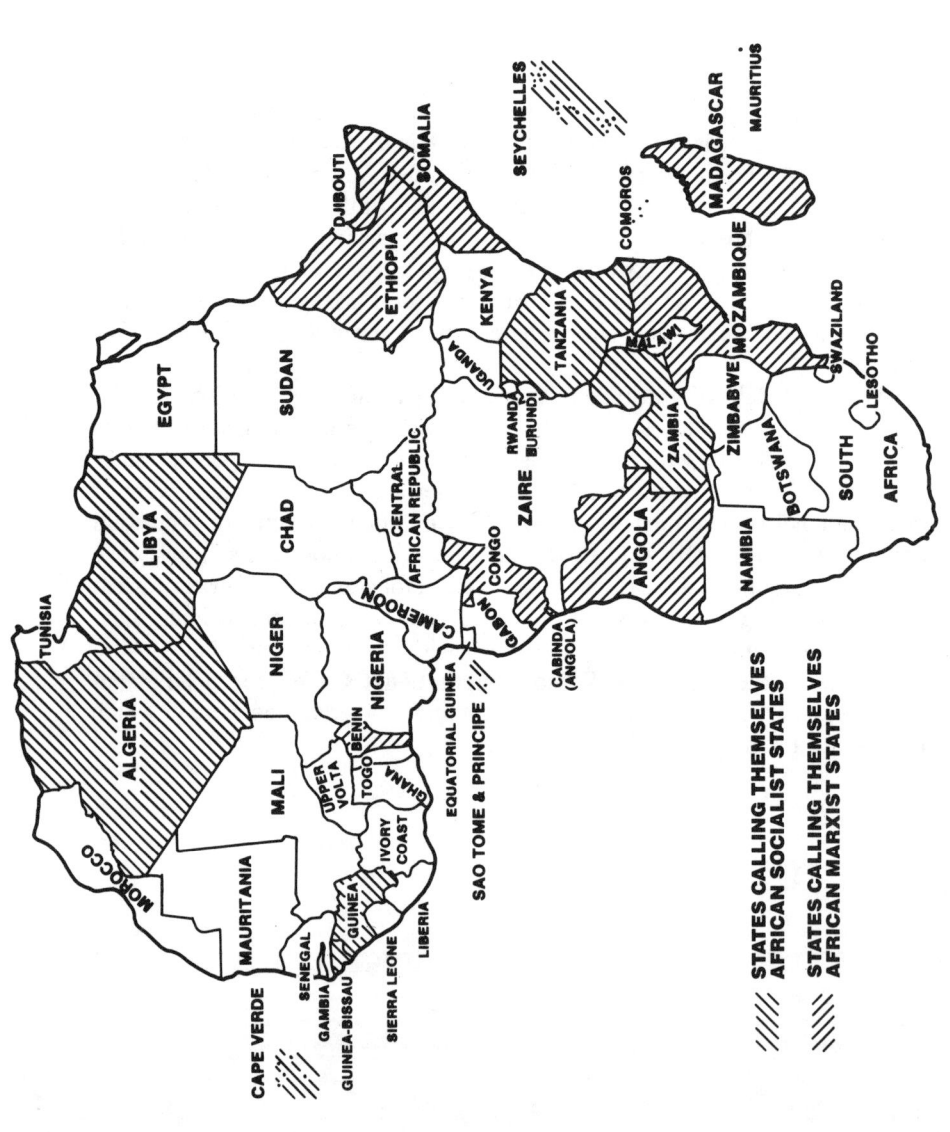

Chapter I
The New Tide of Radicalism

About sixteen years ago, Chinese leader Chou En-lai shocked the West by remarking, while on his first tour of the African continent, that the prospect for revolution there seemed "excellent." As events turned out in the 1960s, his judgment proved largely unfounded, or at least premature, as one after another of the first generation of radical African leaders was overthrown. Comforted by a whole series of Chinese and Soviet setbacks, the West overcame in triumph the first great "red scare." Subsequently, the United States devised a policy conveniently relegating the fate of Africa to the former colonial powers, and for nearly a decade black Africa was simply forgotten. But beginning in the mid-1970s, Western policymakers, scholars, and statesmen were once again reading the African tea leaves and asking themselves whether indeed Africa was finally ripe for revolution and "going communist." For despite enormous adversity, numerous setbacks, and all predictions to the contrary, the appeal of communism was not only stronger than ever before on the continent but Africa's Marxists appeared to be gaining ground rapidly with the help of massive Soviet, East German, and Cuban assistance. The West was again in a state of alarm and the United States transformed into an activist in trying to stem the new red tide.

Probably the most common glib remark about the subject of socialism in Africa among Chinese, Soviets, and Americans familiar with the continent in the 1960s was that "socialism without socialists is impossible." The irony is all the greater, then, that today black Africa seems to have become the breeding ground for some of the most orthodox Marxist-Leninists anywhere in the world, possibly the last of the true believers. An increasing number of African leaders are trying to prove that Marx and Lenin were absolutely right in insisting that there are universal laws of society and development as valid for Africa as for Europe and Asia. At times, their quest has seemed to verge on the absurd, akin to a theory wandering around in the dark in search of a reality that simply does not exist on a continent noted mostly for its absolute poverty, infant working class, and vast rural population living at a subsistence level. The attraction of Marxism-Leninism has also seemed all out of proportion to any concrete evidence of its success on the ground as a formula for either rapid growth or stable political development. Yet faith in the doctrine has not only persisted but grown steadily stronger, and the opportunities have multiplied for the Afro-Marxists to come to power through one or another route.

2 The New Tide of Radicalism

In 1980, seven of Africa's fifty independent black or Arab countries were under the rule of self-professed Marxist-Leninist leadership: Angola, Benin, the Congo, Ethiopia, Mozambique, Madagascar, and Somalia. At least another nine embraced some brand of socialism: Algeria, the Cape Verde Islands, Libya, Guinea, Guinea-Bissau, São Tomé and Principe, the Seychelles Islands, Tanzania, and Zambia. Altogether, these sixteen countries accounted for over one-quarter of Africa's total population of 425 million. A number of them, like Tanzania, Ethiopia, and Guinea-Bissau, were extremely poor, leading critics of African socialism to assert that the doctrine served as little more than a justification for equalizing the poverty rather than any wealth of these countries. But a few were endowed with natural resources of considerable importance, making them presently or potentially among the continent's richest. Such were Algeria, Libya, Angola, Zambia and Guinea. Whether poor or rich, many of these countries were located in positions of strategic importance, either in terms of the East-West geopolitical struggle or of potential intra-African conflicts. Somalia and Ethiopia are part of the so-called Horn of Africa bordering on the Red Sea and Bab el-Mandeb Strait, major international waterways. Mozambique sprawls for 1700 miles along the Indian Ocean just to the north of South Africa, the ultimate prize and battleground for African nationalists and communists alike. Angola holds one key to the future of neighboring Zaire, a main Western client of enormous proven mineral reserves—and of equally enormous political instability. Algeria dominates the northeast Maghreb by virtue of its size and wealth and abuts Morocco, another traditionally pro-Western country in deep trouble at the end of the 1970s because of a war touched off by its annexation of the Spanish Sahara. Madagascar, the largest island off the coast of East Africa, lies adjacent to the Mozambican channel (as does Mozambique itself), whose waters the West's oil tankers regularly ply on their way to Europe and the United States. Finally, the Congo slices from the Atlantic Ocean straight into the heart of Africa and showed its usefulness as a marshaling yard for Soviet and Cuban military activities during the civil war in Angola. Whether by virtue of wealth or geographical location, many of the Marxist-Leninist regimes seem destined to play individually or collectively an important role in shaping the destiny of the entire continent.

The probability of the spread of Marxism-Leninism to other black African countries also seemed extremely high. Leaders of the militant nationalist Southwest African People's Organization (SWAPO) in Namibia and the new leader of independent Zimbabwe, Robert Mugabe, were scarcely hiding their commitment to building new socialist societies on the basis of Marxist-Leninist principles. While South Africa was stalling in its negotiations with the West over the holding of UN-supervised elections in Namibia, it seemed only a matter of time before SWAPO would come to power. In Zimbabwe, Mugabe was moving cautiously to avert a white-led, or white-backed, coup against him and showing an unexpected degree of initial moderation; but he was still asserting he remained a socialist intent upon making his way slowly toward a new society based on Marxist-Leninist principles. The possibility of a band of militant socialist states stretching all across southern Africa appeared very real. On the Indian Ocean island of Mauritius, the largest single political party by the end of the decade was the Marxist-oriented *Mouvement Militant Mauritien* (MMM), whose steady growth and increasing dominance of local city politics put it in a strong position to win at the polls at the next national elections in 1981. In central Africa, Zaire's rotting economic and political situation continued to make that country a natural target for the radical opposition to President Mobutu Sese Seko. In the Maghreb, guerrillas of the Polisario movement, backed by Algeria and imbued with notions of Algerian and Arab socialism, seemed to have a better and better chance of winning their struggle for an independent state in the Spanish Sahara, with far-reaching consequences for King Hassan and his pro-Western Cherifian monarchy. The course of events in Africa is always difficult to predict. Nonetheless, the general economic stagnation in most African countries, coupled with continuing political instability, seemed ideal conditions for more radical leaders to come to power. The growth rate for the forty-five non-oil-producing African states was near zero in 1978 and about the same in 1979. The 1980s hold little promise for a major improvement. Indeed, in the view of United Nations agencies and the US government, the overall economic prospects for most African countries were nothing short of alarming.

In the United States, the expansion of communism in Africa has generally been viewed over the years as the work of outside Communist powers taking advantage of local conflicts and internal political turmoil to put "their man" in power. "When we speak of communism in Africa," remarked Undersecretary of State for Political Affairs David Newsom, testifying before Congress in late 1979, "we are speaking almost exclusively of the role of the Soviet Union, the Eastern European countries under Soviet domination, Cuba, and to a much lesser extent, China."[1] Like a recurring nightmare, one or another Communist country keeps coming back to meddle in the internal affairs of some African country. This, at least, is the image of communism in Africa carefully nurtured by one administration after another. In fact, for Democrats and Republicans alike, black Africa has really only come into sharp political focus when there was a sudden perceived threat from the communist countries to a Western ally or interest on the continent and a heightened sense that they were about to upset the existing status quo in the East-West balance of power there. The outcry of alarm over the Congo in the 1960s, and over Angola and Ethiopia in the 1970s, was the prime example of this attitude. Despite this intense, if only periodic, preoccupation with communist advances in Africa, the United States has never devised a long-term policy and strategy of "containment." Nor has the United States even sought to ask whether there might be some forces internal to the continent at work favoring the spread of communism, or at least Marxist-oriented regimes, the better to deal with them. *Ad hocism* has become the trademark of American diplomacy toward black Africa in reaction to recurring crises that have conjured up the specter of communism. President Carter began his term in office by trying to overcome this *ad hocism* and establish a policy based on another, long-term view of the continent. He at first asserted America had gotten over its "inordinate fear of communism" and accepted Andrew Young's assessment that racism rather than communism was the main threat to the West in southern Africa. Within two years, however, he had slipped back into the traditional American attitude toward communism in Africa, accusing the Cubans of "unwarranted interference" in the internal affairs of the continent and shelving his own initial efforts to promote détente with Fidel Castro. Clearly, the United States was far from being over its "inordinate fear of communism."

United States policymakers, scholars, and the Congress have so far gone through two periods of near hysteria about the spread of communism in Africa, separated by an entire decade of smug conviction that the fright was meaningless. In the early 1960s, they were for a time thrown into a veritable tizzy by what was then seen as a sudden major communist offensive to win the flock of newly independent African states away from their former colonial masters. Such a distinguished writer as Walter Laqueur, writing in 1961 for the American foreign policy elite's journal, *Foreign Affairs,* began an article by commenting that "almost overnight communism in Africa has become an international problem of the first magnitude." The liberated continent had, he said, become "the world's chief trouble center."[2] Proto-Marxist, or pro-Soviet and pro-Chinese, states seemed to be sprouting like mushrooms after a heavy summer rain across black and Arab Africa. First came Ghana under the visionary Pan-Africanist Kwame Nkrumah, whose radical Marxist predilections became increasingly clear with each passing year following his country's independence in 1957. Then Guinea under Sékou Touré broke abruptly with France in 1958 and turned toward the Soviet Union for help, three months before Fidel Castro came to power. In Mali, Modibo Keita, who led his country to independence in 1960, was within two years actively promoting "Marxist socialism" and expressing his admiration for the Soviet model of political and economic development. In 1962, Algeria finally became independent after an eight-year-long nationalist war of liberation and came under the leadership of a militant socialist and anti-Western crusader, Ahmed Ben Bella. He immediately threw Algeria into the East-Westcold war by traveling from the United Nations in New York directly to Havana to express his solidarity with Castro right in the midst of the Cuban missile crisis. Making their radical sympathies known to the entire world, the African militant socialists also banded together to aid Patrice Lumumba and his leftist heirs in their bid to take power in the war-torn Belgian Congo, later to be rebaptized Zaire. The Soviet Union, making use of its new-found allies in Africa, flew arms to the leftist rebels opposing Western-backed leaders in Leopoldville, creating an intense sense of cold war rivalry over the awakening continent.

By the mid-1960s, however, it seemed the "red menace" was beginning to recede. The Soviets and Chinese had overplayed their hand in several countries, and for a variety of other reasons, the club of African radical leaders had begun to shrink. The first reversal in Communist fortunes came in 1961 when the Soviet ambassador to Guinea was expelled for encouraging subversive activities against President Touré. The same fate befell the Chinese ambassador to Burundi in early 1965. He was accused of meddling in the internal affairs of that East African country as well as in those of the neighboring ex-Belgain Congo, where a civil war and secessionist movement were still of major concern to the United States and Western European capitals. Washington had turned to the United Nations to "save" the Congo from chaos, disintegration, and very possibly another Marxist regime under the Lumumbists. Miraculously, the US gambit worked. Lumumba was conveniently assassinated in mysterious circumstances and a pro-Western army officer, Désiré Mobutu, finally came to power. With Belgian-American military and UN backing, Mobutu managed to prevail over both the Lumumbist rebels and the Katanga separatist leader, Moise Tchombe.

While the West increasingly saw events going their way in the Congo, allies of the communist countries began disappearing elsewhere. In June 1965, the first of the Marxist-oriented African leaders, Ben Bella, was overthrown by the military. The coup was led by Colonel Houari Boumediene, who began by vehemently denouncing the "foreign (Marxist) ideology" he accused Ben Bella of introducing into Moslem Algeria with the help of European Trotskyites. Only a few months later, in February 1966, Nkrumah was also summarily deposed by his own army with little sign of opposition from his people. Then in November 1968, it was the turn of Keita to be ousted by the military. Events indeed seemed to be favorable to the West, and the trend continued into the early 1970s. In July 1971, President Jaafar Nimeri of the Sudan survived by a hair a communist coup attempt, the effect of which was to reorient his regime abruptly away from cooperation with the Sudanese communists and the Soviet Union as well. Only a year later, Anwar Sadat, who was already quietly at work dismantling the socialist and pro-Soviet policy of the late Gamal Abdel Nasser, shocked the East and West by ordering thousands of Soviet military advisers to leave the country immediately and cutting Egypt's military ties with Moscow. The only exceptions to a string of setbacks for the communist powers in Africa between 1965 and 1974 were in the French Congo and, most importantly, Somalia. In 1969, the Congo became the first African country to call itself a "people's republic" and formally adopt Marxism-Leninism as its official ideology. The same year, a radical military group led by the Mohamed Siad Barré seized power in Somalia and thereafter moved the country steadily away from the West and toward the Soviet Union. These moves culminated in the signing of the first Treaty of Friendship and Cooperation between Moscow and any sub-Saharan country in July 1974.

The political and economic failings of the radical African regimes, together with the setbacks suffered by the Soviets and Chinese in their initial African diplomacies, led Western scholars and policymakers to the general conclusion that neither the time nor conditions were ripe for socialism on the African continent, let alone for revolution. The highly respected French agronomist, René Dumont, concluded in a 1969 study of various socialist regimes around the world that there had to be a "necessary revision" of the whole socialist endeavor in Africa and noted "the impossibility of a rigorously scientific socialism" given the state of African countries.[3] In the United States, American scholars were similarly skeptical. The theory of African socialism was dismissed as disguised "populism," or even "fascism," and as little more than "a convenient doctrine" to justify government involvement in the process of economic growth.[4] Interestingly, the Soviets were just as skeptical in their judgment of African socialism. After a tortuous ideological debate about how to deal with countries like Guinea, Mali, Ghana, and Algeria, Moscow's Africanists came up with the term "the non-capitalist road of development" to describe their attempt to become socialist and cautiously labelled them "national democracies." While bestowing the Lenin Peace Prize and other honors on their leaders, the Soviet leadership carefully avoided calling them "socialist" and, like Dumont, came to the conclusion that scientific planning in Africa was virtually impossible for the time being. But Africa's socialists were not as discouraged. Instead of giving up hope and faith, they were discarding soft "humanistic" socialism and becoming ever more orthodox in their analysis of the continent and the need for the strict application of Marxist-Leninist principles. Then, just as it seemed the radicals had reached the nadir of their fortunes, a whole series of new opportunities arose for them.

In April 1974, a radical military group seized power in the Portuguese capital of Lisbon, ringing the death knell on Portugal's already crumbling African empire. It set in motion a series of events that would lead within eighteen months to the establishment of orthodox Marxist-Leninist governments in Angola and Mozambique and a dedicated socialist one in Guinea-Bissau. In June of the same year, a cabal of junior army officers began what came to be called a "creeping coup" against Emperor Haile Selassie in Ethiopia and deposed him by September of that year. Within three years, the leaders of Ethiopia had become probably Africa's most orthodox Marxists. Meanwhile in Dahomey (now Benin), Lieutenant Colonel Mathieu Kerékou, in power since 1972, launched a "revolution within the revolution," adopting Marxism-Leninism as official ideology in November 1974. Finally, in June 1975, the commander of the navy on the Indian Ocean Island of Madagascar, Didier Ratsiraka, was elected by his military colleagues to head up the new ruling Supreme Revolutionary Council, heralding a sharp turn to the left in domestic and foreign policy and the embrace of Marxism-Leninism by yet another African country.

While Americans watched events unfolding in Ethiopia with some interest and concern for the country's future, it was really the civil war and power struggle in Angola beginning in early 1975 that aroused the United States from a decade of near total indifference toward Africa. The arrival of large numbers of Cuban combat troops in October and November 1975 to rescue the embattled Popular Movement for the Liberation of Angola (MPLA) from a South African-led offensive by its opponents triggered a visceral anti-communist response on the part of the Ford Administration, or more precisely its secretary of state, Henry Kissinger. Kissinger knew virtually nothing about the affairs of sub-Sahara Africa and had previously ignored the continent in shaping US foreign policy. His sudden interest in Angola arose entirely from an intense preoccupation that in the wake of the Vietnam War the Soviets and their Cuban allies were taking advantage of a weakened American will to expand communist influence. As Laqueur had writter fourteen years earlier, almost overnight communism in Africa became an international problem of the first magnitude—once again.

While the period 1974 to 1975 stands as a watershed in the renewal of the Soviet-American cold war struggle over Africa, it represented no less of an historic turning point in the tortuous development of socialism inside Africa. Within the space of eighteen months, leaders who would eventually espouse Marxism-Leninism as their countries' official ideology came to power in Angola, Mozambique, Madagascar and Ethiopia. Simultaneously, Benin adopted the ideology after a leftward turn in events there. Yet, there is no evidence at all that this happened because of a "grand communist design" for black Africa worked out either in Moscow, Havana, or Peking. Indeed, there is every indication that the Soviets in particular were as much taken by surprise as anyone in the West: they had even cut off all their assistance to the MPLA in late 1973 out of total despair over the factionalism wracking that movement. Neither the Soviets, Cubans, nor East Germans "exported" Marxism-Leninism to Africa in the baggage of the legions of advisers, technical assistants, and combat troops that began arriving on the continent in mid-1975 with the Angolan civil war. In each country, the origins for this phenomenon were rooted in the political developments underway for years and their maturing into an opportunity for radicals to take power. For example, nationalist guerrillas had been at war with the Portuguese in their African colonies for a decade or more, slowly but steadily fighting their way toward the capitls of Guinea-Bissau, Mozambique, and Angola. The long years of struggle had radicalized them in many ways, eventually giving their nationalism a more specifically socialist, even Marxist, content. Years of organizing efforts in their liberated zones during the struggle had convinced many among them of the value of collective rather than individualistic approaches toward solving problems. At the same time, lukewarm Western declarations of support for the principle of self-determination could not offset the fact that the West supported Portugal through NATO while the East provided arms and diplomatic support to the guerrillas. While none of the former Portuguese colonies immediately hoisted red flags over the capital upon becoming independent, they were only waiting for an appropriate occasion to do so. The signal did not come from the Soviet Union or Cuba but from nationalist leaders taking a reading of their own domestic political situation, and potential foreign allies, in the wake of the independence struggle.

Nor were the Soviets and Cubans responsible for Ethiopia and Madagascar becoming Marxist-Leninist states. It was not even members of a local communist party who took power in these two countries, but independent radical military officers, whose embrace of Marxism-Leninism grew out of the internal economic and political deadlocks in which the two countries found themselves. Ethiopia was perhaps a unique case in black Africa in that for the first time a Marxist-Leninist analysis of society naturally fit the objective conditions of the country. That the Soviets and Cubans were in no way responsible for the revolution is made clear by the fact that their involvement came long after the most radical measures had been planned, announced, and executed by the officers and a coterie of Ethiopian Marxist-oriented civilian advisers. In Madagascar, too, the radical reforms grew out of a power struggle among members of the island's military elite and mostly preceded a formal commitment to Marxism-Leninism. Moreover, even adherence to the doctrine did not signal Madagascar's establishment of particularly close relations with the Soviet Union or Cuba. Benin and the Congo had similar tortuous histories of internal power struggles resulting in the most radical elements of the military finally coming to power. In no case could it be said as of 1980 that Moscow or Havana had installed "their man" in any black or Arab African country.

This said, there can be no doubt that the Cubans and Soviets played a crucial role at decisive moments in the mid-1970s in helping to keep in office African leaders whom they knew, or suspected, to be friendly to them as like-minded in ideological persuasion. With a boldness not previously associated with the Soviets in their Third World policy, they seized the opportunity to move into Angola and Ethiopia and had an enormous importance in consolidating the power of their potential allies there. But neither the Soviets nor the Cubans have so far been the primary cause of any Marxist emerging as leader of his country, not even in civil-war-ridden Angola. It is most often forgotten, or deliberately overlooked, that the MPLA had won the battle for the capital against its two pro-Western opponents, and even control of most towns in the central and southern parts of the country, before Cuban combat troops ever became involved. To those Western correspondents covering the civil war, it was clear early on which of the three Angolan nationalist movements had the superior organizing and fighting ability. The Soviets and Cubans simply consolidated the *fait accompli*.

The leftward trend of events in Africa is clearly discernible not only in the increasing number of African governments espousing orthodox Marxism-Leninism but also in the waning of the early African humanistic approach toward socialism. Two decades ago, a separate, third African way of development, different from Western capitalism or Eastern socialism and generally called "African socialism," was very much in vogue. This socialism went hand-in-hand with Pan-Africanism and a nonalignment directed impartially against all the big powers of the East and West and asserting the special identity of Africa and the Third World. By the mid-1970s, however, African socialism was totally discredited intellectually and politically, and its early proponents were rethinking their choices. Some, like Senegal's president, Leopold Senghor, had moved openly far closer to the West and were more vehement than the United States in warning of the Communist danger to Africa. Inside Senegal, socialism remained a theory only. Others, such as Tanzanian President Julius Nyerere, were still maintaining a socialist posture but denying the existence of a separate, third way of development and affirming in an interview with the authors that the only difference between the Tanzanian "African" and Mozambican "Marxist" socialism was one of "rhetoric."[5]

To Western observers, above all to the United States, it appeared that much more than just rhetoric was involved. While Nyerere was still trying to practice genuine nonalignment, the Marxist-Leninist leaders of the 1970s were advocating "proletarian internationalism" instead of neutrality. They considered the Soviet Union and other communist countries to be their "natural allies" in the ongoing struggle against "colonialism, neo-colonialism and imperialism," Communist shorthand for the basic triad of Western evils. Three of the Marxist-Leninist states—Ethiopia, Mozambique, and Angola—were even formally allied to the Soviet Union in twenty-year-long treaties of friendship and cooperation and voting with it on key East-West issues before the United Nations.

Yet even in the hardest of the hardline Marxist-Leninist African states, nationalism was far from dying out as a vibrant force or being totally replaced as a guiding principle by "proletarian internationalism." The nationalist spirit, born of the anticolonial struggle, was being asserted in a variety of verbal and practical ways. "We do not intend to become another Bulgaria," remarked a top political adviser to Mozambican President Samora Machel.[6] In Angola, the late President Agostinho Neto was by 1978 publicly warning his countrymen of the need to "defend the independence of the (MPLA) party" against outside interference, a hardly veiled reference to the country's two main allies, the Soviet Union and Cuba.[7] In Ethiopia, which had earlier given the United States extensive military and communication facilities, the Soviet Union still had not obtained as much after providing the government of Lieutenant Colonel Mengistu Haile-Mariam with upwards of two billion dollars worth of arms. Nor had Mozambique given in to reported Soviet entreaties for a base, despite its close links to Moscow in a Treaty of Friendship. The Soviets were also having their troubles, once again, with Touré of Guinea, who in 1978 terminated their reconaissance flights over the southern Atlantic from Conakry. But the most striking example of the overpowering force of nationalism when pitted against the supposed international solidarity of socialist countries came in the Horn of Africa. Not even the direct personal intervention of Fidel Castro was able to convince Somalia in 1977 that a federation of Marxist states in the region was the correct way to resolve its conflict with Ethiopia over the Ogaden. If the separatist wars being waged by the Somalis and Eritreans against the central Ethiopian government proved anything, it was that nationalism was a far more deeply held conviction than their commonly espoused Marxist-Leninist ideology.

The strain of nationalism so evident in the foreign policy of the Marxist-Leninist states led some, notably the US ambassador to the United Nations, Andrew Young, to conclude that these were not nascent communist regimes but still basically African nationalist ones. Such a conclusion not only dismissed the elements of internationalism in their foreign policy but also overlooked the fact that the kind of political and economic system they were trying to build was visibly different from those created by the early socialist countries. Their ideal was not the idyllic African village community of olden times but the modern factory, the mechanized state farm or, in some cases, the Chinese-style commune. They did not share the African socialists' illusion that conflict was avoidable but instead accepted, and even welcomed, class conflict as a means of promoting radical change. This acceptance was reflected in their rejection of a mass party synonymous with the entire nation and in their efforts to build a Leninist-style vanguard party excluding all but the most committed individuals. Altogether, they were far less romantic about revolution and more aware of the need for blood, sweat, and tears, and above all for a systematic approach to engineering the whole process.

Despite the numerous differences in attitudes, institutions, and policies between the Marxist-Leninist and the early socialist regimes, there has been a general tendency among scholars to focus above all on the similarities brought about by the general conditions of underdevelopment and to conclude that the new regimes are but a variation on an old theme. Such scholars have also noted the difficulties these countries are encountering in building parties, in planning their economies, in resolving conflicts between the military and civilians, or the state and the party. The conclusion often reached on the basis of these and similar observations is that they cannot be considered seriously as Marxist-Leninist. Our contention, on the other hand, is that these countries should be considered as Marxist-Leninist ones, albeit in the initial stages of organization and consolidation. We shall try to show this by comparing the theory and practice of the African socialist countries to those of some of the new Marxist-Leninist ones. But we will go even further to argue that many of the problems the latter countries face stem precisely from their efforts to follow the dictates of Marxism-Leninism in building political and economic institutions. They are, in fact, contending with a series of dilemmas arising from the contradictions inherent in the ideology and the different interpretations to which it lends itself. One central dilemma is a conflict as old as the Soviet revolution itself, namely that between the Leninist centralist interpretation of the revolutionary process and the so-called Trotskyite emphasis on direct democracy and worker participation in the making of a revolution. Other dilemmas result from efforts to integrate the prescriptions of orthodox Marxism-Leninism with the unique experience and conditions of each revolution.

There is, to be sure, no absolute uniformity among the African Marxist-Leninist states. In fact, some are much more orthodox in their thinking and swift in their pace of reform than others. The most orthodox and radical of these countries are Ethiopia, Mozambique, and Angola. They were the only ones where the regimes came to power through a revolution—be it a nationalist one as in Angola and Mozambique or a social one as in Ethiopia. They are the countries where reforms have gone furthest, because of both ideological conviction and the existence of a power vacuum. They are also the three that have established the closest institutional ties to the Soviet bloc. They thus provide the best illustration of what Marxism-Leninism may come to mean in Africa. Some will argue that these are special, unrepresentative cases. They are undoubtedly special at present, but this does not mean that their experiences cannot be duplicated elsewhere: the enormity of the social, political, and economic problems building up in Africa make the prospect of more social revolutions all too likely. Furthermore, Zimbabwe and Namibia may still face a crisis of decolonization creating a vacuum of power similar to that experienced by Angola and Mozambique.

The spreading of Marxism-Leninism on the African continent does not necessarily mean the creation of a string of Soviet satellites there. While orthodoxy is the hallmark of the Marxist-Leninist states at home, they are nevertheless trying to integrate "the universal principles of Marxism-Leninism" with their own unique historical experience. Furthermore, they appear determined to maintain their full sovereignty and to pursue their own policies abroad. They are trying not to become other Bulgarias or Cubas in their relationship to the Soviet Union. This combination of foreign and domestic postures amounts to what we call "Afrocommunism." Like the European proponents of "Eurocommunism," the African Marxist-Leninist states are setting forth the argument that communism does not imply blind imitation of, and enslavement to, the Soviet Union, but can be a choice freely made by independent states, adapted to local circumstances, and implemented with subservience to no foreign power. African Marxist-Leninists have not banded together yet to elaborate and present to the world a common ideology and strategy labeled Afrocommunism. They are nonetheless all of a common mind and working in the same vineyard.

If we are correct in our analysis that Marxism-Leninism is taking hold in Africa and feeding off internal developments more than outside interference, it is a trend that obviously warrants more serious consideration than has heretofore been accorded to it by American scholars, policymakers and politicians. How is the United States going to relate to these increasingly numerous African Marxist-Leninist states and how have we approached them to date? Is the US government going to seek actively to arrest the process, turn its back on the Marxist-Leninist regimes, or find a formula for dealing positively with them? At the turn of the decade, US policy seemed marked mostly by confusion and contradiction. We still had not recognized the MPLA government in Angola, although all member states of the Organization of African Unity, the Eastern bloc and most Western European nations had already done so. Congress had at one point passed legislation to cut off Mozambique, Ethiopia, and even pro-Western Zambia from American economic development assistance. While we still did not have diplomatic relations with Angola, we had them with Mozambique and continued to have them with Ethiopia, despite that country's expulsion of the US ambassador and refusal to reimburse American companies for their nationalized properties. After years of no diplomatic relations with the Congo, the US embassy reopened there in 1977, while Washington's ties to Guinea seemed to be steadily improving after years of ups and downs in American-Guinean relations.

Altogether, American policy toward the African Marxist-Leninist regimes, like our understanding of them, seemed about as confused as their vacillating attitude toward the United States. The only American policymakers sketching and actively promoting a long-term policy toward them were a small group of Africanists led, during the first two years of the Carter administration, by Ambassadors Andrew Young and Donald McHenry and a clique in the State Department's African bureau headed by Assistant Secretary of State for African Affairs Richard Moose. They were calling for a "ride-it-out" policy and arguing that African nationalism would eventually throw off Eastern communism and that all that was needed was time and an alternative source of economic aid in the West, particularly the United States. But few were listening, and American attention was turning elsewhere—to the Middle East, Afghanistan, the deterioration in Soviet-American relations, Cuba, and the 1980 presidential election. As the new decade began, a conservative mood was sweeping Western Europe and the United States. The Africanists were deep in their foxholes, or out fighting a defensive battle on behalf of their relatively radical views toward the African continent.

We have organized this book with a view to explaining not only what Marxism-Leninism is coming to mean in Africa today but also the evolution in the theory and practice of socialism on that continent. Thus, we have first presented an overview of the changes in the concept of socialism prevailing there. Then, we have "revisited" four of the early African socialist countries to establish some benchmarks by which to compare the new Marxist-Leninist states and thereby highlight the differences as well as some of the possible similarities. Finally, we have examined in some detail Ethiopia, Angola, and Mozambique and tried to distill from their experiences the salient characteristics of their economic and political systems. It is on this basis that in the last chapter we present "the case for Afrocommunism," the argument, in other words, that at least some of the new self-proclaimed Marxist-Leninist regimes are not just mouthing a different rhetoric but are seriously attempting to build a communist economic and political order.

Chapter II
From African Socialism to Marxism-Leninism

In the first two decades of African independence, views as to what constitutes "real" socialism on that continent underwent a radical change. In the early 1960s, the notion prevailed that socialism was an economic and social system already deeply rooted in the ways of traditional Africa and that all Africans had to do was to "return to the sources," to their old habits of community-oriented work and thinking. Fifteen years later, this idea had become totally discredited and most socialist African leaders were asserting that there was, and is, only one "true" socialism as set forth in the writings of Marx and Lenin and implemented first as a coherent overall system in the Soviet Union. How this dramatic change in socialist ideology came about is the subject of this chapter.

Much has already been written about the meaning of African socialism by various African, European and American scholars, and we do not intend to retrace old ground in detail. But we are interested in the evolution of certain key notions about socialism and African society among African leaders and thus will review some facets of the early argument in favor of "African" as opposed to Marxist-Leninist socialism. We shall also try to link the two opposing versions of socialism to the historical setting in which they developed, for the setting goes a long way toward explaining why there has been such a radical shift in thinking about the meaning of socialism inside Africa.

Several central themes of African socialism have subsequently been rejected outright or seriously revised by the Afro-Marxists of the 1970s. One of these was the contention that African society prior to the arrival of the European colonial powers was basically classless and communal because there was no private ownership of land and the community was more important than the individual. The corollary of this view held that since there were really no classes or an exploiting and exploited group within the confines of the tribe, there was really no intra-tribal conflict. African tribal society was quite literally one big harmonious family in which all members contributed to the general welfare and were in turn taken care of by the community in case of need. In effect, before the arrival of the European colonizers, there existed an African welfare state based on the principle of communalism.

The most eloquent exponent of this "natural" African welfare state has been Tanzanian President Julius Nyerere, who in the 1960s set forth in considerable detail his view that socialism was the original state of the African man. "The foundation, and the objective of African socialism," wrote the English speaking philosopher-president, "is the extended family."[1] He literally defined socialism as "familyhood," or *"ujamaa"* in the Tanzanian national language of Swahili. This "natural" African tribal man, which Nyerere set out to revive, lived in basic harmony with his brother, and society was free of social conflict. "The idea of 'class,' or 'caste,' was nonexistent in African society," according to Nyerere, because it was only the Agrarian and Industrial Revolutions of Western Europe which gave birth to such social cleavage and thus to such conflict.[2] The task of an African socialist leader, then, was to restore African society to its pristine classless self, and this could be done by ending private ownership of land and other means of production and reestablishing the communal approach to all human activities. It was a question in effect of turning the clock back to Africa's precolonial times. While the economic development of the country remained a primary goal of *ujamaa,* there was no real attempt to show how this could be reconciled with Nyerere's notion of primitive communalism.

This basic view of African society and socialism was shared by almost all of the early African socialist leaders, including Léopold Senghor of Senegal and Sékou Touré of Guinea, the two chief Francophone theoreticians; Kenneth Kaunda of Zambia, and to some extent Kwame Nkrumah of Ghana, the main other Anglophone ones. Senghor sought to give the doctrine a stronger cultural base by rooting it in what he called *Négritude,* the "Negro-African, humanistic" mode of looking at and experiencing reality distinctly different from the Marxist European "materialistic" outlook. But his argumentation was virtually identical to that of Nyerere. Traditional African society, Senghor wrote, was "classless" and "community-based" and the main task for contemporary African socialist leaders was "bringing [traditional African] political and economic democracy back to life"[3] and reestablishing a *"société communautaire."*[4] While Senghor called this ideology "African socialism," Kaunda gave the same set of ideas the name of "humanism," or "African democratic socialism," emphasizing the individual person and the need for his good behavior in a Christian sense in order for socialism to blossom.[5] Touré, for his part, used the language of Marxism in speaking of Guinea's "national democratic revolution," but he thoroughly Africanized the whole concept by explaining that it was based on the "communocratic" character of African society, a characteristic he argued colonial rule had not essentially altered.[6]

This early romantic, or utopian, view of African socialism can be explained on cultural and political grounds. As countries were just beginning to gain their independence, there was a strong thrust throughout Africa to assert the "African-ness" of the continent over and against the former colonial culture and power. This drive took various cultural and political forms. Senghor, as we have already mentioned, erected a whole African philosophy of *Négritude,* based on "Negro-Berber humanism." Kaunda came forth with a political ideology he called "African humanism," although the colonial, Christian imprint on it could hardly be disguised. Even Nkrumah, possibly the most Marxist of the early African socialist leaders, went to great lengths to stress the need to "create our own African personality and identity." The "African personality," he wrote, had to become "a strong driving force within the African Revolution."[7] This same African self-assertiveness can be seen in the Afro-socialists' general rejection of the notion that there is only "one socialism" based on the principles of Marxism-Leninism to which the Africans had nothing to add. "I think that this idea that there is one 'pure socialism'... is an insult to human intelligence," said Nyerere.[8] "In my view, socialism is a vague concept which can have as many different meanings and variations as there are people who advocate it."[9] Touré made essentially the same argument in different terms initially. He spoke of "the African path" toward socialism and warned that "trying to 'Westernize or Easternize' Africa leads to denying the African personality."[10]

On the foreign policy front, this African self-affirmation was probably best embodied in Nkrumah's Pan-Africanism, an ideology and strategy for African unity that aimed at breaking the West's political, economic, and cultural hold over the continent and obtaining the complete independence of Africa from all forms of foreign domination. The emotional power of Pan-Africanism in the 1960s was enormous, leading in 1963 to the creation of the Organization of African Unity and subsequently to an African bloc in the United Nations. The logical extension of this drive to assert African political power was the nonaligned movement which originally sought to mobilize Third World nations against the hegemony of either the East or West and to combat the extension of the Soviet-American cold war outside Europe. As Nkrumah explained at the Second Conference of Nonaligned States held in Cairo in 1964, "We came into existence as a protest and a revolt against the state of affairs in international relations caused by the division of the world into opposing blocs of East and West."[11] Similarly, Touré made it clear that Africa had no interest in becoming entangled in the East-West struggle and should instead use the nonaligned movement to assert its own united force to oblige both blocs to work for the liberation of Africa. Pan-Africanism and nonalignment, conceived as a Third World bloc standing up to both East and West, were the natural foreign policy components of African socialism seen as a distinctive African ideology.

Both the content and institutions of African socialism could also be explained in terms of the domestic political problems facing African leaders immediately after independence. One of the principal tasks was consolidating the mosaic of tribal groupings making up each African country into a single national unit by inculcating a sense of nationalism to replace narrow tribalism. The principal instrument for achieving this was the "mass" party, one of the most distinctive institutions of the early African socialist countries.

The initial overriding concern to create, or consolidate, the sense of national solidarity generated by the independence struggle led all African socialist leaders in the early 1960s to put enormous emphasis on the theme of unity and communality of interest among all segments of their peoples. They had no political interest at all in highlighting existing or potential new divisions, like traditional tribal feuds or emerging class distinctions, that could cause them trouble. Thus, one can explain the stress on the classless nature of traditional African society and its communal values as part of the post-independence crisis of national identity and national solidarity. African socialist leaders desperately needed to present their peoples with a "reconciliation" rather than a "conflict" model of the new national society. The general preference even among the African socialist leaders for a mass party capable of incorporating as many citizens as possible and serving to infuse in them a sense of common purpose and action was a natural extension of this concern. Furthermore, in most African countries, the dominant political party at the time of independence was already a mass organization that had brought together in the nationalist struggle all social groups irrespective of their tribal origin or economic standing. No African socialist leader was anxious to disband this already existing coalition of political and social forces in the name of a hypothetical homogenous vanguard party such as the Marxists proposed. There was also a major political risk in trying to convert a mass party into a small vanguard party as even some of the early Afro-Marxists admitted. For in expelling large numbers of preindependence party members in order to form a vanguard organization, a government might simply end by creating a larger opposition to itself and, as one Afro-Marxist put it, "turn undercurrents into open political struggles" that "could affect the armed forces and impel them to embark on hazardous ventures."[12] The early African socialists thus had good reasons to favor mass over vanguard parties. Explaining to the *World Marxist Review* why Guinea had early on sought to include "all the inhabitants of the country" in the *Parti Démocratique de Guinée,* one of its Political Bureau members remarked: "It was the Party that created the state and the nation by uniting the conglomerate of tribes into a single Guinean people."[13] And a leader of Zanzibar's Afro-Shirazi Party justified that country's mass party to the *Review* in these terms: "We don't think that in our conditions a vanguard party is an indispensable guarantee of effective politics.... To bring about revolutionary changes, the masses building socialism must be able, as we see it, to participate directly in politics. We don't believe this opportunity should be a privilege of the few."[14]

A final aspect of African socialism of particular interest to us here is its "voluntaristic" nature. This voluntarism is revealed in two closely related assumptions common to all these early ideologies: first, that socialism could be brought about without the use of coercion or force; and second, that individuals could be taught new ways of thinking before social structure changed, and that in fact the reformation of the individual was a precondition for the reformation of society. The African socialists originally sought to carry out their programs by persuasion and education and to convince their people that mobilizing to help one another and the whole nation was the traditional African way of doing things. President Kaunda went to great lengths in his doctrine of humanism to stress the notion that the new nation, like the old tribe, was a "mutual-aid society" in which everyone should participate for the overall good of the community. "This means that there must be fundamental agreement upon the goals and all must act together," he wrote in his treatise, *Humanism in Zambia.*[15] By the very nature of his ideology as well as by personal predilection, Kaunda relied totally on persuasion to get Zambians "to act together," and more precisely upon constant preaching to the nation about how the "good" Zambian should act toward his neighbor, village, nation. Always, the emphasis was on individual behaviour as the key to success in the struggle to build socialism rather than on the structures of society and the need to change them first in order for a new socialist person to emerge. Nyerere, who is officially referred to as *Mwalimu,* the Teacher, was similarly voluntaristic in his approach. Socialism, he kept saying, was essentially "an attitude of mind." Once the correct attitude was instilled in the Tanzanians, they would spontaneously and voluntarily join communal institutions, such as *ujamaa* villages. "Socialism cannot be imposed upon people; they can be guided; they can be lead. But ultimately they must be involved," he said.[16] The task of the government, he explained in 1967, "is not to try and force people into communal activity in *ujamaa* villages but to explain, encourage, and participate."[17] Essentially, Nyerere was counting upon examples of success—model *ujamaa* villages—to convince his people of the benefits of socialism. When this failed, he ultimately accepted the use of some force to carry out his program of villagization but only as a temporary measure. Touré, perhaps the most militant of the early African socialists, first publicly stated that Guinea would be the first African government to use "forced labor" to make its program of *"investissement humain,"* or local self-help projects, a success. But the attempt to use it proved highly counterproductive and within a short time he was stressing that "the Guinean revolution is founded on voluntary adherence" of the people and "not on any coercion exerted on the people by a minority."[18] Despite this great reluctance to sanction the use of coercion, force was periodically resorted to in the early African socialist countries, most often to crush one opposition group or another but at times, too, to get people to join various collective schemes. This practice was nonetheless never converted into a tenet African socialism.

"Transitional" Socialism

Alongside this mainstream school of early African thinking about socialism ran a secondary one that slowly gained in importance and acceptance as the difficulties of the undertaking became more apparent. Essentially, this "transitional" socialism was a hybrid mixture of Marxism-Leninism and

African socialism. It represented the link between the African socialists of the 1960s and the Afrocommunists of the 1970s, marking a kind of halfway point toward orthodox Marxism-Leninism. The "transitionals," as we shall call them, were reacting to the problems they were encountering in their efforts to implement socialism in their countries. These included opposition to their policies from various segments of society, most notably capitalist-oriented ones like the traders, businessmen, and aspiring entrepreneurs but also often the very bureaucratic class which was supposed to carry out the reforms. Another major weakness, it came to be realized, lay in the nature of the "mass" party, which incorporated everybody and anybody, including the opposition, and failed to serve as either a secure base of power or an effective instrument for mobilizing the population. At the same time, it became clear to the more serious African thinkers that some of the exponents of African socialism, like Senghor, were doing little to reform their own countries along socialist lines. Instead, they were allowing them to become models of "neocolonialist" African states still closely linked to, and dependent upon, the old colonial power.

Probably the two most articulate representatives of transitional socialists were Touré and Nkrumah, though several others, like Ahmed Ben Bella of Algeria and Modibo Keita of Mali, fell into the same general category. Among them Nkrumah is ideologically more coherent, but Touré is far more interesting because the changes in his thinking closely reflected the political problems he encountered during twenty-two years of laboring to make Guinea into a socialist country. Both Touré and Nkrumah were by training and ideological conviction basically Marxist in their thinking, but modified their views to fit the political, social, and economic situation in their respective countries. Touré was a labor union organizer who before independence led the French Communist-supported branch of the *Confédération Générale du Travail* first in Guinea and then for all of French West Africa. Nkrumah, after spending ten years in the United States, went to London where he became a close friend of George Padmore, a West Indian Communist who lived for some time in the Soviet Union before cutting his ties with Moscow over its policy toward the African liberation movement and becoming a staunch advocate of Pan-Africanism.

Nkrumah began his political career as a relatively flexible socialist but a militant spokesman for Pan-Africanism. He ended it in exile in Conakry as an orthodox Marxist-Leninist advocating revolutionary armed struggle to make all of Africa socialist and linked in a close alliance to the Communist world. There can be no doubt that the military coup that toppled him in February 1966 radicalized his views considerably, but the process was already beginning before his ouster. Early on, Nkrumah made it clear he aimed to establish a socialist society in Ghana even while shunning use of the term Marxism-Leninism to describe his ideology all the time he was in power. Instead, he gave Ghanaian socialism a distinctly personal interpretation by calling it "Nkrumahism" and developing his own philosophy of "consciencism" blending Islamic and Euro-Christian traditions with "the cluster of humanistic principles which underlie the traditional African society."[19] When he finally announced a party program founded on "the basis of socialist production and distribution," after five years in power, he entitled it a "Programme for Work and Happiness."[20] Basically, Nkrumah as president was far less concerned about refining his views on socialism than about devising and promoting a strategy for Pan-Africanism and a union of African state led by Ghana and himself. After he was deposed, however, he turned to more theoretical writings.

The same year Nkrumah was removed from power, he wrote an article in which he violently attacked the whole concept of "African socialism" as basically "meaningless and irrelevant"[21] and called to ideological task not only the already discredited Senghor but even such a highly respected African socialist leader as Nyerere. African socialism, Nkrumah said, "appears to be more closely associated with anthropology than with political economy." Uncertainties concerning the meaning and specific policies of African socialism, he continued, "have led some of us to abandon the term because it fails to express its original meaning and because it tends to obscure our fundamental socialist commitment."[22] He then took direct issue with the view that traditional African society was either classless or imbued with a natural spirit of humanism.

> Such a conception of socialism makes a fetish of the communal African society. But an idyllic African classless society (in which there were no rich and poor) enjoying a drugged serenity is certainly a facile simplification; there is no historical or even anthropological evidence for any such a society. I am afraid the realities of African society were somewhat more sordid.[23]

Nkrumah argued that although there was "a certain communalism" in many African societies and they were imbued with a kind of humanism, they existed a long time ago and were not "co-terminous" with contemporary African ones. A return to the communalistic society of ancient Africa might be a "charming thought," he said, but it offered no real solution because "we are faced with contemporary problems which have arisen from political subjugation, economic exploitation, educational and social backwardness, increases in population, familiarity with the methods and products of industrialization (and) modern agricultural techniques."[24] A return to an idealized notion of traditional African society, he concluded, was "quite unexampled in the evolution of societies."[25] He also took issue with the voluntaristic approach toward socialism. "Socialism is not spontaneous. It does not arise by itself," he asserted. "There is only one way of achieving socialism: by the devising of policies aimed at the general socialist goals." These policies must be based on the universal laws of scientific socialism adapted to the "specific circumstances of a particular state at a definite historical period."[26]

Nkrumah also revised radically his views on the nature of class conflict in Africa, or at least his public statements on the subject. Just before and after independence, he focused on the struggle between the exploited African countries and exploiting Western powers, treating the two as "classes" in conflict. But his own ouster, plus the series of military coups affecting black Africa in the mid 1960s, led him to redirect his attention inward to the state of African society and to take sharp issue with the African socialists, contention that there were no classes in African society. "Nothing is further from the truth," he said. "A fierce class struggle has been raging in Africa. The evidence is all around us. In essence, it is, as in the rest of the world, a struggle between the oppressors and the oppressed."[27] Class divisions in contemporary African society had been "blurred" during the preindependence period, when all groups were fighting together against the colonial powers. This, he said, had led to the African socialist argument that the communalism and egalitarianism of traditional African society still prevailed just below the surface of the present-day one. The fallacy of the argument was exposed, he continued, immediately after independence "when class cleavages which had been temporarily submerged in the struggle to win political freedom reappeared, often with increased intensity, particularly in those states where the newly independent government embarked on socialist policies."[28] Nkrumah then went on to list and analyze the various classes he saw emerging within African society. His social exegesis appeared in one of his last works entitled *Class Struggle in Africa* and illustrated the profound change in his thinking. Needless to say, it was a totally different thesis from that put forth by Nyerere, Kaunda, and Senghor about their own societies.

This theoretical elaboration on class struggle in Africa reflected a very concrete problem Nkrumah had grappled with while in office: how to make a revolution with a mass party incorporating representatives of all groups, including those opposed to socialism. In this, he was not alone. Other leaders, like Ben Bella and Keita, had faced the same challenge and tried unsuccessfully to extricate themselves from it by creating vanguard parties. Like all other African parties involved in the struggle for independence in the 1950s and 1960s, Nkrumah's Convention People's Party (CPP) was open to virtually any adult who supported its nationalist goals and, as its constitution stated, did "not support imperialism, colonialism, tribalism and racialism."[29] Like the others, too, it enrolled practically all adults in the country—it had two million members out of a total population of 4.7 million. The problem after independence for Nkrumah was how to convert the CPP's purely nationalist ideology into a socialist one and get rid of the "national bourgeois" elements in it who opposed socialism and thus his regime.

Nkrumah tackled this delicate political task by trying to create a small corps of "vanguard activists" to lead and educate the rest of the membership. He embarked upon this endeavor relatively late, however, as he admitted with great regret four years after independence. "For twelve years, twelve long years (1949 to 1960), no conscious, consistent effort had been made to provide party members with the requisite education in the party's ideology of socialism."[30] The corps he chose to act as "the custodian of the party's ideology" was the National African Socialist Students' Organization (NASSO), a small wing of the CPP even before independence. NASSO was supposed to provide the "torchbearers" of Nkrumahism and serve as the "bark" of the "mighty tree" which "cements the physical and organizational unity of the CPP."[31] Later, in 1961, he also established an "ideological institute" at Winneba to indocrinate party officials. It is an interesting historical footnote that Soviet President Leonid Brezhnev was present at the laying of the institute's foundation stone. For the Soviets would later push all their Afrocommunist allies with great vigor to set up similar party ideological schools as soon as possible after independence as one tactic in the battle to establish communist-like party organizations. Nkrumah, however, never came fully around to the Marxist-Leninist concept that the entire party should be a small vanguard of only the tried and trusted, as well as thoroughly indoctrinated, militants. He wanted, in effect, a vanguard within the structure of a mass party, and to the end the CPP remained very much a mass party.

Nkrumah was also a "transitional" in his changing attitude toward the notion of nonalignment and of the relations between the African socialist and communist states. Initially, his whole socialist ideology was bound up in Pan-Africanism and the struggle to free the entire African continent from colonial rule and establish a union of African states. This preoccupation, plus the influence of his close friend and mentor, George Padmore, gave a distinctly African and Third World thrust to his whole foreign policy. But the coup that deposed him and his own deep disappointment with the Organization of African Unity led him to a much more radical view in the later years of his life. In fact, he ended by rejecting altogether the notion of a separate Third World and a third, distinctly "African" way of development. In an article written in 1968 for the *Labour Monthly*, he categorically stated that "there is no middle road between capitalism and socialism" and divided the world into two great conflicting blocs of "revolutionary" and "counter-revolutionary" peoples.[32] Nonalignment, he commented, was an "anachronism." What he wanted was an outright alliance between the African socialist countries and the communist ones to wage war in common against "the capitalist world with its extensions of imperialism, colonialism and neo-colonialism."[33] The African socialist revolution, he repeated again and again, "is an integral part of the world socialist revolution," and of the "world revolutionary process."[34] This "realignment" of the African socialist regimes with the communist bloc would become later a clearly stated policy objective of the Afrocommunists.

Touré's thinking reveals some of the same changes, but it has been revised more than once during his twenty-two years in power as he has sought solutions to his country's unending problems. He started as a typical African socialist, stressing the "communocratic" nature of African society, strenuously denying the relevance of class or class conflict to the Guinean revolution and stressing the overwhelming importance of national solidarity as embodied in his *Parti Démocratique de Guinée,* a mass party of practically the entire adult population. Later, he declared class conflict a "universal reality"[35] and produced a tortuous exegesis of the Koran, citing the most famous first verse, the Fatiha, to prove that even Islam "proclaims the class struggle."[36] He also called at one point for the formation of a vanguard party and set up an ideological school to train party cadres for it. He eventually backtracked, however, reviving the notion of a mass party of "all the people" in the country "without distinction of religion and philosophy," whose main purpose was to distill a "collective conscience" at the village, regional and national levels.[37] The culmination of his ideological peregrinations was the concept of the "party-state" first enunciated in the late 1960s and subsequently embodied in the local institution known as the *Pouvoir Révolutionaire Local.* Even before Guinea had reached socialism, it appeared, Touré had decided to force history and provoke the "withering away of the state." Speaking to a visiting Common Market delegation in 1976, he proudly proclaimed that "very soon we are going to pass historically to the phase of the party-state. Nowhere in the world has anyone reached this stage. It is an original enterprise."[38] In practice, he explained elsewhere, "this means merging the organs of the party and the state into single organs of revolutionary power, delegating to them political and administrative functions and gradually extending the responsibility of local authorities."[39] Such a concept of party and state in a socialist country can only be considered heretical from a Marxist point of view. Touré, after toying with Marxism, had thus gone back to a very independent formulation of socialism.

Like Nkrumah, the Guinean leader eventually also rejected the notion of a specific African personality favoring African socialism, and, as a result, he also ended up rejecting the concept of Pan-Africanism as he and other socialist expounded it in the early 1960s. At the Sixth Pan-African Congress held in Dar es Salaam in June 1974, Touré launched a violent attack upon what he termed the "parochial identity" of the original concept and particularly its identification with Senghor's idea of *Négritude,* which he contemptuously rejected as "the most harmful, the most alienating form" of Pan-Africanism."[40] "*Négritude* has in fact become the ideological and literary form of the policy of native reserves practiced by the Pretoria administration against Africans," he told the Congress. "The racists of southern Africa and the poets of *Négritude* all drink from the same fountain of racial prejudice and serve the same cause—the cause of imperialism, exploitation of man by man, and obscurantism." Senghor's philosophy of Negro-Africanism, he continued, "is fatal to Pan-Africanism and should therefore be destroyed and its offshoots made to parch in the burning sun of Africa."[41] Touré proposed instead a new definition for what he called "revolutionary Pan-Africanism" in which Africans would identify themselves "not by the color of our skin ... but in terms of our goals." Africa should identify its friends and enemies accordingly, he said, posing at the same time a question the Afrocommunists would reply to in the affirmative without hesitation: "Was not [Salvador] Allende [of Chile] closer to the exploited black than certain Afro-Americans or African leaders?" And, he added, "Is it not true that our friend, the great revolutionary leader of Cuba, Fidel Castro, is more hated by the imperialists, colonialists, segregationists, and fascists than black leaders who have become the accomplices and devoted and servile agents of those who exploit their brothers and generally scoff at the rights of African people?"[42] Like Nkrumah and the Afrocommunists later, Touré was coming to see the world divided essentially along East-West rather than North-South lines.

A last example of non-Marxist socialism in Africa worthy of note here is the Algerian brand, which has undergone two phases in its history. Under Ben Bella, it was an example of transitional socialism similar to that of Nkrumah and Touré in trying to integrate Marxist and African elements. After a coup in June 1965 and the rise to power of Colonel Houari Boumédiène, Algerian socialism took on a uniquecharacter, violently rejecting Marxism even while following Soviet tenets in the organization of the state and economy. Ben Bella, like Nkrumah, rejected the notion that African society was classless and strove to transform the wartime *Front de Libération Nationale* (FLN) from a coalition of nationalist but ideologically diverse groups into a vanguard party with a quasi-Marxist ideology. Like Touré, he reiterated that Islam and Marxism were not necessarily in conflict and that Algeria thus was not foregoing its Arab and African personality by turning to socialism.[43]

The evolution in Algeria toward outright Marxism was interrupted by a power struggle involving the rejection by Ben Bella's military opponents of what they regarded as an alien ideology being spread inside Algeria by his foreign "Trotskyite" advisers and the Algerian Communist Party. This anti-Marxist stance did not imply a return to any romantic notion of African communalism, however. Boumédiène's socialism looked very much toward the future, not to the past. It meant the building of a strong centralized state based on an industrialized economy. To Boumédiène, Marxism was simply too dogmatic and did not take into account the specific conditions of Africa. His regime's main ideological document, the National Charter of 1976, argued that there was no "single, obligatory model" a Third World country had to follow to qualify as socialist, and that every nation must derive its own "national socialism" from its specific experience.[44] "Socialist ideology is not an immutable dogma. It cannot be reduced to lifeless clichés and interchangeable slogans. Socialist ideology requires a permanent theoretical refinement which is continuously enriched through contact with experience,"[45] the document asserted, quite obviously taking issue with the Marxist-Leninist notion of "one socialism." Continuing in the same independent vein, the Charter noted that because of their acute underdevelopment, newly independent countries scarcely had a working class to lead the process of socialist transformation. Instead, this task befell a "vanguard of all revolutionary patriots," also referred to as "the revolutionary national cadres," who are drawn from all segments of society, namely workers, military men, intellectuals and "political militants."[46] Contrary to extolling the workers as the prime movers of socialism, the Charter argued just the reverse, that only the process of industrialization and modernization of the country along socialist lines could eventually create a working class. Not only did the Charter reject the glorification of the working class or any notion of proletarian dictatorship, it also defined a "worker" in a very broad, non-Marxist manner. A worker, it said, was "any person who lives from the fruits of his labor, whether it be manual or intellectual, and does not employ for a profit other workers in his professional activity."[47] Thus, an intellectual, a small-holding peasant, a factory worker, were all lumped together as "workers."

The only aspect of the Algerian National Charter that owes anything to Marxism-Leninism is the one concerning the party, conceived of as a vanguard organization. It is also the part of the Charter which bore the least relationship to reality; the FLN under Boumédiène played a minor role, let alone serving as vanguard of the revolution. It underwent repeated attempts at reorganization, but it never held a congress in the thirteen years of his rule. From the very beginning, Boumédiène was concerned above all with the creation of a "stable and efficient state."[48] Algerian socialism essentially led to a state-dominated industrial system in which technocrats and bureaucrats had much more power than party officials.

In foreign policy, however, Algeria's new ideology under Boumédiène appeared very similar to that of the early African socialists (and different from the later Afrocommunists). For Boumédiène, the Third World was very much a separate entity with its own interests and causes different from those of the industrialized nations of the North, both capitalist and socialist ones. The world was far less divided between the East and West than the North and South. "The vast movement for the emancipation of Third World countries has engendered an important contradiction between underdeveloped and industrialized countries, since the latter are interested in maintaining by any means the present international economic order," the Charter stated.[49] It called, as Boumédiène had already done at the United Nations, for a "new international economic order" to do away with this conflict and establish a better equilibrium between the developing and industrialized worlds.[50] It also rejected the notion of a world political order dominated by the Superpowers. "The solution of today's international problems can no longer be the monopoly of a closed club where a small number of states dictate their will to the whole world. It implies a democratic organization of international relations and presupposes a real will to readjust more equitably relations between industrialized and Third World countries."[51]

From this fundamental view of world relations grew Algeria's definition of nonalignment as "the expression of our will for total independence vis-a-vis all foreign powers."[52] As for the nature of Algeria's relations with the communist world, this was outlined only last, after a long discussion of its historical ties with the other North African, Arab, and African countries.

Algeria's policy of cooperation with other socialist states, the Charter said, "continues to develop and expand in all domains" and was based on "an equilibrium of interests."[53] Significantly, no mention was made of any special ideological affinity between Algeria and the Eastern bloc. Finally, while affirming the Algerian commitment to the struggle against "colonialism, neo-colonialism and imperialism," the document noted with approval the willingness of a number of Western countries to establish "a new kind of relationship" with Algeria, making it possible to conceive of even expanded cooperation with them.[54]

The Theory of Afrocommunism

What do the Marxist-Leninists believe, in theory at least?

First of all, they hold unanimously to the view that there is no "African," or "Asian," or "Latin American" socialism distinct from Marxism-Leninism, the only "true" socialism. Mozambican President Samora Machel has perhaps been most emphatic on this point in reaction, ironically, to a description of Mozambique as Africa's first "Afrocommunist" country. It was a label he totally rejected as belittling his government's efforts to carry out an authentic Marxist-Leninist revolution, albeit in an African context.

> Frelimo identifies with Marxism-Leninism as it is ... as a science of the workers ... as a fundamental instrument for the analysis of society ... as the greatest instrument for understanding class struggle. The divergencies are secondary. The great thing about Marxism is that, it being a science, it can adapt to all conditions. There is no African Marxism, Asian Marxism, European Marxism. There is only one Marxism.[55]

The leadership of the *Movimento Popular de Libertação de Angola* (MPLA) has been just as emphatic on this point. Lucio Lara, regarded widely as the party's chief theoretician, has castigated just as sternly as Machel what he called "these original species of socialism."

> Clearly for the MPLA there has always been only one expression of socialism, known precisely as scientific socialism. Experience has shown that all that rhetoric [about African socialism] has not led to concrete steps showing a true socialist option ... the colonial presence, the presence of neo-colonialism, is obviously in all of them. Their capitalist orientation is clear.... These 'socialisms' are basically disguises for one or another form of colonial exploitation.[56]

Virtually all the Marxist-Leninists, even the military ones most suspect in their depth of conviction, vie with each other to show their orthodoxy. Somalia's military leader Mohamed Siad Barre, who dropped references to Marxism-Leninism after his break with the Soviet Union in late 1977, was no exception. Explaining earlier the Somali option for socialism, he said that "our socialism cannot be called Somali socialism, African socialism, or Islamic socialism.... Our socialism is scientific socialism founded by the great Marx and Engels."[57] The central tenet of the African Marxist theory of revolution is that society can only be understood in terms of class analysis and with the acceptance of class conflict as the moving force. All the Marxist-Leninist leaders talk of their political problems and of their countries' history in class terms. They refer constantly to the "petty bourgeoisie," the "working class," the "national bourgeoisie," and the "peasantry" as the basic social units of their societies. They see the postindependence period as marked by inevitable bitter conflict among these classes, or even, as the *Frente de Libertação de Moçambique* (Frelimo) asserted in one party document, "the intensification of the class struggle."[58] A crucial aspect of this struggle is the role of the petty bourgeoisie. What for Marx was a residual category of fence sitters, siding at times with the bourgeoisie and at times with the proletariat, becomes central in these countries where the national bourgeoisie has been stifled by colonialism and the working class kept miniscule by underdevelopment. Civil servants, traders, small businessmen, university graduates, intellectuals, middle-ranking military officers, and school dropouts tend to be lumped together in the petty bourgeoisie. This class is both glorified and vilified, particularly in the Portuguese colonies. It is acknowledged that the initial leadership and impetus for the liberation struggle came from its ranks.[59] Yet, in the postindependence periods "the petty bourgeoisie tend to go astray," in the words of Lucio Lara of the Angolan MPLA. "It has very strong propensities toward opportunism and personal ambitions" and "lacks the kind of maturity which makes for consistency in the analysis of problems."[60] Opponents of the MPLA, both within the government and outside, are inevitably labelled as petty bourgeois who have lost their way. Similarly, individuals and groups opposing Frelimo in Mozambique, or the regime of Colonel Mengistu Haile-Mariam in Ethiopia, are regularly condemned as "reactionary petty bourgeois" who must be dealt with ruthlessly. The progressive petty bourgeois, on the other hand, are seen as having an important role to play in the revolution.

Just how the African Marxist-Leninists should go about transferring the leadership of the revolution from the petty bourgeoisie to the working class has been the subject of a considerable amount of writing. The first leader of the nationalist guerrilla struggle in Guinea-Bissau, Amilcar Cabral, argued, like Franz Fanon, that the petty bourgeoisie must "be capable of committing suicide as a class in order to be reborn as revolutionary workers," a rather voluntaristic notion.[61] None of the Marxist-Leninists in power at the turn of the decade advanced such a thesis, however. In a distinctly less voluntaristic approach, they have generally argued that the working class must be strengthened, instead, to the point where its representatives can be eased into positions of power and "neutralize" progressively the petty bourgeois elements.[62] It is not clear in this analysis how the temporary vacuum is to be filled until the proletariat is ready to assume its historical leadership role.

Much of their writing stresses, however, the need for a broad coalition of all progressives pending the day the working class takes power. Frelimo has explained the process in these terms:

> The Mozambican proletariat, the peasants, particularly those in cooperatives, revolutionary intellectuals, artisans, workers in general, are in the process of gaining a clear awareness of their situation and their historic destiny. They are gradually organizing themselves, under the leadership of the working class, to mould society in accordance with the interests of the Mozambican proletariat.[63]

The immediate postindependence stage of the revolutionary process is thus seen as a struggle to create the correct political, social, and economic conditions "for the development of the dictatorship of the Proletariat." This stage is variously referred to as "people's democracy," or "national democratic revolution."

> People's democracy is the historical phase in which the laboring masses, under the leadership of the working class, strengthen their Power, establish the dictatorship of the Proletariat and put into effect the Power of the majority in all spheres of social life.[64]

The fact that the working class did not usually play an important role in the national liberation struggle is a point that clearly troubles the Marxist-Leninists of the former Portuguese colonies. They remain convinced nonetheless that no real revolution can take place without this class in control. "It has always been and still is the working class which gains true political consciousness in the struggle and which grasps the process of the revolution and of the transition to socialism with the required degree of reliability and consistency," remarked Lara in a discussion of this issue with the South African Communist Party organ, *The African Communist*.[65] In his view, the Angolan working class, which he admits played a minor role in the nationalist war, began to take a more significant part during the "Second Liberation War," the MPLA struggle against the two pro-Western Angolan nationalist groups and the South Africans in the period 1975 to 1976. With the conversion of the MPLA into a "Labor Party" in late 1977, the working class in Angola was beginning to assume its proper role in the revolution. "We are already in the phase in which our working class begins to take hold of the reins of the revolutionary process," remarked Lara.[66]

The African Marxist-Leninists differ quite emphatically from the earlier African socialists in insisting that the social basis of the revolution, and thus of the party, has to be the working class rather than a broad coalition either of the entire population, as in Guinea, or of revolutionaries drawn from all segments of society, as in Algeria. They are ready with a good Marxist explanation for why the worker is so important to the process of building socialism, even in African countries where the vast majority of the population is peasants and the workers a small minority of relatively privileged people. It is only the worker, they said, who does not own any means of production and "lives by the collective property" of the state. It is the working class alone that can teach the peasants and other groups "the collective spirit, the spirit of organization and the spirit of collective property."[67] Progressive petty bourgeois, civil servants, intellectuals, nurses, and teachers, are too influenced by the ideas, customs, and tastes of the bourgeoisie to be entrusted with the leadership of the revolution. These elements, explained Frelimo, have first "to wage internal combat within themselves," absorb the values of the working class, and acquire a new mental outlook "whereby they renounce the bourgeoisie and identify themselves with the working class."[68]

There is complete agreement among African Marxist-Leninists that the revolution must be led by a small vanguard party whose social base is the working class and whose ideology is Marxism-Leninism. Since they see society as essentially wracked by irreconcilable class conflict, there is no question of a mass party incorporating the entire adult population. Socialism, they fully realize, does not represent the subjective interests of all groups in society. Certain classes are inevitably opposed to it, and thus they must be excluded from the party. One of the first things the MPLA and Frelimo did after independence was to undertake the conversion of their wartime fronts and movements into proper vanguard parties by tightening criteria for membership, limiting severely their size to thousands rather than millions, and setting up a party school to educate the chosen few in Marxist-Leninist theory. Even Ethiopia, which as of 1980 still had no party, accepted the theory of a vanguard party and had set up its preliminary structures, including an ideological school to train its cadres. It was quite clear that the model these countries were following was that of the Soviet Communist party, and in fact Soviets, Cubans, and East Germans were providing assistance and encouragement to the point of pressure to help them establish as quickly as possible a correct type of vanguard organization.

In addition to believing in a single scientific socialism, class conflict, the dictatorship of the proletariat, and a small vanguard party to lead the revolution, African Marxist-Leninists also distinguish themselves from the early African socialists by their acceptance of coercion as inevitable in the process of socialist transformation. It is true that the early African socialist and "transitional" leaders often had recourse to the use of coercion either to carry out their reforms or to repress their oppositions. Touré, for example, earned the reputation of being an African "Stalin" and even Nyerere condoned the use of force by his party to resettle several million peasants into villages in the mid-1970s. But, as we noted earlier, none of them came forth with a theory of coercion as a legitimate part of revolution. The Marxist-Leninists, on the other hand, are much more ready to justify the use of coercion and even "terror" as a legitimate means of forcing along the revolutionary process. The most dramatic example of this has been seen in Ethiopia, where Colonel Mengistu has openly resorted to what he called "red terror" to crush a wide variety of his own personal as well as the revolution's numerous political enemies whom he accused of employing "white terror" against the military government. "It is an historical obligation to clean up vigilantly using the revolutionary sword," said Mengistu following the execution of his own vice-chairman, Colonel Atnafu Abate, in November 1977. "Your struggle should be demonstrated by spreading red terror in the camp of reactionaries. Turn the white terror of reactionaries into red terror," he added.[69] It is not surprising that such a doctrine of terror should emerge from a revolution wracked by separatist and opposition movements on all sides. Violence was endemic to the Ethiopian revolution almost from the very beginning, and both its partisans and opponents were fully prepared to use force to prevail. The land reform proclaimed in 1975 pitted peasants and farm workers against landlords, and the wars in Eritrea Province and the Ogaden pitted the heartland of the old empire against the periphery. Marxist doctrine coupled with the historical circumstances led to the glorification of victory through violent struggle. As Mengistu told Fidel Castro, who visited Ethiopia in September 1978, "Victory is always the fruits of struggle. This is what Marxist-Leninist practice has taught us. This is what the great October (Soviet) Socialist Revolution has taught us."[70]

More surprising, perhaps, was the acceptance and advocacy of violence by some other African Marxist leaders in far more peaceful countries where the revolution was not really that contested. One such example was President Didier Ratsiraka of the Malagasy Republic, the military officer responsible for making Marxism-Leninism the official doctrine of that Indian Ocean island. "Revolutionary violence," he remarked in early 1978, "is necessary to confront and defeat counter-revolutionary violence, in order to prevent the reactionaries from taking back control of the revolutionary power."[71]

In foreign policy, the African Marxist-Leninists have similarly come a long way from the early African socialist preoccupation with Pan-Africanism and Third World nonalignment. Pan-Africanism is scarcely mentioned in their speeches and writing, and nonalignment has assumed an entirely different meaning under the impact of "proletarian internationalism." Like Nkrumah in his later years, the African Marxist-Leninists see the world divided primarily between socialist and capitalist countries, imperialist and antiimperialist ones. This is the primary contradiction in the alignment of international forces, at least in theory. Thus, the socialist countries of the East are declared to be the African Marxist-Leninist states "natural allies," the term used by Frelimo in Mozambique. These are the countries with which the African Marxists believe they should have the closest economic, political, and military ties. Mozambique, Angola, and Ethiopia all have signed treaties of friendship and cooperation with Moscow. This "natural" alliance between the Soviet bloc and the African Marxist-Leninist states is seen in the former Portuguese colonies as already rooted in the history of their nationalist liberation struggles and thus simply an extension of what already existed before independence. "The socialist countries were on our side and gave political, diplomatic, and military support to the armed struggles for national liberation," explained Machel reviewing the history of the nonalignment movement as Frelimo saw it. "The socialist countries were and are at all times our safe rearguard."[72] This view has profoundly influenced the African Marxist attitude toward nonalignment, a movement to which they still adhere. To the Marxist-Leninists, however, nonalignment means primarily the struggle against "imperialism, neo-colonialism, and colonialism," evils they attribute solely to the West. Thus, nonalignment and proletarian internationalism are seen as going hand-in-hand without contradiction in purpose or objective. President Tito of Yugoslavia had a hard time convincing the African Marxist-Leninists of his theory that nonalignment implies equidistance between the East and West. At meetings of the nonaligned group in the late 1970s, Yugoslavia found itself waging an uphill struggle to incorporate in its documents the original principles of the movement. At the end of the decade, the nonaligned movement was the scene of a bitter struggle between pro-Eastern and pro-Western countries, and it seemed all too symbolic that its 1979 summit meeting should have taken place in Cuba, an extremely close ally of the Soviet Union and a vociferous advocate of the thesis that the Third World should link up with the Eastern bloc in a worldwide struggle against Western imperialism.

Origins of Afrocommunism

Marxism-Leninism quite obviously did not spring from the soil of Africa. Not only did it originate in Europe, it also stemmed from socioeconomic conditions completely different from those prevailing in Africa. How then does one explain its increasing appeal today, after its general rejection as a "foreign" ideology in the early 1960s? What have been the conduits by which Marxism-Leninism spread across the continent?

The first point that ought to be made clear is that the expansion of Marxism-Leninism inside Africa really owes very little to the work of African Communist parties. By the calculations of the Soviets themselves, the number of official, Moscow-aligned Communist party members throughout the continent, including the Arab countries, had only grown from 5,000 in 1939 to "over 60,000" in 1971.[73] Of this number, 20,000 were said to be in Senegal and another 22,000 in Nigeria; in both, the Communist party has had negligible influence over the first two decades of independence.[74] The largest party, according to the Soviets, was on Madagascar, where the Independence Congress Party (AKFM) was said to have "over 30,000" members by the early 1970s.[75] Madagascar was one of only two African countries, Senegal being the other, where a Communist, or Marxist, party was officially allowed to operate as of 1980. It was the only African country where, after Ratsiraka's rise to power, the Communists were participating in the government as party members, having two representatives in the ruling coalition known as the National Front for the Defense of the Revolution. Without exception to date, Marxism-Leninism has been made the official ideology of African states by independent nationalist or military leaders. The

Soviets are only too well aware of this, and it is one of the reasons for their doubts about the steadfastness of their new African Marxist-Leninist allies.

While African Communists have not been directly responsible for the growing number of Marxist-Leninist states in Africa, it is nonetheless true that Western European Communist parties have played a significant role in the development of this trend. It seems no mere coincidence that all of the Marxist-Leninist regimes are former colonies of France, Italy, or Portugal, countries with active Communist parties (the one in Portugal was long clandestine). Britain, with a stronger Fabian than Marxist tradition, has so far spawned regimes oriented toward African socialism rather than Marxism-Leninism. Students from the Portuguese and French colonies who studied in the *métropole* were exposed to Marxist thought more systematically and thoroughly than those from the British colonies going to England. In the Portuguese colonies, a very large proportion of these students were either whites or *mestiços* (mixed race individuals). The *mestiços* were few in number, less than 100,000 in Angola or Mozambique, but played a very important part in the nationalist struggle and later in shaping the ideology and running the government. Portuguese whites who opted for Angolan or Mozambican citizenship at independence were mostly staunch Marxists and also played a vital role relative to their tiny number. While figures for this group are hard to come by, no visitor to either country can help but being struck by their visibility in many top positions. The presence of these whites and *mestiços* has provided a social stratum generally supportive of Marxist-Leninist regimes in Angola and Mozambique. A comparable group simply does not exist in any of the ex-French or ex-British colonies.

In trying to assess the impact of the European Communist parties in the diffusion of Marxism-Leninism in Africa, it is imperative to make a distinction between their role in the 1960s and that in the 1970s. The record of these parties in the initial African struggle for independence beginning in the 1950s was extremely mixed and sometimes outright negative. The French Communist party distinguished itself in this regard, opposing the independence movements in the various French colonies. This led a number of West African nationalists to break with it over this issue. In Algeria, the French Communist party was extremely late in coming over to the side of the National Liberation Front, a fact the Algerians never forgave or forgot after independence and which vastly complicated the attempt by Algerian Communists to stage a comeback. Padmore, one of Nkrumah's closest friends, has written in great passion and detail about the failings of the European and American communists in their relations with the African liberation movements and castigated their initial attacks on Pan-Africanism as well as black nationalism. His book, *Pan-Africanism or Communism*, helps explain the strong anticommunist feelings practically all of the early African socialist leaders held and the lack of influence of the African Communist parties in the politics and ideology of the independence movements in the 1950s and 1960s.[76]

In the 1970s, however, the Western European Communist parties had a good deal more impact on the later African liberation movements and even some of the radical military men who came to power. The Italian Communist party, for example, had considerable influence on the Somali revolution under Siad Barre. A number of his civilian Somali advisers, like Mohamed Adan, were extremely close to that party as a result of their studies and stays in Italy, and they became the principal conveyors of Marxism-Leninism into Somalia after Barre came to power. Similarly, the French Communist party indirectly influenced the Ethiopian revolution. Several of Colonel Mengistu's top civilian advisers, most notably Negede Gobeze and Haile Fida, were French-educated intellectuals who had developed strong ties to it during and after their student days in France. Probably the closest association any European communist party enjoyed with the later liberation movements was that of Portugal's with the nationalist leaders in Angola, Guinea-Bissau, and Mozambique. It was not only because these nationalists went to school in Lisbon and came there into contact with the Portuguese communists. In Portugal, unlike the other African colonial powers, the Communist party was outlawed and engaged in the same kind of clandestine struggle against the Salazar government as the African nationalists themselves. The two struggles thus went hand-in-hand. Portuguese Communists in Angola were involved right from the beginning in the launching of the liberation war, while Agostinho Neto and other Angolan nationalists maintained contacts with members of the underground Portuguese Communist party during his student days and early political career.

While there were differences at times between the founders of the MPLA and both Angolan and Portuguese Communists, there was no disagreement concerning the necessity for Angolan independence. Moreover, a large number of MPLA leaders, particularly those of mixed African-Portuguese blood, were Marxists by intellectual conviction even at the beginning of their long struggle in the mid-1960s. The common ideological heritage of most MPLA leaders and the Portuguese Communists helps explain why after the April 1974 coup in Lisbon the Communist party provided as much help as possible to this nationalist faction. Such assistance was particularly important during the three-way civil war that broke out in early 1975 and from which the MPLA emerged victorious despite its initial military disadvantages. Individual Portuguese Communists actively participated on the side of the MPLA in this period. Furthermore, the transitional government set up by the Portuguese to prepare for independence was for a time under a Communist governor, Rosa Coutinho, known as the "Red Admiral," who closed his eyes to shipments of arms into the country for the MPLA. The nationalist movements in Guinea-Bissau and to a lesser extent in Mozambique also had contacts with the Portuguese communists, although the latter's involvement was far less extensive in these two countries.

It was not just the European Communist parties that changed in their attitude and tactics toward the national liberation movements of the 1970s.

Both the Soviet Union and Cuba did, too. The policy of befriending African nationalists and extending all kinds of diplomatic, moral, and military aid to them began for both these Communist countries only in the early 1960s, after the first great wave of independence had freed from colonial rule all but the Portuguese colonies and the white-ruled countries of southern Africa. The Soviets used seminars, visits, and conferences held under the auspices of the Afro-Asian People's Solidarity Organization (AAPSO) to weld links with the nationalist leaders, whom they described in their carefully constructed lexicon as "revolutionary democrats." By the end of the 1960s, the Soviets had picked out the groups they regarded as most legitimate or closest to their ideological thinking among contending nationalist factions in the various Portuguese colonies and white-dominated southern African countries. These included the MPLA in Angola, the *Partido Africano de Independência da Guinée Cabo Verde* (PAIGC) in Guinea-Bissau, Frelimo in Mozambique, Joshua Nkomo's Zimbabwe African People's Union (ZAPU) in Rhodesia, the South-West Africa People's Organization (SWAPO) in Namibia, and the African National Congress (ANC) in South Africa. These groups were invited to all of AAPSO's conferences, and many of their representatives helped to run the organization. The Soviets also provided some military assistance to a number of these nationalist movements, though not to all and not usually to the extent they themselves hoped for. The MPLA was one main beneficiary, but Frelimo, on the other hand, owed very little to the Soviets. By the late 1970s, the Soviet Union had become the major arms supplier to SWAPO in Namibia and ZAPU in Zimbabwe and was providing far more than it had to either the MPLA or Frelimo during their nationalist struggles. This may have been partly because of criticism about the limited extent of its earlier assistance to the nationalist movements. But it was doubtlessly, too, out of cold political calculation concerning how best to extend its political influence among those African groups still engaged in an independence struggle in southern Africa. It is difficult to assess how much influence the Soviets had in spreading Marxism-Leninism through their growing contacts with African nationalists in the 1970s. By the latter part of the decade, groups like ZAPU, the ANC, and SWAPO were being exposed to Marxist doctrine through many other channels as well, most particularly the frontline countries in which they had their headquarters or bases, particularly Angola and Mozambique.

Cuba, too, played a role in extending Marxism-Leninism inside Africa, though again it is difficult to determine the importance of Cuban influence as compared to that of European Communist parties or the African Marxist-Leninists themselves. Its earliest and closest contacts with any of the nationalist groups came with the MPLA in Angola. By the end of the 1960s, Cuban military advisers were aiding the MPLA in training guerrillas, and even doing some fighting inside Angola. By contrast, Cuban contacts with Frelimo were negligible throughout its struggle for independence, probably for the same reason the Soviets failed to help it—its association with, and military assistance from, China. Cuban assistance to the remaining nationalist movements on the continent in the latter half of the 1970s was far more significant. The Cubans were staffing guerrilla training camps for SWAPO and ZAPU inside Angola and even helping Robert Mugabe's Zimbabwe African National Union (ZANU) through the intermediary of Ethiopia, where this group began sending its recruits for military instruction in 1978.

While the Soviet and Cuban presence grew steadily in Africa during the 1970s, Chinese influence declined. In the 1960s, the Chinese were viewed in the West as the predominant Communist "threat" on the continent because of their highly activist policy and of the appeal that the Chinese experience held for such rural-based nationalist movements as Frelimo and ZANU. By the end of the next decade, the Chinese had almost completely withdrawn from Africa, partly because of the political turmoil inside China and partly because of a series of diplomatic blunders that put them on the side of losing causes. Obsessed by their anti-Sovietism, they had backed the CIA-supported *Frente Nacional de Libertação de Angola* (FNLA) during the civil war; supported the regime of President Mobutu Sese Seko in Zaire—much despised in radical African circles; refused, like the United States, to recognize the MPLA government in Angola; and chosen to assist diplomatically isolated Somalia after its break with the Soviet Union in late 1977 and its invasion of the Ethiopian Ogaden region. The clearest evidence of the Chinese withdrawal from Africa was Peking's failure to meet ZANU's arms request at a time when this nationalist faction appeared to be winning the war not only against the whites but against the Soviet-backed ZAPU. The most dramatic example of declining Chinese influence came in Mozambique; after establishing itself as the primary Communist supporter of Frelimo, China was edged out by the Soviet Union after independence as that country's most important ally.

While foreign communist influence played a part in the diffusion of Marxism-Leninism inside black Africa, it was mostly indirect and filtered through indigeneous African Marxist elements. In no case did either the Cubans or Soviets impose a regime or ideology on an African country, not even in Angola as we shall try to make clear later. By the time of their independence, the Portuguese colonies had a large number of dedicated local Marxists in their nationalist movements. The process of ideological conversion from pure nationalism to Marxism-Leninism had already taken place inside the MPLA, Frelimo, and even the more moderate PAIGC in Guinea-Bissau. In a very real sense, Marxism-Leninism became a part of the nationalist ideology of these movements, although the word was never used prior to independence. Furthermore, all kinds of institutions—people's shops, collective villages, various forms of cooperatives—set up in the liberated zones of these three Portuguese colonies, embodied the socialist principles their independent governments would later adopt officially. This interlinking of nationalism and Marxism-Leninism prior to independence represented a major difference from the early African socialist countries, where independence came first and socialism was superimposed later in the midst of great controversy. The best example of such a crisis was Algeria, where the FLN fragmented into rival groups at independence. While there were other causes as well, there can be little doubt that the ideologically heterogeneous nature of the Front was a major cause of the split. Leaders of the three nationalist movements in the Portuguese colonies were all frequent visitors to Algeria and witnessed firsthand its postindependence crisis of conversion from pure nationalism to socialism. The lesson doubtlessly was not lost on them.

The same process of "Africanization" of Marxism-Leninism we have described above also took place elsewhere on the continent. Somali and Ethiopian intellectuals were responsible for introducing Marxism-Leninism into their respective countries and pressing the military regimes there into adopting it as the official ideology. In other countries, like Madagascar, Benin and the Congo, the personal conviction of the military leader and of a small clique of military and civilian associates, accounted for the conversion to Marxism-Leninism. In all cases, the role of Soviet, Cuban, or other outside foreign advisers seems to have been initially minimal; their time came later when they helped Marxist-inclined military leaders to consolidate their power and implement socialist policies. The two contemporary examples where direct and prolonged Soviet, East German, and Cuban contacts may have played an important role in infusing Marxism-Leninism into the ideologies of a nationalist movement are ZAPU and SWAPO. As these two groups sent more and more guerrillas and cadres to Eastern Europe, Cuba, and camps in Angola staffed by Cuban instructors, they became noticeably more Marxist in their thinking and pronouncements, notwithstanding Joshua Nkomo's careful avoidance of Marxist terminology when addressing Western audiences. The exact extent to which their foreign communist allies were really responsible for this radicalization, however, as opposed to their even closer relations with the Marxist-Leninist states, becomes virtually impossible to determine. The two were quite obviously mutually reinforcing in the spread of Marxism-Leninism throughout southern Africa after the collapse of the Portuguese African empire in the mid-1970s. The other major source of influence in the diffusion of Marxism-Leninism has been the concrete experience of the early African socialist countries, whose problems and failures have not gone unnoticed by the Africa Marxists. Indeed, their orthodoxy grows, at least in part, out of the lessons they have drawn from these countries' labors at implementing socialism. Thus, it is to an examination of the early socialist experience that we shall next turn.

Chapter III
African Socialism Revisited

We have seen in the preceeding chapter how in the last fifteen years socialist ideology has undergone a considerable evolution away from humanistic "African socialism" and toward orthodox Marxism-Leninism. This ideological evolution was not the only change taking place among the African socialist countries. Their policies, in fact their politics, also underwent a metamorphosis over the years. States which started out in the early or mid-1960s with a remarkably similar ideological approach ended the 1970s as quite distinctly different political and economic systems. This process needs to be examined because it highlights the difficulties of socialist transformation on the African continent and points to some of the critical factors affecting the outcome. There is no reason to believe that Marxist-Leninist countries will be immune to these same difficulties. While we believe that the different ideological choice may be extremely important, it is only one among a number of factors determining the end result. We will discuss here four African countries which consider themselves socialist: Zambia, Tanzania, Guinea, and Algeria. They are the longest surviving experiments in socialism anywhere in Africa and have some of the oldest regimes under the same leader on the continent in general. Because of this continuity, they are particularly good case studies of what non-Marxist socialism has meant in practice. The four countries are all the more interesting since they are extremely different from each other today. Tanzania has remained relatively faithful ideologically as well as politically to the original concept of African socialism. Zambia, on the other hand, has strayed far away from it, in our opinion, to become basically a welfare state for the upper class. Algeria has turned into a highly centralized and bureaucratized country, single-mindedly pursuing a policy of industrialization; while it has rejected Marxism and extolled Islam, it is the most statist of all the early socialist countries. Guinea has become more Marxist in its ideology and continued to adhere to policies aimed at mobilizing the entire population. By creating the "party-state," however, Touré has opened the way for the eventual triumph of the state over the party, the very institution he had tried to build into the main pillar of his regime.

It is not possible to explain the different roads these countries have traveled in terms of their ideologies alone. Tanzania and Zambia are both prime examples of the African socialist ideology: Nyerere's *ujamaa* and Kaunda's humanism are almost indistinguishable from each other, yet the two countries have evolved into very different types of socioeconomic systems. Guinea is a perfect example of what we have called a "transitional" ideology, but the economic policies of the country do not reflect such a concept of socialism. Algeria, which has moved in the other direction, away from Marxism-Leninism, still is following a Soviet approach to economic development. Whatever their ideological similarities and differences, the four countries constitute today four quite distinct models of socialism in Africa: Zambia has become an example of perverse socialist development leading toward an "upper class welfare state"; Tanzania is a case study of "development without growth"; Algeria typifies a policy of "economics in command"; while Guinea is the protype of just the opposite, "politics in command."

Zambia: "The Upper Class Welfare State"

In October 1978, President Kaunda decided to reopen the border between Zambia and Rhodesia to rail traffic in order to facilitate the export of Zambian copper and the import of essential commodities. The border had been closed since January 1973, and the difficult situation created for landlocked Zambia had further deteriorated by 1978 because of chronic congestion at the port of Dar es Salaam and the inefficiency of the Tazara railroad, the main alternate rail link to the sea at the time. Making matters even worse, the country was gripped by drought and the upcoming crop of maize, the basic staple, was expected to be 300,000 tons short of what was needed to feed its five million people. Already, the Zambian public was badly suffering from acute shortages of such everyday goods as salt, cooking oil, soap, milk, and sometimes even maize. Long lines outside shops had become a common sight and Zambians, particularly the poorer ones, spent hours in them every day just to get enough food to survive. Yet among the first consumer goods to appear on store shelves after the reopening of the border were rows of bottles of wine and whisky selling respectively for $8.00 and $33.00. This was not the only evidence of the government's concern to satisfy first the demands of Zambia's already well-to-do elite. A few months later in May 1979, the government announced a substantial increase in the ceiling on car loans available to its upper-level employees to "ease the life of civil servants" in the midst of the country's worst economic crisis.[1] Instead of 3,600 kwacha ($4,740), the government would provide up to K6,000 ($7,900), or 75 percent of the recipient's annual salary. In addition, the period for repayment was extended from three to five years. Highly generous though it seemed under the prevailing conditions, the announcement met with a howl of disapproval from civil servants who argued that the increase simply were not enough. A few days later, the government dutifully hiked the maximum a bit more.

The same government and parastatal employees who raised such a ruckus over the car loan issue were already housed in pleasant European-style homes and villas for which they paid only a token rent, one among a wide variety of benefits available to them. Their enviable lot stood in sharp contrast to that of the vast majority of Zambians. Half the urban population, including most lower-echelon government employees, lived in "squatter compounds" at the edge of the cities in one- or two-room, sun-dried, mud-brick shanties without water or electricity. The better off were housed in cement block homes of the same size, sometimes with water and electricity but not usually. Transportation, sufficient food for large families and a place in school for their children were the main preoccupation of these lower class urban dwellers. Many took to growing plots of maize and vegetables near their homes just to make ends meet. For all the hardships and shortages of city life, however, residents of the compounds were still far better off than their compatriots living in the countryside, as countless studies confirmed and reconfirmed throughout the 1970s.[2]

A growing gap between rich and poor, the city and the countryside; a stagnating economy as dependent on copper mining today as it was at the time of independence in 1964; a rapidly growing urban population with an insufficient increase in food production to feed it; a mass party specializing in control and demobilization rather than mobilization, and dispensing patronage to the faithful in the best Tammany Hall style; an ideology few took seriously, and a well-cared-for urban elite; such was Zambia fifteen years after its independence—an excellent study in "perverse" African socialism. For all its inequalities, Zambia was not a capitalist country, however. The government, through 113 parastatals grouped under one enormous octopus-like holding company known as *Zimco,* controlled over 80 percent of all economic activity.[3] Kaunda periodically launched tirades against the evils of capitalism and private enterprise, even while pleading for foreign private investment. A leadership code forbade top party and government officials from engaging in business or renting out homes, and a highly progressive income tax took 70 percent of every kwacha earned above 12,000 kwacha ($15,800). Nonetheless, Zambian socialism spawned a well-off and highly secure elite assured of high salaries; subsidized housing; car, house, furniture and even radio loans; free education and medical care; and above all, job tenure. The benefits available to the rest of the population were much more modest. Almost all children were in primary school, but few from rural areas and urban slums could go any higher. Medical care was free for the entire population, but the clinics in the countryside were poorly staffed and supplied as were those in the squatter compounds. There could be no doubt that Zambia had become a welfare state. But the major beneficiary was the upper class.

Perhaps the most polite but nonetheless firm indictment of Zambia-style African socialism came in a 1977 study by the International Labor Office appropriately titled *Narrowing the Gaps.* The figures and findings contained therein sketched a picture of an extremely inequitable society. It found, for instance, that just 2 percent of all Zambian families accounted for 20 percent of the national household income, roughly the same share as that of the poorest 50 percent.[4] Half of all households were estimated as of the period 1972 through 1973 to be living at below the poverty line.[5] Despite a rapid increase in wages since independence, wide disparities had persisted and even gotten worse. The ratio between the lowest wage of workers in industry and the highest salaries of managers and administrators were 1:18–20 while within the civil service the ratio was 1:25. The minimum wage for farm laborers was about half that of unskilled workers in industry.[6] Independent small farmers had also fared poorly because producer prices had been kept very low; in fact, according to the ILO study, they had actually declined in real terms. "Estimates show that between 1964 and 1973, the purchasing power of the typical unit of peasant produce has fallen by 20 percent. In other words, a peasant farmer who responded to party and government calls for higher productivity, and increased his volume of sales of produce by 20 percent, would have been no better off in 1973 than he was in 1964."[7] The study concluded that there was "an urgent need in Zambia to narrow the gaps; gaps between policies and their implementation, between words and action, between rich and poor, between rural and urban areas, and between this (government and party) elite and the mass of the people—mainly rural."[8]

The growing inequalities in Zambia could not even be justified on the grounds of vigorous economic growth. After an initial impressive spurt immediately after independence, the country's economic situation had deteriorated rapidly. An AID study calculated that the growth rate of the Gross Domestic Product in real terms had actually lagged behind that of the population between 1965 and 1975.[9] By the end of the decade, the rate was negative. Agricultural production in particular had been disappointing. In the subsistence sector, output between 1970 and 1977 grew only by about 1 percent a year, not enough to keep pace even with the tiny 1.5 percent increase in the rural population.[10] White commercial farmers even in the late 1970s were still providing the bulk of the food for urban areas. The economic plight of the country at the end of the decade was summed up by its serious indebtedness, well over $1.5 billion; its arrears of $400 to $500 million in payment for imports; and its turning to the International Monetary Fund for a $400 million loan to keep the country afloat.

What had gone wrong? In 1967, President Kaunda had launched what he and other Zambian leaders regarded as a model African socialist revolution aimed at creating a more just and egalitarian society. On the face of it, Kaunda's humanism seemed a perfect example of the African socialist approach. Explaining what it meant to "interpret humanism into action," President Kaunda initially declared back in 1967 that all the government's efforts would be aimed at the "creation of a man-centered society" such as Africans had known in the past. "Our ability to maintain and develop the traditional community based on mutual-aid society principles demand that we recognize the village," he told his countrymen, "as the most important political, economic, social, scientific, and cultural unit for development."[11]

The flourishing of the Zambian "common man" in his "natural" rural setting went to the very heart of humanism. "Humanism in Zambia," he said in elaborating on the country's forthcoming economic development strategy," is a decision in favor of rural areas."[12] An "agrarian revolution" aimed at uplifting the countryside was the heart of this strategy, and the 450,000 small and medium-sized family farms located there were to be the basic units of the country's overall development.

Just how "man-centered" and "cooperative" Zambia's past may have been is a complex and controversial issue which we shall avoid discussing here. But certainly conditions in Zambia in the mid-1960s were far different from the rural-based society of the idealized Zambian past. The country was, and had been increasingly so for several decades, dominated by mining and therefore the cities. Copper alone traditionally accounted for 90 percent of all export earnings and a third or more of the total Gross Domestic Product. The mines, like a powerful magnet, had attracted Zambians to the cities, whose population grew by about 9 percent a year after independence. By the end of the 1970s, nearly 50 percent of all Zambians, the highest proportion anywhere in black Africa, were living in urban areas. Furthermore, mining had accustomed the people to wage jobs to the point where wages and work had become synonymous. For example, many craftsmen and market traders interviewed in the squatter compounds of Lusaka in 1979 declared themselves to be "unemployed" because they were not earning a wage.[13] Such an ethos was hardly conducive to a socialism based on traditional rural values.

The problem was compounded by the fact that Kaunda did not have a clear concept himself of what humanism should mean in practice in a society like Zambia. The policies enacted by the government following his initial 1967 Mulungushi declaration on humanism were more in the nature of *ad hoc* responses to immediate problems than part of any coherent overall plan inspired by his own ideology. They were, in fact, far more influenced by the urban orientation of Zambian society. In this respect, it is instructive to compare the First National Development Plan covering the years 1967 through 1970 and designed before the Mulungushi statement and the Second Plan spanning the years 1972 through 1976 and thus presumably aimed at carrying out Kaunda's humanist revolution. The first one was unabashedly urban-oriented. While it sought to diversify the economy by reducing its dependence on copper, it did so by focusing on construction, services, and manufacturing rather than on agriculture. Infrastructure and transport were allocated over 38 percent of the total investment, industry and mining 21 percent and social services 18 percent, while agriculture received only about 12 percent.[14] The second plan did not change this distribution of resources in any significant way, despite the fact the country was supposedly in the midst of a radical humanistic revolution. Agriculture still only received about 11 percent of the total.[15] It is true that rural areas benefited by some of the investment in infrastructure and social services. Agriculture and the rural sector nevertheless were given low priority. Even in the industrial sector, the pattern of investment was not in keeping with Kaunda's humanist goals. Indeed, the ILO report reprimanded the government for encouraging the growth of a consumer goods industry aimed at a "luxury market" rather than producing basic necessities for Zambians. "Thus we find that Zambia assembles Fiat (and is considering the Fiat-130—even more expensive than the Mercedes it is intended to replace) and Land Rover motor vehicles, but has no plant to manufacture bicycles or hoes."[16] By the end of the 1970s, Zambia had gone ahead to produce both Fiat-132s and Fiat-131s but was just beginning to build its first bicycle assembly plant.

To be sure, there was a whole raft of new programs and institutions set up, or proposed, after Kaunda's call for an "agrarian revolution" to uplift the village and the small peasant family. These included administrative decentralization; village productivity committees; cooperatives; an agricultural extension service; rural service centers; a tractor mechanization program; village regroupment; intensive development zones and rural reconstruction centers. With a disturbing consistency, each proved ineffectual, or even a complete disaster, and left the countryside strewn with the wreckage of nonfunctioning institutions (and tractors) often overlapping each other to create a bewildering mumbo jumbo. It is not possible to present here a comprehensive analysis of all these schemes and institutions, but a brief review of what happened to a few of them is sufficient to provide a general idea of the approach and ensuing problems.

First, there were those programs that were announced but never saw the light of day. Such were the rural service centers first spoken of by Kaunda in his 1968 speech, "Zambia's Guideline for the Next Decade." By 1980, he said, every Zambian peasant should have "easy access" to a "substantial service center" no further than 10 miles from his home.

> At these primary service centers, which on the average I estimate will serve a population of about 10,000, we will aim to provide by 1980 a health center, well-stocked shop, an agricultural depot where there will be implements, an extension office together with some sort of facilities to improve the cultural amenities of the region, a football stadium, a place ... to perform traditional festivities or show films, a local government office. . . .[17]

In 1980, there was not a single such center in operation anywhere in the country, or even planned for that matter. There were, however, village productivity committees. They were supposed to promote agricultural production and peasant participation in rural development, but they had no funds or revenue-producing capability. Furthermore, their authority was unclear and clashed with that of the traditional chiefs who were still officially recognized as the main local government authority. Not surprisingly, these committees either did not function at all or were taken over by village elders and integrated into the very economic and social structure they were supposed to shake up.[18] Fewer than one half of the 25,000 village committees planned had actually been created by October 1977.[19]

The cooperative movement, also launched after the Mulungushi declaration, was initially much more successful, dramatically so in fact. But the accomplishment was short lived. In 1964, there were 220 registered cooperatives. By 1969, the number had mushroomed to 1,114 with over 50,000 members.[20] Many of these cooperatives collapsed soon afterwards, however, leaving behind heaps of unserviceable and often unpaid-for trucks and tractors, huge debts, and a long-lasting suspicion of cooperatives among Zambians. When asked about the state of the movement in 1979, an official in the department of cooperatives declined to give any figures, explaining that very few of those registered in his books were still functioning.[21]

An indirect admission that the Zambian peasantry was not responding spontaneously to Kaunda's call for an agrarian revolution came with the launching of the rural reconstruction centers, in mid-1975, to teach unemployed school dropouts farming skills so that they would be equipped to return to the countryside. The centers were organized and run by the army, with one in each of the country's 53 districts. The results were a national embarrassment. "Many of the recruits who thought the rural reconstruction centers were military camps, deserted; while a few compared them to concentration camps."[22] It was not just the recruits who regarded them as such. Zambian officials discussing the centers on the state-run television service in 1978 also decried their reputation as concentration camps. Conditions were apparently pretty bad, for foreign journalists were never allowed to visit the centers.

It is about as difficult to identify a system embodying the principles of humanism in the political as in the economic sphere. A multiparty state until 1972, Zambia under the Second Republic became a "one-party participatory democracy," a system in theory meant to assure a high level of popular participation while at the same time safeguarding the country's unity. The United National Independence Party (UNIP) was envisaged as a mass party because, as Kaunda himself put it, "the people are the vanguard of the revolution."[23] In practice, UNIP has served as an instrument for control over the population more than one for mobilizing it or assuring its participation in anything other than national elections. This tendency is most obvious in the urban areas where UNIP literally runs the squatter compounds in place of the town or city authorities. Party officials in each township decide, for example, who can live there and who can build a shack; they allocate stalls in the local market, the economic hub of the townships; they maintain law and order and see to it that no other organization springs up to challenge UNIP; and, above all, they make sure the residents buy party cards and go to the polls when told to do so. UNIP plays no similar role in the high income suburbs of the cities, however, and in fact is scarcely visible there, though this is precisely where high party officials mostly live. In the rural areas, UNIP officials and traditional authorities are often the same people, thus assuring the perpetuation of the status quo rather than mobilizing the peasantry for change.

The failure of the party to serve as a catalyst for political and economic mobilization is apparently a longstanding one. Already in the early 1970s, scholars were pointing to UNIP's lack of success in transforming itself from a "vehicle of political liberation" to "an agency of economic development" and noting the total absence of trained party cadres to carry out its assigned tasks in this respect.[24] This statement seemed as valid at the end of the decade as it was at the beginning. During the two years the authors spent in Zambia, the party undertook no national campaigns to mobilize either the peasantry or the townfolk for any task whatsoever. The only burst of activity came at the time of the 1978 presidential and parliamentary elections when UNIP worked extremely hard, and successfully, to get out voters to reconfirm Kaunda as president and just as hard to stamp out the last vestiges of opposition to him within the party. First, UNIP changed its own constitution to make it impossible for any of the other declared presidential candidates to run. Then in the parliamentary elections, the Central Committee banned 28 candidates who had won in the local party primaries but were known as dissenters. Clearly there was little "democracy" in Zambia even within the definition of this term in a one-party system.

The fact that UNIP did not mobilize the population greatly strengthened the statist tendency within Zambia. This trend was probably inevitable given the special character of the Zambian economy as almost a "company country" dominated by the copper mines, which by necessity had to be run by technocrats and bureaucrats in a centralized fashion. Right from the time of independence, the notion prevailed that the economy had to be organized under the control of large parastatals and that the central government was the prime mover of change. Kaunda repeatedly decried this tendency and warned his countrymen that they should not wait for the state to do everything. "Why should the state get more and more involved in activities which individuals or cooperatives could perform at least as well and probably better than the state? As things stand," he told a conference on rural development in 1970, "the state is being obliged to undertake activities which should ideally be left to private initiative."[25] But given UNIP's inability or unwillingness to organize and mobilize Zambians for any purpose other than elections, the state continued to do almost everything. Zambia's one-party participatory democracy was in practice a highly statist system.

Zambia at the end of the 1970s bore little resemblance to the ideal humanistic society Kaunda had envisaged, and he was well aware of this. He blamed the failure on "external forces' such as the drop in world copper prices and the closure of the border with Rhodesia. He also blamed it on the moral shortcomings of Zambians, variously accused of being lazy, drunkards, immoral, and imbued with the spirit of capitalism. "What we have been doing is not humanism—it is capitalism. We have missed the course," he thundered in his famous 1975 Watershed Speech, "Somewhere we have gone wrong. That animal in me, in you, him, or her has been growing—now it is almost uncontrolled."[26]

Kaunda's explanations were not satisfactory. The "external forces" had certainly aggravated Zambia's economic problems but were not the crux of them. The moral shortcomings he cited certainly existed but were hardly exclusive to Zambians. The heart of the Zambian malaise was that the doctrine of humanism never affected the goverment's actual policies and probably could not have because it bore so little relationship to the conditions prevailing in the country. Kaunda refused to see this connection, however, and instead focused on individual conduct as the sole cure of the disease. From his numerous pronouncements, it appeared he viewed humanism more as an ethical stance, a mode of personal behavior, than as a guideline for reorganizing society into socialist structures. Somehow he seemed to expect this reorganization to take place spontaneously once Zambians were converted to humanistic principles. Such an expectation of a spontaneous conversion to socialism was common initially to all the African socialist states. It was disappointed in all, leading to a serious crisis usually within a few years after independence and often to a redirection of policies. In Zambia there was a crisis but no subsequent redirection of policy. Fundamentally, this was due to the fact that it was impossible to translate humanism into concrete action in Zambia; the ideology just did not fit the society and thus could not be used to transform it in the direction humanism pointed. The ideal of the old African community was simply too far removed from the reality. It is difficult to see how Zambia could have been radically transformed into a new socialist society except by dealing first with the most vital, central sector of its economy, the urban one tied to the country's dominant mining interests. It is equally difficult to see how the ideal of the traditional African village community could have ever served as a model for transforming the urban and mining sectors. We are not arguing here that the economic and social conditions of Zambia made radical change impossible. What we would maintain is that the specific interpretation Kaunda gave to socialism was just too far removed from those conditions to help change and remold them along socialist lines. Th end result was the transformation of Zambia by default into a perverse upper class welfare state serving a small elite and presided over by a president relentlessly exhorting his countrymen to behave in a manner to which they were no longer accustomed or motivated to imitate by any concrete rewards.

Tanzania: "Development Without Growth"

It has become fashionable among liberal social scientists to bemoan the Third World phenomenon of "growth without development." This term denotes a situation where the "growth" of a country's Gross National Product does not translate into any significant improvement in the standard of living for the vast majority of the population, most notably those living in the rural areas, and where, therefore, there is not really any "development" in the larger sense. The expression also implies that the economy of a country, although expanding, remains highly dependent on outside financial sources and foreign-owned economic interests and is still thus incapable of self-reliant or self-sustaining growth. The danger of such growth without development is one of the arguments most often used by Western and African radicals to defend the need for socialism in Third World countries. Tanzania has been perhaps the African country that came closest to following a correct "development" strategy, stressing the equal distribution of wealth, the provision of basic needs to the poorest and the goal of national self-reliance. By the end of the 1970s, however, the performance of Tanzania was beginning to raise a lot of serious questions about the viability of Nyerere's approach and whether the Tanzanian strategy was not ironically leading to a situation of "development without growth." While living standards for the bulk of Tanzania's peasant population have improved somewhat due to the government's emphasis on the delivery of social services and the satisfaction of basic human needs, the productive base of the economy has remained weak, growth erratic, and self-reliance a myth. Nyerere's enormous stress on development has led to a serious imbalance between government revenues and expenditures, between the country's mainly agricultural export earnings and its import needs. Furthermore, Tanzania has become extremely dependent on outside, predominantly Western, economic and financial assistance to continue the pursuit of its socialist goals.

Mwenda Pole, a village some 30 miles from Dar es Salaam, is a place to which visitors to Tanzania are often taken.[27] It is a relatively prosperous *ujamaa* village favorably located on a main road and has a population of some 8,000 peasants. To all appearances, it is a comfortable, clean village with a relatively well-supplied cooperative store, a school, a cashew nut storage shed, and a poultry yard. All around the village lie small family plots tucked away under the cashew trees. At the farthest reach of the village land, past all the family fields, lies the communal *ujamaa* farm, a 47-acre expanse of orange trees. The grass under most of the trees had not been cut for many weeks, or months, at the time of our visit. Back in the village, the local secretary of Tanzania's ruling *Chama Cha Mapinduzi* Party explained how Mwenda Pole was saving up the money raised from selling chickens in the capital and the small commission it got from the state for collecting cashew nuts from individual villagers. With that money, he said, the village would buy its first farm-to-market truck, expand the orange plantation, and set up a small canning factory for orange juice. All this sounded admirable enough. But it was 15 years after the village was founded, and its economy was still very much in the pre-take-off stage. As for the communal farm, it had grown in size by exactly 13 acres in 10 years. So far as production was concerned, Mwenda Pole had made no big breakthrough. But the village had its store and its school, its water system where water was piped to public fountains at various points in the village, and a dispensary. As in the rest of Tanzania, development in Mwenda Pole had clearly outrun growth.

Tanzania came to independence as the poor relative of the East African British colonies. Kenya and Uganda had the wealth and infrastructure, the developed settler farms on the highlands and around the lakes, and the big coffee plantations. Tanzania, much less attractive in climate and resources, had very little by way of modern agriculture or British-inspired development projects. The urban population accounted for less than 5 percent of the total and was concentrated in Dar es Salaam, the capital and main port. Most of the 9.5 million Tanzanians lived scattered on isolated homesteads. Of the estimated 2.5 million farms, 83 percent were less than five acres in size and 97 percent less than 12 acres, while European settlers had taken only 1 percent of the land.[28] Agriculture accounted for 47 percent of the Gross National Product, while the infant industrial sector provided just 7 percent.[29] It is with these concrete conditions in mind that Nyerere's rural development strategy of *ujamaa,* launched with the Arusha Declaration in 1967, must be understood. In this context, it can be seen not simply as a nostalgic hankering after a utopian past but as an attempt to tackle some of the country's pressing problems while taking into account the concrete conditions existing at the time. Different approaches were certainly possible but that is not the point we wish to underline here. What was important and remains so is that *ujamaa* bore a fairly close relationship to reality. When Nyerere asserted, as he did in the Arusha Declaration, that it was a mistake to think development begins with industries, he was simply acknowledging what he had and didn't have to work with. Nyerere's *ujamaa* fit the conditions of peasant Tanzania, much more so than Kaunda's humanism fit the copper and urban-oriented society of Zambia.

The ideology of *ujamaa* translated into a series of policies: nationalization of banks and major industries to strengthen the government's control over the economy; lack of encouragement for private enterprise and later the adoption of a "leadership code" which directly forbade party and government officials to engage in business; a reform of the educational system to expand it greatly at the elementary level; and above all, the *ujamaa* village policy. This last policy had several goals. Minimally, it was an attempt to bring peasants together in villages so that it might become possible to provide them with schools, clinics, and clean water. More ambitiously, it was an attempt to prevent the spread of excessive individualism and of capitalism among the peasants, so that development would not result in the enrichment of a few and the impoverishment of the many. Finally, it was also an attempt to spur productivity by encouraging the peasants to cultivate together. All this was to be accomplished, declared Nyerere, through persuasion and not through coercion.

By late 1973, persuasion had failed to bring about any spontaneous resettlement of peasants on a large scale. A mere 18 percent of the rural population was in villages by that time.[30] The government's initial efforts to attract them by setting up 22 model *ujamaa* villages, well supplied with sevices, had only succeeded in creating unrealistic expectations of what help the state was ready to provide. Abandoning the idea of noncoercion, Nyerere abruptly set 1976 as a target date for completing the villagization, or *vijijini,* campaign and even defended the use of force. The amount of coercion used by party officials anxious to show their accomplishments varied from place to place. In some cases, people moved easily; in others, they moved only after the army or local militias burned down their huts and loaded their belongings into trucks. Most of the resettlement involved short moves, since the objective was only to regroup peasants into villages, not to redistribute the population on the national territory. A massive four to six million people were resettled in 1974 alone, despite the fact that the country, caught in the middle of a devastating drought, was facing a serious food shortage.[31] With the help of normal rainfall in the following years, the villagization program was completed without disastrous repercussions on food production. Some 8,200 villages were thus created. With this task accomplished, Nyerere once again reverted to a less coercive approach to socialism. The villages were not pushed to collectivize, but were allowed to move at their own pace toward communal farming, while the government concentrated on delivering services to the rural population. Further elaborating on his approach the Tanzanian president told the authors in an interview in early 1979 that what mattered was not the collective cultivation of traditional subsistence crops such as cassava but that of cash crops, so as to prevent the growth of a "kulak class" and capitalism generally. As a result, the pace of collectivization has been extremely slow. When the government began carrying out a census of all villages in 1978, formally registering as *ujamaa* villages only those where 50 percent or more of all economic activity was collective, only two of the 8,200 met this requirement.[32]

The results of the *ujamaa* policy so far have thus been less than spectacular, as Nyerere himself has admitted in a candid analysis published in 1977 and entitled "The Arusha Declaration Ten Years After." He began by noting that he had thought originally that it would take Tanzania 30 years to become a socialist country, but added: "I was wrong. I am sure that it will take us much longer." "Ten years ago after the Arusha Declaration," he said, "Tanzania is certainly neither socialist nor self-reliant."[33] He went on to enumerate the country's various economic and political failings and acknowledged its continuing dependence on outside nations, "upon economic and political decisions taken by other peoples without our participation or consent."[34] But he also argued that Tanzania had succeeded in stopping the drift toward a class society, in establishing "some of the attitudes which are necessary to the development of socialism as well as some of the required institutions, and in making "reasonably good progress" toward providing the entire population with services. "We are learning to take pride in the extension of basic public facilities to the mass of our people rather than in grandiose public buildings or the evidence of personal prosperity for a few."[35]

While taking enormous pride in the strides made in extending basic services to the countryside, Nyerere was frank to admit that the "growth" in the economy had been disappointing and warned that the country would have to "produce more wealth" if the government was to continue its rural-oriented policies. "It is as true now as it was in 1967 that the calf can only suck the amount of milk which its mother produces."[36] He said that the growth of the economy before the implementation of his *ujamaa* program had actually surpassed that following it, and that there had been only "a negligible real improvement in the per capita standard of living. The improved living standards of the majority of Tanzanians comes from better distribution of what we do produce more than from an increase in the amount of production."[37]

Nyerere's own frank assessment of the situation is amply supported by the evidence provided in numerous economic studies. It should be remembered that Tanzania is one of Africa's, and the world's, poorest countries and that no government could have worked dramatic changes in just ten years. Still, the rate of economic growth has been disappointingly low. By Nyerere's own account, the per capita growth rate in real terms averaged only 1.4 percent between 1967 and 1975 taking account of the population increase of 2.8 percent a year.[38] Other accounts studying the 1970 to 1977 period estimated the growth rate in per capita GDP to be just slightly higher, 1.9 percent.[39] The performance of the agricultural sector was perhaps most disturbing. UN Economic Commission for Africa data showed the average annual growth rate to be only 3.5 percent between 1970 and 1977, only marginally greater than the population increase.[40] Particularly worrisome was the drop in production of cash crops for export, the basic source of the nation's foreign exchange earnings. While the value of Tanzania's agricultural exports increased by 12.7 percent over the 1970 through 1977 period, this was only because of the sharp increase in world prices.[41] The export volume of four major commodities—cotton lint, cashew nuts, sisal, and pyrethrum—actually decreased by 40 percent during this time.[42] Moreover, the increase in the value of exports did not offset that in the cost of imports, resulting in a deterioration of the country's balance of trade.

The poor performance of the agricultural sector, particularly the failure of the *ujamaa* villages to meet the urban demand, has led Tanzania to seek a solution in the creation of state farms and ranches. Ministry of Agriculture officials see such farms as basically the answer to feeding the cities while the villages satisfy their own needs.[43] With the help of foreign donors, including the World Bank and Canada, Tanzania in 1979 was investing tens of millions of dollars to establish a nationwide network of state farms to produce wheat, maize, and rice and to raise dairy cattle and chickens. This assumption, that the state can succeed where the peasants have failed, is common to most African socialist countries; whether it is warranted or not is another matter. In Tanzania, where the state has come to dominate the industrial sector, the performance of the 316 parastatals has not been impressive. It is true that industrial production has averaged a seemingly healthy 7.8 percent growth rate per year between 1964 and 1975.[44] But economists regard this as a relatively poor return given the fact the government invested over 20 percent of its Gross Domestic Product over most of this period.[45] Management of the parastatals is notoriously poor, to the point where many have not even kept their books in proper order. Overemployment is rife. Nyerere himself has decried the failure of the parastatals to generate sufficient profits—6.5 percent of gross sales between 1967 and 1974—to finance more than 20 percent of new investment. "The fact is that we have been, and still are, grossly inefficient in our factories and workshops," he remarked.[46] He also noted that output per worker had actually fallen despite the enormous increase in capital investment.

If "growth" has been disappointing in Tanzania, "development" has been considerably more successful, although the picture is somewhat mixed even here. The government did succeed in preventing the growth of income inequality and actually reduced it in the state-controlled sector of the economy. The ratio between the lowest and highest government salaries, for instance, shrank from 20:1 in 1967 to 9:1 after taxes in 1976.[47] Another relative success was the government's ability to keep the difference between rural and urban incomes from growing even wider, an unusual accomplishment for a developing African country. On the other hand, studies showed that there has been very little improvement in the real income of poor peasant households.[48] What the figures on various income levels in Tanzania tend to demonstrate is that the government has been among the most successful in Africa in preventing the growth of a well-off privileged elite and in narrowing the income gap. But whether this greater overall social justice and equality is sufficient compensation for the lack of any improvement in the income of the poorest Tanzanian peasants remains a thorny question.

The most positive aspect of the Tanzanian development strategy has been the improvement in government services aimed at satisfying basic needs for education, health, and clean water at the village level. The effort has been remarkable and widely acknowledged as such by the international community. By the end of the 1970s, Tanzania had virtually achieved universal primary education, several years ahead of the initial target, and had enrolled five million adults in literacy classes. One of the adverse consequences of this crash campaign, however, was the drop in the quality of education as hastily trained teachers were sent to makeshift schools without an adequate supply of books and other materials. The results of the drive to extend health services to the rural poor were very similar. The government made a major and successful effort to channel health care away from urban hospitals serving a privileged minority and to rural clinics instead. According to Nyerere, the number of rural health centers increased from 42 in 1967 to 152 in 1976. (The number had increased to 181 a year later.) There were 610 more maternal and child-care clinics in 1976 than a decade earlier, while the number of rural medical aids had increased 200 percent and that of medical assistants 270 percent.⁴⁹ But the government's capacity to keep these clinics functioning properly was still quite limited in the late 1970s. For instance, it was not unusual for vaccines to spoil before inoculations could be given because of the lack of refrigerated depots in the rural areas. Another incident that raised questions about the rural health services was the major cholera epidemic that hit Tanzania in 1977 and lasted well into 1978, forcing a ban on all travel out of the capital for months. Despite this and other strict measures, the government was extremely slow in bringing the epidemic under control and thousands died.

The campaign to provide clean water to all villagers ran into major financial and mechanical problems almost from the beginning. By 1976, three million of Tanzania's thirteen million people living in the rural areas had access to clean water, according to Nyerere, and the government was working to meet a 1991 deadline to provide the entire rural population with the service. But the scheme was providing horrendously expensive and maintenance a serious problem. The cost of the entire project, according to a World Bank study, would reach $400 million (at 1976 prices), a figure representing almost 25 percent of all capital investment planned for the third five-year plan.⁵⁰ In addition, a large number of the existing water systems, in some areas up to 75 percent, were not functioning because of technical breakdown or lack of interest among the villagers themselves to keep them operating.⁵¹ Nyerere himself cited the enormous problem encountered in trying to keep village pumps operating and admitted that in some instances the peasants were worse off then before because the old wells had been sealed off in the name of hygiene.⁵²

What then has been the overall effect of the Tanzanian concentration on "development"? There can be little doubt that it has resulted in a redistributive bias in favor of the rural areas. But Tanzania's "great leap forward" in development has created new problems and raised new questions about the wisdom of its approach. The two major ones are the impact of the emphasis on social services on the political system and the economic viability of the whole enterprise. Development in Tanzania has come to mean the delivery of services by the state to the people, and villagization has only increased the pressure for this. It is the state that staffs the clinics and schools, provides the medicine and books, and installs and repairs the pumps. Maybe it could not be otherwise. But these services have tended to be the major improvements in the life of the villagers. Thus, the major agent for change has been the state, not the people through their own efforts as originally foreseen in the *ujamaa* doctrine. Not surprisingly, popular participation has been low, as long argued by radical critics of Tanzania and substantiated by a recent study of the *ujamaa* villages.⁵³ Contrary to the popular image, there is a far stronger statist than participatory tendency afoot in Tanzania, a trend that has served to weaken considerably the party vis-a-vis the government bureaucracy. What the study cited above found was that while the party remained a "mass" one of three million members, or 25 percent of the total population in 1970, it was being steadily infiltrated and dominated by civil servants, and decision making was concentrated within the higher levels of its bureaucracy.[54]

The second question concerns Tanzania's ability to continue financing its ever-expanding public services while the productive base of the economy lags behind. By 1975, the growth rate in expenditures on public administration and services was more than three times that of the Gross Domestic Product, 15.3 percent compared to 4.6 percent.[55] The deficit in the government budget for combined recurrent and development expenditures grew from 800 million shillings (around $100 million) in the period 1970 to 1971 to 2.5 billion ($360 million) in the period 1976 to 1977.[56]

How has Tanzania managed to sustain this growing imbalance for so long without encountering a major crisis earlier? The answer is as simple as it is troubling for a country propounding an ideology of self-reliance: foreign aid. Thanks to Nyerere's personal charm and his obvious serious commitment to fulfilling the basic human needs of his countrymen, Tanzania has been able to attract enormous amounts of foreign grants and low-interest loans. This assistance grew steadily from about $25 million in the period 1967 through 1968 to more than $450 million a year in the late 1970s. During the first five-year development plan, foreign assistance has accounted for 30 percent of capital expenditures. The figure increased to 50 percent in the second plan.[57] By 1976 through 1977, foreign loans and grants covered 67 percent of total government spending,[58] and by the end of the decade, foreign donors were seriously debating whether they should shift part of their assistance from launching new projects to financing the recurring costs of old ones. Tanzania, in other words, had received gifts it could not afford.

The crisis which had been brewing for years was finally precipitated by the war with Uganda in the years 1978 and 1979. Forty thousand Tanzanian troops were mobilized and sent into the neighboring country to topple the bloody dictatorship of Idi Amin in April 1979. Following the war, Tanzania appealed to foreign donors for $375 million in additional loans to help it defray the $500 million cost of the confrontation with Uganda. A few countries, like Sweden and Holland, provided some additional help but scarcely enough to fill the gap, and Tanzania found itself obliged to turn to the International Monetary Fund for a major loan. The IMF made it clear, however, that before it would provide any additional assistance, Tanzania would have to scale down some of its development projects, slow down others, and simply forego a few grandiose ones, like the steel mill complex it was planning, until its finances were back in order. As Nyerere interpreted these conditions, they amounted to gross IMF interference in Tanzania's domestic policies and an attempt to force him to abandon the emphasis on rural services so central to his own *ujamaa* strategy. He refused. At the time of this writing, it was not clear what the outcome of the conflict with the IMF would be, but there could be little doubt that Tanzania was facing a full scale crisis in its whole "development" strategy.

Tanzanian socialism has so far not lived up to expectations. What was supposed to be a highly decentralized village-based, participatory and self-reliant system has turned into an extremely dependent one marked by a low level of participation and incipient statism. After a decade of effort, there were only two official *ujamaa* villages, and the peasants were showing remarkably little enthusiasm for collectivization or mobilization. We argued that in Zambia the statist tendency stemmed fundamentally from the lack of "fit" between the existing conditions, ideology, and policies. This was not the case in Tanzania. There, the fit between the ideology of *ujamaa* and prevailing conditions was very good, and the policies pursued were congruent with the other two for the most part. The problem was that the conditions existing in the country at the time of independence were not such as to provoke widespread demand for radical change among the peasants. They had neither lost a large portion of their land to white settlers nor were being exploited ruthlessly by Tanzanian landlords. As a result, an ideology and policy that called upon them to take the initiative evoked little response. This inevitably led to the state taking over as the agent of change with the consequences we have discussed.

Guinea—"Politics in Command"

> If for some, politics is the art of playing, of deceiving, and of using other people, we do not view it in the same light. We define politics for our part as the science from which all other science originates, as essentially the capacity of making possible what is necessary for the people.[59]

Nothing could sum up more eloquently the Guinean approach to socialism than this statement by Sékou Touré himself. From 1958, the year Guinea became the first of the French African colonies to gain its independence, until the present time, Touré has counted on politics to make what he regards as "necessary" become "possible." The result of such total dependence upon politics has been a nearly total economic disaster for the country and the flight of two million Guineans, more than one third of the total population, to neighboring countries.[60] The most sympathetic analysts credit Touré with having built possibly the most effective party anywhere in black Africa, albeit at the expense of the country's economy. His sharpest critics denigrate his rule as amounting to little more than "Banana Stalinism" or "Stalinism minus economic development." In 22 years of socialist endeavor, Guinea has become famous as the land of the "permanent conspiracy" aimed at overthrowing its own leadership and of "hyperpoliticization" as the result of Touré's endless Maoist-inspired efforts at mass mobilization. At the same time, it stands out as a classic example of a horribly mismanaged African economy: growth has lagged behind the population increase; agriculture has slipped backward toward the subsistence level; and the country's main source of wealth, the world's largest bauxite deposits, has come to be exploited primarily by foreign multinational corporations. Although trucking with the capitalist devil abroad, Touré has done everything in his power to curb and even stamp out capitalism at home, including the step, unprecedented in Africa, of imposing a total ban on retail trade for nearly a decade. While preaching a doctrine of self-reliance, Touré had by 1977 allowed Guinea's foreign debt to reach such gigantic proportions that it just about equalled its Gross Domestic Product of $1.1 billion.[61]

The explanation of how Guinea, a country with enormous agricultural potential and French West Africa's richest mineral wealth, got to this state of affairs has to include considerations of several factors: Touré himself; the conditions under which Guinea reached independence; the ideology he has elaborated over the past 20 years, and above all, the difficulties he has encountered in translating that ideology into effective policies. In a sense, the tragedy of Guinea stems from Touré's attempt, and failure, to solve a crucial problem affecting many African attempts at socialist transformation, namely the lack of a built-in tension in the society and the difficulty of bringing about radical change without one.

Since before Guinea's independence in 1958, Touré has been the sole pivot of his country's politics, even more so than, say, Fidel Castro in Cuba, whom he preceeded to power by a few months. To use a trite political expression, he is the prototype of the charismatic leader. Not only the state, but the Guinean nation, is Touré. Officially, he is referred to as Guinea's "Great Elephant" or even "Messiah." With almost religious fervor, he has relentlessly imposed upon Guineans his own personal vision of society and the world, immortalized in tome after tome of his speeches and writings. The official organ of the *Parti Démocratique de Guinée* (PDG), known as *Horoya,* prints little else than the word of Touré. Virtually every decision of even the slightest consequence is made by Touré himself, from the twists and turns in economic and political policy to such minute administrative details as the approval of personnel changes and the issuance of visas to those wanting to go abroad. Despite this obsessive concentration of power in his own hands, Touré has worked harder and longer than any other African leader to build a party that would become the dominant political institution of the land and wield more effective, day-to-day power than the state. The end result has been a party that serves primarily as a direct extension of Touré himself rather than as a self-perpetuating body serving to institutionalize the revolution.

Touré started his political career as a labor organizer within the French Communist-dominated *Confederation Générale du Travail* and by 1950 he was responsible for all CGT branches in French West Africa. With an education in Marxist ideology and Communist organizing techniques, he was inclined from the beginning to think in terms of global solutions and structural change rather than piecemeal reforms. But he did not accept Marxism in its entirety and eclectically applied those principles which fitted the Guinean political and social reality or served his purpose. Until the mid-1960s he doubted the applicability of the concept of class struggle to African societies, as we have already seen, and he never rejected Islam even in his most radical Maoist phase. He was furthermore concerned, like many African intellectuals, with the problem of discovering and preserving an authentic African culture and personality. Nevertheless, his ideological approach showed time and again his attempt to adapt Marxism to African and Guinean realities rather than to pursue a romanticized vision of some primitive African communalism.

The historical conditions under which Guinea acceded to independence also served to favor radical solutions. While Guinea did not fight an armed liberation struggle, it broke suddenly with France by opting for immediate independence in 1958 rather than accepting President de Gaulle's proposal for a federation of France's West African colonies in a community still closely tied to the colonial power. Infuriated by Touré's cheek, de Gaulle cut all of France's ties with Guinea and tried to force its collapse by withdrawing all 3,000 technical assistants, financial aid, and all other forms of help. Even telephones were ripped out of the walls by departing French personnel. Thus, Guinea started its independence in the midst of a massive disruption and with few cadres of its own to take over from the departing French. It was a struggle for survival that lent itself to radical decisions and helped Touré to keep his people mobilized behind him initially.

Despite the circumstances of independence and Touré's own natural radical inclinations, the concrete domestic policies he initially followed were not noticeably original or even unusually radical for a socialist-oriented country. They were characterized by nationalization or forced closure of French companies in the modern sector of the economy; the establishment of state monopolies over banking, insurance, exports, imports, and transportation; a consolidation of the party's rule throughout the country; and, above all, the mobilization of all Guineans in the name of self-reliance and rural development. The essence of this initial strategy was the program known as *"Investissement humain,"* self-help projects carried out at the village level on a collective basis to improve the everyday lot of the peasant. Initially, this approach to socialism was enormously successful. Under the direction of the party, Guinean peasants en masse undertook thousands of self-help community projects during the first two years after independence. They built roads, schools, and clinics, erected new mosques and public buildings, and planted acres of new rice fields and trees. Then problems began to set in. Schools and clinics remained unstaffed and ill-equipped because the government had neither personnel nor money to operate them. Hastily constructed roads were washed away in the first rainy season. Collective fields were left unattended or unharvested as the peasants concentrated their efforts on their private plots first so that they would be certain at least of enough food in the midst of the national crisis. Finally, party and government officials turned to using forced labor to keep the program going and concentrated on putting up buildings for themselves, sometimes even their own homes, rather than carrying out projects that would directly benefit the participants. By the early 1960s, this human investment strategy had run out of steam and Touré was rethinking his policies. Such revision was given added impetus by growing opposition to his policies from the country's traders and entrepreneurs and, most disturbingly, from within the ranks of the government and civil service.

Space does not permit a detailed account of Touré's herculean efforts to build the party into an effective ruling instrument and to find some means for the sustained mobilization of his people. He experimented with an enormous variety of institutions in his painful search for an overall system which would embody his vision of socialism. He repeatedly changed his concept of the PDG, envisaging it first as a mass organization, then as a vanguard one, than again as a party of 'all the people,' and finally as a "party-state." With a population of about three million people, Guinea had 1.8 million party members in 1961.[62] It was an amorphous, all-inclusive body, indistinguishable from the entire nation. Beginning in 1967, Touré began talking about the need for converting the PDG into a "vanguard" party, or at least creating a vanguard within it. He placed enormous stress on ideological education in the vastly expanded school system in hopes of producing socialist-thinking Guineans, and he also opened a party school to train and indoctrinate cadres. At the same time, he turned from a voluntaristic approach to mobilization to a more militaristic one, creating a number of corps and auxiliary bodies to ensure the involvement of Guineans in the revolution. These included the party youth wing, called Revolutionary Democratic African Youth Movement (JRDA), the Pioneers, the *service civique,* the production brigades, and a militia. He put the army to work building roads and running farms and factories, and enrolled women through their own organization in similar nation-building tasks. For the workers, there were "management committees" and "improvement committees" through which they were to participate in the running of state companies. He experimented with so-called *chantiers de la révolution,* "revolutionary work projects," set up *Collèges d'Enseignement Rural* and *Centres d'Education Révolutionaire* to raise the political consciousness of the youth, created cooperatives and communal farms to increase production, and launched a "cultural revolution" inspired by China. Virtually every Chinese and Soviet technique and institution for mobilizing people was tried in one guise or another in Guinea, and abandoned as soon as it failed.

The problem Touré was trying to overcome through this plethora of institutions was that of creating some dynamism in Guinean society to arouse the peasants to accept, and seek, change. Initially, such tension had arisen from the struggle to obtain independence from France and then to survive after the abrupt break with the former colonial power. But it wore off as time passed and the crisis subsided. Otherwise, there was very little natural dynamism in the existing social and economic conditions. Like Tanzania,

Guinea was basically a country of small independent farmers and pastoralists, poor but not oppressed by exploitation. There is no indication that revolution was a widely felt need. Touré's objective was to artificially produce such a need, and the various schemes he experimented with were part of this strategy. His perennial announcements of a "plot" or foreign-supported "conspiracy" to overthrow the revolution, and himself, were used at least in part for the same purpose. So, too, was his periodic promotion of class struggle throughout the country.

Central to Touré's efforts to instigate a revolution was the party. His concept of the party, however, changed repeatedly in response to the problems he encountered and his perception of his society. When he saw it as classless, he opted for a mass party. When the existence of a widespread opposition convinced him there were classes in Guinea, after all, he turned to a vanguard party. When persistent dissatisfaction with his rule among civil servants continued, he decided the struggle was between the people and the bureaucratic elite and invented the party-state. He was constantly castigating state officials for "seizing effective leadership" of local party institutions and "subordinating party activities to the administrative power."[63] He carried out extensive and repeated purges of state and even party officials he regarded as "counterrevolutionary," earning in the process the reputation of being an African Stalin. The International League for Human Rights, for instance, called upon the United Nations in 1977 to investigate what it called the "reign of terror" and "massive violation of human rights" in Guinea, documenting in a 300-page report the death, disappearance, or imprisonment of around 1,000 Guineans, including two former Guinean ambassadors to the world body, the first secretary-general of the Organization of African Unity, and more than twenty government ministers. Other groups alleged there were between 3,000 and 15,000 political prisoners in the country.[64] Paradoxically, the final outcome of Touré's unrelenting struggle against the state was a plan for its total merger with the party.

His "party-state," which he boasted was a completely new concept, appears in fact to be simply a version of the old Marxist dream of the withering away of the state. As he defined it at one point, the party-state meant the following: "At first, the people commanded the party and the party controlled the state. Now the party has become identical to the state or is the state."[65] The idea of a party-state first surfaced with the announcement of a cultural revolution in August 1968. The lynchpin of the new system was to be a village- and neighborhood-level institution called the *Pouvoir Révolutionaire Local* (PRL). This was essentially a local assembly of the entire population, run by committees, whose members were elected from among party-picked candidates. The PRLs were supposed to perform virtually all administrative tasks as well as some judiciary ones, mobilize the people through voluntary labor, ensure local security, and spur development generally. Each PRL had its own 100-person militia and a production brigade used to cultivate the village collective field. These new revolutionary bodies were organized very slowly with a major effort coming only in the mid-1970s. By 1978, they reportedly numbered around 2,500, each controlling a population of between 1,500 and 2,000.[66] The PRLs were an impressive attempt to institutionalize a system of local democracy that allowed villagers to decide and take care of all local affairs and even part of the national one of defense. With a meeting every week and a number of corps like the militia and production brigades involving the peasants in all aspects of daily life, the PRLs created the potential for a high degree of grassroots participation. Whether they were working any better than the myriad of other local institutions Touré has experimented with remains unclear in the absence of any detailed study. Equally uncertain was whether in the long run the new party-state would end in the triumph of the party over the state or in the demise of the party. According to one study, the PDG was heavily staffed by civil servants "detached" from their state duties; at the intermediate section and regional levels 70 percent of party officials were civil servants.[67] Whether these individuals regarded themselves first and foremost as "party" or "state" officials is not known.

Despite the numerous caveats one feels compelled to make in judging the party-state, it seems the party has evolved into a very effective instrument of personal rule with a fairly effective organizational structure. Perhaps the most obvious indicator of its success is the fact it has kept Touré in power 22 years despite innumerable attempts to unseat him. One former U.S. ambassador to Guinea, somewhat overawed by what he witnessed there, compared Touré to a spider sitting at the center of a vast web, the PDG, covering the entire country, from which he could pull the appropriate string in order to reach the most remote village instantaneously.[68] The web enabled Touré to turn out crowds for visiting dignitaries at a moment's notice and mobilize his supporters for the defense of the country and himself. But it is much less clear that the party even today can mobilize Guineans on a sustained basis for either "development" or economic "growth." Touré even rejects the notion that economic performance is a criterion by which to judge his revolution, stressing instead such values as solidarity, nationhood, political consciousness, and even cleanliness. From the late 1960s until a revolt of the market mammies in August 1977, Touré amply demonstrated this disdain for economics by forbidding the functioning of an internal market system to the point where there was practically nothing to buy in the capital city of Conakry. Touré's attitude toward economics is summed up in his oft-repeated comment that Guinea must "build its economy to suit its politics and not its politics to suit its economy."[69] In practice, it has done neither. The two have become almost divorced from each other and the attempts to harness politics for any economic or even social development purposes have been abortive. Although endowed with agricultural resources and initially with sizeable export crops of coffee, bananas, palm oil and pineapples, Guinea has slipped back almost totally to subsistence level, struggling to produce enough to feed itself and exporting little. In the case of some crops, like bananas and coffee, production has fallen to a quarter or less of its preindependence level, when Guinea was Africa's leading banana exporter. According to the government's rare statistics, the index of per capita food production dropped from 110 in 1964 to 86 in 1972, despite the enormous political emphasis Touré has put on the rural sector.[70] None of his schemes, including the production brigades established at the village level and a subsequent system of state-run farms, has succeeded in overcoming the agricultural production crisis.

The economic survival of the country hinges as a result on its vast bauxite deposits and on the foreign corporations exploiting them. Stridently anti-capitalist in his domestic policy, Guinea turned unabashedly to the world's giant multinationals, many of them American, to develop the mining sector and entered into joint ventures with them generally as a minority partner. Until the early 1970s, Guinea had practically no control over their operations and received remarkably little in terms of either government revenue or foreign exchange. The situation did not change substantially even after Guinea gained a 49 percent interest in two mining consortia, the *Compagnie de Bauxite de Guinée* (CBG) and FRIGURIA, and totally owned a third, the *Office de Bauxite de Kindia* (OBK). The world's largest exporter of bauxite with more than ten million tons annually, Guinea in 1979 only received $75 million back in revenues because of the unfavorable terms of the agreements.[71] The accord reached by Guinea with the Western consortia confirmed the darkest radical contentions about international capitalist exploitation of the Third World. The deal that Touré struck with the Soviet Union over the Kindia mine was hardly more favorable, however. Guinea was in theory entitled to two thirds of the profits from both CBG and FRIGURIA, but the books were manipulated in such a way that neither had any.[72] Moreover, the Guinean government itself was entitled to only 10 percent of their production. In its partnership with the Soviets in OBK, Guinea had to guarantee delivery to the Soviet Union of 90 percent of the production for 30 years and sell the bauxite at well below the world price, only 60 percent of it in 1978.[73]

The economic future of Guinea was increasingly tied to the exploitation of its mineral resources at the end of the decade. There were three other large bauxite schemes in the works, one huge iron ore mining project costing $800 million and expected to produce 15 million tons a year, and several diamond and uranium ventures. (Guinea's iron ore reserves had proven to be enormous, estimated at 600 million tons at least). Yet, there was little evidence Touré was coming to terms with the implications of this dependency on minerals. He continued to act as if these huge mining complexes sprouting up inside the country could be sealed off from the rest of the economy and their social, economic, and political consequences totally avoided. He had tried neither to harness this mineral wealth to industrial development nor to plow its dividends back into the agricultural sector. Industry still accounted, as it had a decade earlier, for only about 4 to 5 percent of the Gross Domestic Product. As for the agricultural sector, the amount of money invested in it under three different development plans spanning the years from 1960 to 1978 steadily decreased from 11 to 5 percent of the total.[74] Paradoxically, the little that was being devoted to agriculture was as much in contradiction with Touré's philosophy as was the growing reliance on mining. Faced with the continuing failure of the various rural development schemes to boost production, Guinea was setting up 200 state farms around the country.

The most recent trends in Guinea—the merging of party and state, the growing reliance on mining, and the creation of state farms—all point to the onset of a by now familiar phenomenon: statism. And yet no African leader has worked harder than Touré to prevent just such a trend by insisting that politics take command. He did set up local institutions making direct participation possible. This did not result in any significant change in the economic realm, however. As in the case of Tanzania, peasants left to their own devices did not opt enthusiastically for economic development through collectivization, but continued to cultivate for the most part as they had always done—only somewhat worse since Touré's anticapitalist efforts destroyed any incentive to produce for the market. "Politics in command" ravaged the economy. For all his Marxist inclinations, Touré never learned that any political system must have a sound economic base to survive and that economics cannot be totally divorced from politics. Touré saw socialism as "necessary" for his people and relied wholly on politics to make it possible. The lesson from the Guinean experience is that such a path to socialism is more likely to lead to disaster.

Algeria—"Economics in Command"

> The high and rapidly growing levels of centrally planned public investments have provided the principal stimulant for economic growth in Algeria. Following the sharp increases in oil prices in 1974, projected public investments have suddenly increased by 61.6 percent in 1975 and have continued to increase by 36.5 percent a year in the following three years. Reflecting this change, the ratio between gross fixed capital formation and GNP passed from 43.1 percent in 1974 to 48.1 in 1977.[75]

The technical language and cold figures of an IMF report provide perhaps the best introduction to the nature of Algerian socialism at the end of 1970s. When discussing socialism in Algeria, in fact, one must talk first and foremost of a strategy for economic growth and for attaining economic independence. Only secondarily can one talk of ideology and political mobilization.

Algerian socialism must be understood at least in part against the background of the country's wealth. While undoubtedly underdeveloped, as an oil-producing country, Algeria enjoys a very high revenue, particularly since 1974, so that it can devote billions rather than just millions of dollars to investment. With a population of 17 million, Algeria in 1978 had a GDP of $24.6 billion and a per capita income of $1,374. By contrast, Tanzania, with a similar population (16 million), had a GDP of $3.1 billion and a per capita income of $198 in 1977.[76] Algeria's economic strategy centers on the development of "industrializing industries," or heavy industries in turn generating the impetus for the growth of secondary ones. The basic concept of using the country's oil and gas revenues to build the basis for a self-sustaining process of economic growth is well summarized in the Algerian slogan "to plant oil so as to reap industry." The ultimate goal is to free Algeria from its dependency on the industrialized capitalist countries, and in order to attain it, the leadership is willing to pay an enormous price in terms of economic imbalances and risks. The social and political costs of the policy have been high: a centralized, bureaucratic system, the development of a technocratic elite, the accentuation of income inequality and regional imbalances as the standard of living in the industrialized cities grows much faster than in the rural areas. Algeria has been accused by radicals of betraying socialism by being blind to the political implications of its economic policies. It has also been accused by more moderate critics of risking disaster by being blind to the economic implications of its drive for independence from the industrialized world. In reality, the Algerian leadership has not been blind at all to either; it has made a quite deliberate and acknowledged choice in a huge gamble that its strategy will pay off in the long run by creating the basis for a successful model of socialist development.

Algerian socialism did not being with its present statist character; it only took this on after a coup in June 1965, which put an end to the initial participatory and voluntaristic approach of President Ahmed Ben Bella. At independence in 1962, Algeria faced a chaotic situation, even worse than the one Guinea had gone through in 1958 and Angola and Mozambique were to experience later. One million French settlers poured out of the country in the course of a few months, leaving behind thousands of farms and factories paralyzed by lack of qualified manpower as well as by outright sabotage. Socialism emerged from this chaos in the form of self-management, originally a spontaneous effort by the workers to run the abandoned enterprises in order to save their jobs and means of livelihood. While initially the choice of self-management had not been a deliberate one reflecting a specific concept of socialism, Ben Bella within a few months seized upon the approach, codified self-management into the 1963 March Decrees, and gave it an ideological base. By the end of that year, over five million acres of the best farm land and some 450 industrial enterprises were under the new system of worker control.[77]

By necessity more than by choice, Algerian socialism started out by being a highly participatory system. Not only were the workers involved in the management of the enterprises they worked for, but the entire population was called upon to participate through the party and other mass organizations and by offering volunteer labor for all sorts of endeavors, from literacy campaigns to reforestation. As in most African countries which chose socialism, participation was initially high and spontaneous, yet it accomplished little in the long run because it was so poorly organized and directed. A major problem in Algeria was the weakness of the party. The *Frot de Libération Nationale* (FLN) had the greatest difficulty after independence in reorganizing itself and redefining its role. A coalition of diverse groups tenuously held together during the war, the FLN had to make a controversial political choice about socialism after 1962. Different groups contended for the leadership. The membership was not only socially and ideologically heterogeneous, but it had been swollen just before and after independence by a variety of opportunists jumping on the bandwagon. Ben Bella's efforts to reorganize the FLN as a vanguard party with a quasi-Marxist line had not come to fruition when the army finally overthrew him in June 1965 and Colonel Houari Boumédiène took over as president. The early period of Algerian socialism thus fell into the same pattern we have observed in all the other countries discussed so far: revolution by fiat of the leadership and the spontaneous efforts and good will of the people. The statist tendency which developed covertly in these countries in response to the failure of such a voluntaristic approach was openly heralded in Algeria by the June coup.

Boumédiène made no pretense of hiding his intention to reverse his predecessor's approach to socialism, relegating the party to the sidelines and depending primarily upon state power to carry out a revolution. Nowhere in Africa has there been such a glorification of the state as in Algeria under Boumédiène. From the beginning, he declared that his primary objective was to establish a "serious, democratic state, governed by laws and based on an ethic, a state which will be able to outlive men and events."[78] The colonel regarded the "resurrection of the Algerian state" destroyed by the French invasion of Algeria in 1830 as "the first objective" of his government.[79] It was above all the state, in his view, that must be relied upon to carry out a well-planned, coherent socialist policy, while political participation and mass mobilization were of very secondary importance. As a result, the party gave way to the state and politics generally yielded to economics under Boumédiène.

The economic policies of his regime can be summarized fairly easily, since they have been so consistent over time: a continuation of the nationalization of all important foreign-owned property, started under Ben Bella; reliance on the creation of over 360 parastatal companies in the industrial sector, with the slow atrophy of self-management there; emphasis on industrialization, and particularly on development of the oil, gas, steel, and petrochemical industries; and, until 1976, very little attention to the problems of agriculture. The structure of the country's development plans clearly reveals these choices. The three-year development plan (1967 through 1969) saw 48.7 percent of investment going to industry, 10.1 percent to infrastructure, and only 16.9 percent to agriculture. The first and second, four-year plans (1970 through 1973 and 1974 through 1977) showed a similar pattern of investment.[80] Equally significant is the distribution of investments within the industrial sector. In the first four-year development plan, oil and gas received the lion's share with almost 37 percent of the total devoted to industry. This is not surprising since the sector was key to growth in all other spheres. More revealing is the fact that other heavy industries (petrochemicals and steel) altogether accounted for another 40 percent of industrial investment, leaving only about 21 percent for consumer goods industries.[81] The second four-year development plan saw an almost identical distribution of investment among different industries, although total investment quadrupled to $27 billion.

The effect of this "industrializing industries" policy has been somewhat mixed. On the positive side, Algeria has achieved an impressive real growth rate, estimated at 10.4 percent in 1976, 7.8 percent in 1977, and 9 percent in 1978. It was expected to remain at the latter level throughout the early 1980s.[82] On the negative side, most of the new industrial plants in Algeria produce greatly under capacity for three main reasons: technical and managerial problems; the low level of demand within the country; and the failure to break into European markets upon which the planners had been counting to absorb surplus production until internal demand arose. As a result, many industries have been producing at a loss and essentially been subsidized by state oil and gas revenues. The official Algerian response to this problem has been its acceptance as an inevitable but temporary phase of a strategy which will eventually make the country economically independent. The government has rejected criticism of its industrialization policy, and suggestions that heavy industry should be deemphasized, as simply part of a Western attempt to keep Third World countries forever in a dependent state. Boumédiène's own statements show how the Algerian leadership looked at this problem:

> The essential goals of a policy of industrialization are not manifested only through the creation of more jobs. They go beyond that. They include the need to foster, through the development of our national forces of production, a process of internal accumulation of our material and human resources, essential for us to emerge into the technological era.[83]

Boumédiène also justified nationalization in a similar perspective:

> ... nationalization is in itself a step toward development. It forces us to face the realities and the responsibilities of complex industrial operations and thus permits us to acquire real management experience.[84]

From this point of view, the fact that many of the industries created still produce at a loss indeed appears as a secondary problem and the industrialization policy pursued by the Algerian government justifiable.

It is more difficult to understand, let alone justify, the neglect of the agricultural sector, which has made Algeria dependent on imports for about half its staple food needs. Agriculture was bound to be a difficult sector. Relative to the size of the population, arable land is scarce, and much of it is not irrigated, leaving the country vulnerable to the vagaries of irregular rainfall. Making the problem even more acute, the population is growing by a hefty 3.2 percent a year. All of this would seem to argue for special attention to agriculture rather than its neglect. The official explanation is that significant agricultural development can be achieved only through mechanization and the intense use of fertilizers and thus that industrial growth was a necessary precondition to rural development. The cost of this approach has been high both to the rural population and to the country at large. Between 1973 and 1977, Algeria imported over a million tons of wheat alone every year. The average annual bill for all food imports was $700 million during this period.[85] Employment in the rural sector increased by only 1 percent a year, far less than the rate of population growth. This compared to the 9 percent increase each year in the number of new jobs available in the urban areas.[86]

Whatever the official Algerian rationale, the stagnation of agriculture was partly due to the lack of a clear policy. Before the promulgation of the Charter of the Agrarian Revolution in 1971, there was not even any public discussion of a rural strategy. The Charter led to a moderate land reform and a modest attempt to push collectivization by forming "socialist villages." State lands as well as private land expropriated from absentee landlords and excessively large estates were distributed to landless or semilandless peasant families. A maximum limit was placed on the size of remaining private holdings, depending on the quality of the land, whether it was irrigated, and where it was located. By the end of 1978, the National Land Fund created under the reform had acquired 4.6 million acres and redistributed 3.1 million acres of this to over 100,000 needy peasants. Some 6,500 cooperatives of various kinds had been registered. The formation of the "socialist villages," however, had run into serious problems; less than 200 had actually been established and these were experiencing a drop-out rate of about 20 percent.[87] State intervention and control created "an army of rural bureaucrats" trying to run the cooperatives and socialist villages as well as to distribute the land. While a definitive judgment on the Algerian land reform may be premature at this point, it seems clear already that it does not represent a sharp break with the overall statist approach to development but simply an extension of it to the rural sector: the "agrarian revolution" was being engineered by the central government and implemented under bureaucratic control. Moreover, the land reform was not even accompanied by any shift in investment away from industry to the agricultural sector; in fact, the share of agriculture in the second four-year plan, covering the reform, did not increase.

For a full decade, the Boumédiène regime devoted itself to economic growth, the building of a strong state apparatus, and administrative reform.

Participation, such as it was, came indicatively through the creation of new state bodies—people's assemblies at the village or town, regional, and national levels—and occasional public debates over major government-produced policy documents. The subordinate of the party position, was perhaps best illustrated by the delay in the adoption of any ideological platform until 1976 and the failure to hold a single FLN Congress before Boumédiène's death in December 1978. A nationwide discussion of the *Charte Nationale,* as the official ideological document was called, was the major exercise in political participation of the Boumédiène era. The debate did not lead, however, to any significant alterations in the charter, which amounted to a justification of the regime's policies ever since 1965. The charter contained many candid admissions of the problems being encountered by the country in the economic and political realms, yet only sought to justify them as inevitable stages in the process of development. While the charter rejected "all rigid dogmas," and thus Marxism by implication,[88] the concept of socialism it upheld was much closer to the Soviet than to the early African socialist models, stressing the need for an "overall and harmonious development on the basis of planning which is scientific in its origin, democratic in its formulation, and imperative in its application."[89] A central idea of the charter was that the process of national liberation would only be completed once Algeria had full control over its resources, did not depend upon other countries to exploit them or provide technology, and had a solid industrial base capable of sustaining growth without outside assistance. Independence was thus synonymous with economic development, and development with industrialization. The charter acknowledged that a policy of rapid and centrally planned economic development encouraged the growth of a bureaucracy. While decrying this trend, it offered no real solution: "The most effective antidote to the bureaucratic phenomenon is the involvement of the public and the best remedy is the propensity of the state apparatus and of the structures of management to improve themselves."[90] There was absolutely no evidence of any such propensity on the part of the Algerian state bureaucracy and little effort by the Boumédiène regime to involve the public.

Until Boumédiène's death in late 1978, Algeria seemed to be locked into a set of ideological and policy choices which reinforced each other, and the mounting problems resulting from a very unbalanced model of development were not being corrected. The colonel's death and the election of a much weaker president,Benjedid Chedli, provided the opportunity for a period of cautious reconsideration of priorities and analysis of the consequences of the country's industrial strategy. There were signs of disquiet over "the lack of vertical and horizontal integration" within the huge socialist sector and the "absence of coordination" of the massive investments in industry, as well as talk of the large foreign debt ($12.3 billion in 1978) "threatening the national will for economic independence."[91] There were reports that the new government intended to devote more attention to the sorry state of agriculture in the country and also to some of the long neglected needs of the public, above all the critical one for urban housing. It was also reported that some of the grandiose industrial schemes were to be scaled down and others canceled. Confirmation of these reports awaited the publication of the third four-year plan, which had been postponed. While it seemed likely that there would be some changes and that the frantic pace of investment would slow down to allow for consolidation, no reversal of policy appeared imminent. The official weekly *Révolution Africaine,* for example, hardly mentioned agriculture throughout 1979. It did devote voluminous articles to the problem of housing, but it indicated the government intended to tackle this problem as it had all others: through a nationwide program undertaken on the massive scale of 100,000 units a year and by setting up an entire industrial sector devoted to the production of building materials, including prefabricated elements. The basic character of Algerian socialism seemed to have been permanently etched across the face of the country. It would take a revolution to destroy the statist system erected under Boumédiène, and there was no indication that such a revolution was in the making.

Lessons From the African Socialist States

By 1980 and after anywhere from thirteen to twenty-two years of laboring to build socialism, the four countries we have briefly analyzed above offered some interesting lessons about the outcome of such an endeavor in the special conditions of the African continent. All four had evolved in unexpected directions and drifted away from their original vision of socialism, sometimes undermining the very goals they had set out to fulfill. The models that have emerged, which we have discussed above, are all "distortions" of one or another aspect of the African socialist ideal of participation, egalitarianism, and self-reliance. Touré may have checked capitalism and created a strong party, but his woeful neglect of the economy alienated a large portion of the population and eventually made Guinea into the epitome of the Third world country caught in the grip of multinational corporations. Nyerere made his society more egalitarian and marginally more collective, but he made a mockery of the principle of self-reliance in the process. Under the leadership of Kaunda, Zambia grew to become a society which was neither egalitarian, nor participatory, nor self-reliant. Finally, Boumédiène's Algeria turned its back on self-management and participation, sacrificed egalitarianism by neglecting the rural areas and allowing the growth of a bureaucratic and technocratic elite, but it did build a base for economic self-reliance through rapid industrialization.

Perhaps the most striking distortion of the initial concept of socialism in all four countries has been the drift toward statism. The initial aspiration to create highly participatory democracies was embodied in insitutions such as the *ujamaa* villages in Tanzania, the *Pouvoirs Révolutionaires Loucaux* (PRLs) in Guinea, the village cooperatives in Zambia, and self-management in Algeria. But within a few years of experimenting with the approach to revolution and these kinds of institutions, all four countries reached a crisis point because of either apathy, mismanagement, or outright failure, and turned to the state for salvation. The specific reasons why this trend toward statism emerged differ from country to country, and they are worth pondering here because they highlight some of the dilemmas facing countries aspiring to socialism in Africa.

In the case of Algeria, statism was a deliberate choice: the growth of a large bureaucratic class and the lack of political participation were a direct consequence of priority given to rapid industrialization as a means of overcoming economic dependency. It was this concern that led to centralized planning, the development of a technocratic elite, and increasing inequality between rural and urban areas. Radicals have been highly critical of Algeria, arguing that its statism is a betrayal of socialism. This criticism flows from the radical brief for socialism in the Third World, which assumes that this system—in fact, only this system—can simultaneously check the growth of social classes and thus of income inequality, assure a high level of political participation, and allow a developing country to overcome its dependency on the world capitalist order. The example of Algeria suggests that these goals may not be compatible, a conclusion that seems further confirmed when we consider that countries placing a high premium on stopping class formation, like Tanzania, and on fostering political participation, like Guinea, have actually increased rather than decreased their dependency on the world capitalist order. None of the early African socialist countries has succeeded in simultaneously promoting equality and participation while at the same time building a sound basis for a nondependent economy. This suggests that the requirements for the former are in conflict with the latter, if not in theory then at least in practice. In theory, it is conceivable that a country might develop an industrial base while at the same time narrowing the urban-rural gap; that it might build a strong party while improving the state's capacity to plan and administer; that it might train the technocrats and bureaucrats it needs to develop the economy while checking the growth of an elite. In practice, this is extremely difficult anywhere and particularly in underdeveloped African countries where there is an acute shortage of financial resources and manpower. Algeria may not so much have betrayed socialism as simply chosen one horn of a dilemma.

The emergence of statism in the other countries was not the result of a deliberate choice and cannot be explained in the same way. In Zambia, it was related to the centralized nature of a copper-dominated, urban-oriented country and the total lack of "fit" between humanism and these conditions. The cases of Tanzania and Guinea are more interesting because they challenge another common assumption about socialism cherished by radicals, namely that political participation automatically assures far-reaching change in a society. Yet in both countries, statism emerged as a direct result of the failure of participatory schemes to spur lasting change. Both the *ujamaa* villages in Tanzania and the PRLs in Guinea were intended to put power in the hands of the people and let them take responsibility for the economic and social transformation of the villages. But left on their own, the peasants did not take the initiative, and in the end the state stepped in to fill the vacuum. The question remains why the peasants were not motivated to take the initiative. One major problem was the low level of inherent social conflict within the peasant societies of these two countries. Their societies were certainly not models of primitive communalism as the early African socialist leaders tended to view them. But they were not sharply divided into classes, either. There was no class of exploiting landlords or of exploited sharecroppers anxious to break the chains of bondage. At most, there were some kulaks. Thus, there was nothing in the existing social conditions to spark revolutionary change. On the other hand, the socialist policies pursued by Touré and Nyerere deliberately removed, or held in check, the incentives for change built into a capitalist system, namely the possibility of personal gain and enrichment. Touré virtually prohibited the functioning of a free market, Nyerere for years kept down producer prices, and both discouraged the kulaks in favor of cooperatives and communal farming. With neither class conflict nor the possibility of personal gain to motivate the peasantry, there was no natural dynamic element in the villages to spur participation, change, or development. The task of introducing dynamism fell upon the two countries' mass parties which were afflicted by the same inertia as the societies they largely incorporated. This left only the state.

The early African socialist experience reveals a set of crucial issues affecting the outcome of the socialist endeavor on the continent: distortions arising from the lack of congruence among ideology, policy and conditions within the country; weaknesses caused by the lack of a solid economic base; dilemmas emerging from the impossibility of attaining all goals at once; and the difficulty of sustaining participation in the absence of any inherent, or for that matter artificially generated, dynamism in the society. Underlying all of these have been the omnipresent shortcomings of underdeveloped countries, such as the acute shortage of capital, personnel, and managerial experience and the strong proclivity toward elitism in situations where anyone with a high school diploma, or even with a regular wage job, by definition belongs to a privileged minority. All these problems are bound to affect the Marxist African countries, too. The issue that must be examined is whether their more orthodox approach will lead to a substantially different outcome.

Chapter IV
Mozambique

Independent only since 1975, Mozambique quickly became southern Africa's first "People's Republic," creating a storm of controversy which to this day obscures an understanding of its socialism. To the 150,000 Portuguese stampeding from the country at independence, Frelimo was a hardcore Communist party bent on nationalizing everything, including children, as some refugees reported, and making life unbearable for whites and blacks alike. To its foreign admirers, Mozambique was a rare example of a country successfully combining socialism and democracy in a nonrepressive, egalitarian, and immensely appealing village-based system. But Mozambique has also been busy proclaiming itself a follower of Marxism-Leninism, signing a Treaty of Friendship and Cooperation with the Soviet Union, and setting up gigantic state farms with the help of Bulgarian and East German agronomists. Clearly, there are great contradictions in the country at the present time. Some trends are beginning to be discernible, however, and they are quite understandable if one considers both the dedication of Frelimo's leadership to Marxism-Leninism and the specific problems the country faces. Commitment to this ideology, but also changing views within the Party as to how Marxism-Leninism should be translated into practice, are combining with the pragmatism dictated by a very difficult concrete situation to give rise to a unique configuration. For all its ideological orthodoxy, Mozambique is not, nor is it likely to become, a replica of the Soviet Union. It is also distinctly unlike any of the early socialist countries we have described, although it shares with them specific problems and dilemmas. It is not an example of African socialism, but of the new phenomenon we have called Afrocommunism.

The War Legacy

The war of national liberation in Mozambique started officially in 1964, two years after Frelimo was founded through the merger of three smaller nationalist organizations. The conduct of the independence struggle was from the very beginning heavily influenced by geography, and geography in turn had political repercussions. A long, narrow strip of country extending along the Indian Ocean for more than 1,000 miles, Mozambique was fenced in to the south and much of the west by white-controlled South Africa and Rhodesia. By necessity, the war had to start in the northern part, where guerrillas could penetrate relatively easily from Tanzania and Zambia. Furthermore, the Portuguese presence was at its weakest in these regions, since the settlers were concentrated further south, particularly in and around the capital of Lourenço Marques (now Maputo) and in the fertile valleys of the Zambezi and Limpopo rivers. Sparsely settled by the Portuguese, the northern regions were also weakly administered and poorly serviced by roads or any other infrastructure. In fact, they were scarcely integrated into the rest of the country. The result was that the war in the north made very swift progress, but also that its repercussions were contained. Four years after the launching of the armed struggle, the two northern provinces of Niassa and Cabo Delgado were largely "liberated zones," where Frelimo had set up its own administration and even held its second congress. Until the end of the war, however, Frelimo had the greatest difficulty in penetrating further south or into the cities.

The early liberation of the northern provinces had a deep impact on Frelimo, forcing it to face very early on in the struggle the issue of its ultimate goals other than independence. Like all African liberation movements, Frelimo had started as a front in the literal sense of the term, a conglomeration of disparate groups with various political orientations sharing only the common objective of national independence. The initial character of Frelimo's leadership varied greatly in terms of race, level of education, and political orientation. The more highly educated tended to be *mestiços,* Mozambicans of Goan descent or *assimilados;* these were the Mozambicans who had studied and traveled abroad, were better read and informed, and had been exposed to the greatest variety of ideas. Eduardo Mondlane, Frelimo's first president, was an American-educated *assimilado* who had been teaching at Syracuse University before being called upon to head Frelimo. Others were Portuguese and French-educated *mestiços* and Goans: among the most prominent of these were Marcelino dos Santos, soon to emerge and remain the number-two man in the Front, Sergio Vieira, Jorge Rebelo, and Oscar Monteiro. These four figures were probably the most instrumental in influencing Frelimo in a Marxist direction, although Samora Machel and other blacks among the top guerrilla commanders were coming to the same ideological convictions based on their own personal experiences inside the country. Whatever the interaction between these two groups, the Front was not yet clearly a socialist movement when the issue of how to organize the liberated zones first arose in 1968. As Frelimo documents officially tell the story, there existed within its ranks at that time a "counterrevolutionary" and "bourgeois" faction which wanted to allow a Mozambican elite to fill the vacuum created by the withdrawal of Portuguese administrators and businessmen, thus opening the way for African capitalism and neo-colonialism. The majority within Frelimo opposed this approach, and at a meeting of the Central Committee in April 1969 the "bourgeois" position suffered its final defeat. From this time on, the Front was fighting for socialism as well as for independence.

Frelimo's initial concept of socialism was influenced by ideology but also by the very special characteristics of the liberated zones. Ideologically, the Front was already moving very close to the explicit adoption of Marxism. But this Marxism had to be adapted to the reality of areas where there were no industry, no cities, little political consciousness, in fact hardly anything other than peasants living at the subsistence level. The Front's main wartime ideological document was written after the triumph of its radical faction and was first published in early 1971 under the title of "The Process of the People's Democratic Revolution in Mozambique." For the first time, the war was viewed as revolution, and revolution as a dialectical process in which periods of unity and periods of conflict, or "criticism," inevitably followed each other. The Front, the document claimed, had already undergone two periods of criticism. The first one concerned the decision of whether to launch an armed struggle for independence. The second phase of criticism, crucial to the subsequent emergence of Frelimo as Marxist-Leninist party, dealt with very major, long-term issues:

> How production should be organized, how the population should be administered, which types of relationships of production should exist in the liberated zones, which relations should be established between the population and the leadership of Frelimo, between the army and the population, these are all urgent problems, requiring immediate, clear and concrete solutions.[1]

In tackling these problems, Frelimo deliberately decided to forge a whole new socioeconomic system. It would not imitate that created by the Portuguese, merely replacing the settlers with a Mozambican elite. Nor would it try either to restore a society in the image of the precolonial one, as Tanzania and Zambia were theoretically attempting to do. Traditionalism was rejected as emphatically as neocolonialism. Tradition was seen as synonymous with feudalism, gerontocracy, male domination, and a society which did not give full rights to all its citizens. It was not, as Kaunda or Nyerere claimed, characterized by cooperation, mutual aid, and sense of community. As Frelimo put it:

> A liberated zone, in the real sense of the term, is a zone which has been liberated from colonial-capitalist domination and from feudal-traditional domination. In other words, at the administrative level power is exercised neither by the colonial administrators, nor by traditional customs.[2]

In order to create a new society freed from the bonds of colonialism and tradition, Frelimo proposed to establish "the structures of people's power," namely a system of rural democracy based on elected committees at the village and higher levels within the liberated zones.[3] A new economy emphasizing communal production would have to be developed. Education would be provided to all and its main objectives would be to "inculcate in each person an advanced, scientific objective, and collective ideology allowing the revolutionary process to go forward."[4] In the field of medicine, "the Frelimo political line puts health care in the service of the masses," giving the priority to general preventive measures.[5] There was, to be sure, a lot of revolutionary rhetoric in Frelimo statements that outstripped its actual accomplishments. But there was more than just words, for the Front was indeed faced with a multitude of "urgent problems requiring immediate, clear, and concrete solutions." It had at once to wage the war, provide administration for the liberated zones, grow sufficient food, provide medical care for its wounded, and set up workshops to support its growing army of guerrillas. It set about solving these problems in a clearly socialist manner, forming communal villages and cooperatives and stimulating a high degree of political participation. But since all these tasks had to be carried out in a very decentralized fashion and in small communities due to war conditions, the end result was a kind of village socialism which resembled *ujamaa* more than Marxism. In other words, while the ideological writings of Frelimo already showed a strong Marxist imprint and a clear rejection of the vision of African communalism on which *ujamaa* was based, the practical steps taken by Frelimo in the villages could have been suggested by Nyerere.

The history of the liberated zones during the war remains to be written in detail, and existing accounts are either Frelimo's own or those of wartime visitors favorably predisposed. While there remain some doubts about the magnitude of Frelimo's accomplishments, there can be few about the basic thrust of its efforts. The Front did not try to run the liberated zones from the top down, imposing its own authority in a "commandist" fashion. How much this was due to conviction and how much to shortage of personnel we do not know, but it appears that in fact Frelimo did encourage the peasants to organize themselves and elect their own leaders, relying generally on persuasion rather than coercion to stimulate collective endeavors. It could scarcely have been otherwise. In 1968, when the problems of organizing the liberated zones first arose, Frelimo only had 8,000 cadres,[6] by its own admission, and with these it had to defend and organize the territory it had already conquered and open new fronts to the south, in Tete and Mozambique provinces. The liberated zones covered one fifth of the national territory and contained a population of perhaps 800,000. It was inevitable that Frelimo should rely heavily on the peasants to run their own affairs, favoring a form of direct democracy.

The key institution created during the war was the *aldeia communal*, or communal village, originally the very symbol of Mozambican socialism and later the center of a covert controversy within Frelimo. In the original wartime concept, communal villages were very similar to the Tanzanian *ujamaa* villages; in fact the first president of Frelimo, Eduardo Mondlane, reportedly declared once that independent Mozambique would look like Tanzania. Politically, the communal villages were governed by representatives elected by the population; economically, they combined individual and collective farming, starting with a small communal plot which was supposed to expand progressively to become the major economic unit. One element which helped in the growth of communal fields during the war was the participation of the guerrillas, who needed food for themselves. The extent of communal farming has probably been exaggerated, however. There is scant evidence that it ever became the primary system of cultivation in the liberated zones, expanding beyond the existence of a communal field in each village. Food, though, seems to have been produced in sufficient quantities, and there was even some surplus of crops exported from the northern provinces. Peanuts, cashews, and sesame seeds were transported to Tanzania by women walking at night on bush trails with bundles on their heads. Frelimo also tried to develop some social services in the villages under their control. Schools were set up whenever possible, and by 1968 the party claimed 100 schools with 12,000 pupils in Cabo Delgado, although it admitted that the instruction imparted there was most rudimentary: for lack of pencils and books, students were often taught to write by tracing letters on slabs of wood with cassava roots.[7] By 1970, 30,000 children were in school in the liberated zones.[8] Some health care was also introduced, particularly vaccinations. In absolute terms, the services did not amount to much, but for areas which had been severely neglected by the Portuguese, it was definitely progress.

The other great achievement of Frelimo during the war was the preservation of unity within its leadership. This went largely unnoticed at the time and was only fully appreciated later when Mozambique was spared the factionalism and struggle for power that rent Angola at independence. The Front managed its two major internal crises successfully through institutional channels. The elimination of the "bourgeois" faction led by Uria Simango and Lazaro Kavandame was decided upon after a series of long meetings by the Central Committee. The succession to President Mondlane, killed in February 1969 by a package bomb probably sent by the Portuguese secret police, was also smoothly handled within the Central Committee and did not provoke any major rift. In May 1970, the leader of Frelimo's guerrilla army, Samora Machel, was elected as president and Marcelino dos Santos as vice president. These two men would continue to occupy these top positions even after independence. Machel's election furthermore helped to avoid a problem afflicting many other liberation movements, namely the conflict between military and civilian leaders. Frelimo argued that "given the circumstances under which we operate, there is not, in fact there cannot be, a clear separation between a strictly military and a strictly political sector."[9] Frelimo militants were both guerrillas and party members. "In our midst, there are no 'politicians' and 'military,' no 'politicians' and 'technicians,' "[10] a party document explained. Perhaps more than in other African liberation struggles, there was in fact little or no division between the two.

There was also a great weakness in Frelimo's wartime legacy. Despite the Front's obvious successes there, the liberated zones represented only a small part of the entire national territory. Elsewhere, the Front was poorly implanted. The original plan had been to enlarge progressively the guerrilla-controlled areas until the whole country was infiltrated. This did not happen, however. A third front was opened in Tete Province in 1968, but the region was never fully liberated, and the building of the huge Cabora Bassa hydroelectric dam continued uninterrupted until the end of the war. In the southern half of the country and the cities, Frelimo scarcely existed. To be sure, as a nationalist movement fighting against the Portuguese, it had sympathizers everywhere, but no real organization. It is also doubtful that most Mozambicans understood that Frelimo identified national liberation with socialism.

Conditions at Independence

Independence came, in a sense, before Frelimo was ready for it. What had been envisaged as a slow process of expanding the liberated zones to establish firm control over the entire population and to implant a solid political structure turned into a landslide into independence because of internal political events in Portugal. In April 1974, the Caetano regime was toppled by the Armed Forces Movement; in September 1974, a transitional provisional government was set up in Mozambique; and in June 1975, Frelimo found itself governing the entire country. The initial problems were acute. The most obvious was the departure of the Portuguese, which Frelimo did nothing to discourage. Only 20,000 to 30,000 Portuguese stayed in the country out of the 170,000 who had been there before independence. In the long run, their departure was probably a blessing for a country determined to bring about a radical change. In the short run, it led to severe disruption and a dramatic decrease in production in all sectors. Since the Portuguese had occupied virtually all managerial and technical positions, their flight left an enormous vacuum. To this must be added the effects of deliberate sabotage and of the uncontrolled export of machinery and vehicles.

Economic decline started in 1974 and continued for several years. While there are few precise statistics, there is enough information to indicate the general magnitude of disruption. Industrial production, for example, had accounted for 15 percent of the GDP in the early 1970s, but declined to 10 percent by 1975, although the GDP itself had also shrunk.[11] Moreover, the decline was still continuing. Employment in the industrial sector declined by 40 percent, from 120,000 in 1973 to 73,000 in 1976.[12] Agricultural production in the modern sector was similarly badly affected as most Portuguese farms and plantations were abandoned. These farms apparently numbered 3,000 to 4,000 and occupied four million acres of land, of which 800,000 were under cultivation. The area cultivated by the Portuguese was roughly 10 percent of the country's total, and accounted for a substantial part of urban food supplies and some export crops.[13] Furthermore transport ground to a standstill, as the fleeing Portuguese destroyed or took with them 25,000 vehicles. Consequently, the export of agricultural commodities declined drastically. One major export crop, cashew nuts, was affected not so much by a drop in actual production—cashew trees grow wild—as by the disintegration of the marketing network. The intermediaries in the collection process had been the Portuguese village storekeepers who had bought the nuts from the peasants, or most often bartered them against overpriced consumer goods. With the shopkeepers gone, the nuts were simply not collected any longer. Cashew exports, which reached a peak of 185,000 tons in 1973 dropped to around 75,000 tons in 1976. Cotton, the most important export in terms of value, plummeted even more disastrously from 43,000 tons in 1973 to 13,000 tons in 1976 and to 3,800 tons the following year. The overall value of Mozambican exports declined from $200 million in 1974 to $150 million in 1977.[14]

In trying to reactivate the economy, Frelimo had very little to work with. While most studies agree that Mozambique's long-term potential for economic development is good, it has no easily exploitable resources affording a quick accumulation of capital for development. Land and water are abundant, but agriculture is still mostly at a subsistence level. The Portuguese did not develop a particularly large modern farming sector, but relied instead on forced cultivation of cash crops by peasants to bolster their exports. Cotton in particular was cultivated in this way. As a result, Portugal left behind little developed land and even less knowledge of modern farming techniques. The country's mineral wealth also had not been exploited and developed on a large scale. Mozambique mined and exported coal, but the Portuguese had not taken advantage of what economists consider one of the country's main assets, namely the fact that "the industrial base minerals of iron ore, high-grade coking coal, and bauxite are located within close proximity to natural gas, extensive forests, inexpensive electricity (Cabora Bassa), a railhead (Moatize), a navigable river (the Zambezi) and the finest deep water port in East Africa (Nacala)."[15] The potential for this central region to become an "African Ruhr" could not help in the short run a country which did not have the capital necessary to develop it.

The political problems of the immediate postindependence period were also quite serious. As we have already pointed out, Frelimo was poorly implanted in all but the northern provinces, and particularly weak in the cities; yet it was in the cities that the principal problem lay. It was here that the greatest opportunities existed for Mozambicans to step into the shoes of the departing Portuguese, and thus that opposition to socialism was likely to be strongest at first. Moreover, the policies followed by the Portuguese just before independence, and particularly in the transitional period, had created expectations among the urban workers which risked leading to discontent or opposition to Frelimo. The transitional government had given in to workers' demands for pay increases ordering an across-the-board raise of $20 for wages under $200 a month, and it had provided for compulsory arbitration of labor disputes. Wage increases resulting from such arbitration fell in the 40 to 100 percent range.[16] A Frelimo document argued that these "demagogic wage increases," bearing no relationship to the company's productivity, were part of a maneuver to confuse the workers. And it concluded: "The roots of indiscipline, liberalism, and corruption, which disorganized the working class and resulted in the fall in production and productivity, can be traced to the capitalist strategy during the collapse of colonial rule."[17]

Production and political organization were thus the two most urgent problems Mozambique faced at independence. Frelimo initially relied heavily on the involvement of the population to solve them, as it had done in the liberated zones. The conclusions reached by some observers that Frelimo was basically an African "populist" rather than a Marxist-Leninist movement were based mostly on this early period. The principal institution used by Frelimo at this time was the *grupos dinamizadores,* or "dynamizing groups." Created first in 1974 during the transitional period, they were committees of Frelimo sympathizers, but not necessarily members, upon which the Front counted to organize people in a given neighborhood or enterprise. The members of the dynamizing groups were not selected by Frelimo, but by the people involved. Party cadres participated only to a limited extent, providing the initial incentive to mobilize and organize and making sure that the groups would be pro- and not anti-Frelimo organizations. In this objective, Frelimo did not always succeed initially, and in fact some of the groups became clandestine centers of opposition. By and large, however, they performed their role as links between the party and the population as well as accomplishing practical tasks ranging from creating urban consumer cooperatives to organizing communal villages. The activities of the dynamizing groups did not fit into an overall plan for the transformation of the country, but rather simply responded to the host of immediate problems.

In the economic realm, too, Frelimo's efforts immediately after independence were dictated above all by expediency. The most urgent need was to relaunch production, reorganize transport, reopen stores. Solutions varied greatly. Abandoned plantations were grouped into state farms, very often huge ones. In areas of peasant agriculture, Frelimo continued to encourage the organization of communal villages. By and large, operating Portuguese enterprises whose owners were still in Mozambique were not taken over by the government, which already had its hands more than full with the abandoned ones. It would be difficult to characterize precisely Frelimo's economic policy in this period; while it was not encouraging private enterprise, it was not trying to destroy what was left of it either. And the socialist sector consisted of everything—state enterprises and farms, cooperatives, communal villages. Expediency prevailed.

When one looks at these first years of independence in Mozambique, one is struck by the similarities with the corresponding period in Algeria and Guinea. There, too, independence had led to a mass exodus of the settlers, with a consequent massive dislocation of society and economy. There, too, the new regime was not sufficiently organized and in control to tackle systematically the various problems. In all cases, the first solution was an extreme degree of decentralization, an effort to achieve through mobilization and enthusiasm what could not be achieved immediately through systematic organization. Principles, to be sure, played a part in shaping the policies followed by Frelimo initially. The choice of socialism was clear, as was the intention of creating an entirely new socioeconomic system rather than trying to preserve the old one, with Mozambicans replacing the Portuguese. But a lot of the specific solutions adopted were the result simply of necessity and expediency. In Algeria and Guinea, this period of what we have called "voluntaristic" socialism led to disillusionment and chaos, and in the former, finally, to a coup d'etat. In Mozambique, there was no real chaos, to a large extent because Frelimo was united and faced no serious opposition. However, even in Mozambique there soon emerged a group within Frelimo convinced of the limitations of the voluntaristic participatory approach and determined to make Mozambican socialism more scientific,even if less democratic. The first sign that the meaning of socialism in Mozambique was undergoing change came at the Third Frelimo Congress when, in a great display of unanimity and revolutionary fervor, the Front proclaimed itself a Marxist-Leninist party, adopting new statues and elaborte documents on ideology and policy.

The Adoption of Marxism-Leninism

Frelimo's Third Congress met in Maputo in February 1977, when the country was finally beginning to settle down after the initial disruption at independence. It was preceded by a remarkable effort to familiarize the population with the basic concepts of Marxism-Leninism, and to explain why the choice was being made and what it meant for Mozambique. The preparation of the congress undoubtedly showed that Frelimo took political participation seriously. A set of seven "theses" widely circulated for discussion before the congress was remarkable for its clarity and simplicity, particularly when compared to the ideological writing from other African countries, for example Algeria or Ethiopia. These theses, the Central Committee's report, the party statutes, and the "economic and social directives" approved by the congress are the documents which most clearly indicate how Marxism-Leninism was interpreted in Mozambique, and it is on these documents that the following discussion is based.

Frelimo went to great lengths to demonstrate that Marxism-Leninism was not a foreign ideology, artificially implanted in the country by a group of ivory tower intellectuals, but rather an answer to specific Mozambican problems formulated in the heat of a prolonged struggle. Officially, the party's ideology was declared to be a synthesis of "the revolutionary experience of the Mozambican people and the universal principles of Marxism-Leninism."[18] What this meant, according to President Machel, was that "our movement's revolutionary ideology was forged in each of the political battles which it was necessary to wage, in each of the options it was necessary to choose."[19] Machel has been at times very critical of Mozambicans who are afraid of departing from dogma to adapt the meaning of Marxism-Leninism to the particular conditions of their country. Despite this emphasis on flexibility and even originality, Frelimo insisted that its ideology was true Marxism-Leninism and not yet another variety of African socialism.

> It is necessary for us to be always on guard against the chauvinistic deviations of 'specific socialisms.' We reject the idea that there can be an "African socialism" or a "Mozambican socialism." We consciously affirm that there can be no socialism other than scientific socialism.[20]

This insistence on both originality and orthodoxy, on the necessity of elaborating an ideology reflecting the Mozambican reality while at the same time avoiding "chauvinistic deviations," would lead to a great deal of tension, since the two were not as easily reconciled as the party statutes and Machel's statements suggested. While the wartime tradition of Frelimo had been marked by a great deal of flexibility, adherence to universal principles suggested that the correct political choices were by necessity predetermined and not the result of a conscious process of adaptation. For example, Marxism-Leninism prescribed the dictatorship of the proletariat and Frelimo adhered unquestioningly to this idea. Yet, the proletariat constituted a tiny segment of the Mozambican population, and historically Frelimo's own roots were in the rural areas rather than the cities.

A socialist revolution, in Frelimo's view, could not take place immediately in Mozambique, but had to be preceded by two preliminary stages: a "national democratic revolution" and a "popular democratic revolution."[21] The first having been achieved with independence, Frelimo was now launching the popular democratic revolution devoted to the "intensification of class struggle," the creation of a "New Man," and the development of the economy under state control. The idea of class struggle occupied a central place in the congress documents and was by far the most problematic concept set forth there, deriving much more from pure theory than from an analysis of the society or an evaluation of Frelimo's experience. This difficulty of applying class analysis meaningfully in Mozambique was reflected in the ambiguity surrounding the various definitions of class struggle found in Frelimo documents. One of the seven "theses" circulated before the party congress described it not as a struggle against a properly defined, established "class" which most Mozambicans could easily perceive as their enemy, but as an effort to prevent the growth of an exploiting stratum. Three groups of exploiters were singled out for special attention. The first was the colonial bourgeoisie, the mainstay of the former Portuguese regime bearing ultimate responsibility for the war. This bourgeoisie essentially no longer existed with the flight of most Portuguese at independence. The second was an aspiring national petty bourgeoisie, or "certain individuals, although not possessing many assets, who have tried desperately to replace the colonial bourgeoisie and to occupy the positions left vacant by them."[22] This stratum was regarded as having been defeated in the liberated zones during the war but still a potential threat. The third group, a rather pitiful class enemy, was made up of individuals who "although born of the people, became corrupt and betrayed the people," such as wartime collaborators and "all lawless, professional criminals, thieves, murderers, drug addicts, prostitutes, gamblers, and others."[23] Frelimo admitted that all these class enemies were weak, but Machel warned that they must nonetheless be watched closely because they acted as a "connecting link" to external foes. "We must constantly see in our enemy imperialism," he declared, "and think of ways of fighting imperialism.[24] Thus, class struggle had two aspects: it was an external battle against imperialism and a internal one to prevent the formation of an exploiting stratum.

Class struggle was given an inordinate amount of importance for a second reason, namely because it was viewed as the key to the process through which a proletariat would be strengthened to the point where it could play a leading role in the revolution. Frelimo was entirely orthodox in its acceptance of the notion that the working class had to become the dominant political force. But it was also totally cognizant that in Mozambique this class was not yet ready to lead, given its small size and low degree of political consciousness. Class struggle was regarded as the main solution to both these problems. Through it, Frelimo declared, "the conditions are brought into existence for the development of the dictatorship of the proletariat."[25]

Frelimo was similarly aware that it had to justify the idea of a proletarian dictatorship in a predominantly rural and peasant-based society. The argument it used was quite elaborate. Thesis Number Four stated that the workers must constitute the leading class because their consciousness was "collective" by definition. This was so, in Frelimo's view, because they did not own the means of production and, above all, because they realized they could only make a factory operate collectively. The situation was inherently different for the peasantry:

> The peasant class, by its sheer numbers and the riches it creates, is the basically of the working class. It also wants the socialist revolution, but the truth of the matter is that, in order to make the socialist revolution, it must learn from the working class the collective spirit, the spirit of organization and the spirit of collective property.[26]

Such a concept of the peasants as at best apprentices in the revolution stood in sharp contradiction to the recent history of Mozambique, where it was the peasants who had provided the main support for Frelimo during the war while the urban proletariat had proven irrelevant to the struggle. It is very difficult, in our opinion, to relate Frelimo's theoretical conclusions about class struggle to the concrete situation in Mozambique. This difficulty was well symbolized by the cartoon character, Xiconhoca, the class enemy, which appeared widely in magazines, newspapers, school books, and wall posters. Xiconhoca's sins ranged far and wide. He was the worker shirking his duty, the citified dandy in bell bottom pants and dark glasses afraid of dirtying his clothes, the bureaucrat harassing people with his incompetent paper-shuffling, the male chauvinist, the collaborator with the imperialists. Yet Xiconhoca was not clearly a member of a well-defined class. His sins appeared subjective, the result of bad attitudes; in the final analysis this class enemy was a rather shapeless, though quite despicable, figure.

The concern for the creation of a "New Man," is much easier to relate to the Frelimo experience. Creating a new man meant in practice asserting the Mozambican identity and socialist commitment without looking to the past. This was a concrete problem Frelimo faced. In the liberated zones, the Front had seen how the departure of the Portuguese was interpreted by traditional authorities as a chance for regaining their lost authority. This, to the Frelimo cadres, was unacceptable, since they did not believe that the precolonial society was characterized by a form of primitive communalism. "The traditional feudal society is a conservative, immobile society with a rigid hierarchy.... It is a society which excludes youth, excludes innovation, excludes women. The correct term is gerontocracy."[27] The new man would reject both tradition and the colonial mentality. He was the man of the future, who could only arise out of a restructured society since attitudes are dependent on social structure.

> The creation of the New Man is not primarily a subjective factor, but the change in objective conditions. If it were to be the contrary, we would fall into idealism. We have to change the economic and social base, we have to change the infrastructure of society in order to create the New Man. If not, we would be like the priests and would fall for the thesis of the internal transformation of the person and we would have a saint.[28]

Throughout Frelimo documents, it was stressed that the creation of a new man and a new society could only be achieved if the traditional relations between men and women were radically transformed. The emancipation of women was seen not as "an act of charity" but as a "fundamental necessity of the revolution, a guarantee that it will continue, a condition for its triumph."[29]

The new party statutes and economic and social directives issued by the Third Frelimo Congress were also quite orthodox in their Marxist-Leninist orientation. Frelimo itself was supposed to be converted from a liberation "front" into a "vanguard party of the worker-peasant alliance"[30] subscribing to the idea of "proletarian internationalism"[31] and guided in its operations by the principle of "democratic centralism."[32] The economic and social directives for development outlined the following goals:

> Taking agriculture as the base and industry as the dynamic and decisive factor, in this phase we must:
> a) promote the increasing socialism of agriculture and launch the basis for its industrialization;

b) accelerate the process of industrialization and promote the creation of heavy industry;
c) develop and consolidate the role of the state in the economy;
d) guide the process of development through overall economic planning;
e) form a powerful working class that, organized and led by its vanguard Party, will assume the leadership of the society.[33]

The achievement of these goals required the creation of "a state apparatus to plan and direct the economy" and the consolidation of "a state sector that will determine and dominate the economic process."[34] In the rural areas, however, "our strategy for development should be carried out basically through the communal villages."[35] Interestingly, Frelimo gave far more importance in its program to production than to the immediate improvement in living standards and social services. The increase of "material production and productivity in work" was seen as "the indispensable precondition for the improvement in living conditions and for the revolutionary transformation of society. Our basic resources and efforts will thus be mainly applied to the economic sectors."[36] In theory at least, Frelimo totally rejected the Tanzanian identification of socialism with the welfare state.

In examining the Third Congress documents, one is struck by the manner in which the acceptance of Marxism-Leninism concretely influenced policy objectives. The basic principles of the ideology were taken very seriously and objectives spelled out within a logical systematic Marxist approach. Socialism required the dictatorship of the proletariat, and if this class was a negligible force in Mozambique it simply would have to be built up until it could play its proper role. This meant that all policies should aim at creating this proletariat, thus giving priority to industry and socialist agriculture. Similarly, since socialism was seen as the result of a structural transformation of society through economic development, all efforts were to be concentrated on the economy, even if that meant postponing the immediate betterment of living conditions.

Despite this very clear commitment to the path prescribed by Marxism-Leninism, Frelimo also assumed that these ideologically correct solutions were compatible with the "experience of the Mozambican people" during the war of liberation, meaning reliance on the communal villages to promote both participation and collectivization. This assumption was not only explicitly stated in the party statutes but also incorporated in its social and economic directives adopted at the Third Congress. While this stress on the *aldeias communais* was certainly in accordance with past Frelimo policy, it was not necessarily the best means for pushing collectivization or proletarian consciousness, for, in practice, the amount of truly collective economic activity in the communal villages had been quite limited. After the congress, it became increasingly clear that there was an underlying tension between Frelimo's new ideological commitment and its wartime experience. In fact, the history of Mozambique since the congress has been to a large extent that of the conflict between the more centralizing tendency deriving from a Soviet-type interpretation of Marxism-Leninism and the more decentralized and direct participatory tradition deriving from Frelimo's wartime experience. In the very attempt to implement the principles set forth in the various congress documents, the contradictions in the stance of Frelimo have become more obvious.

The Policies

We will consider here policies being implemented in Mozambique in three major areas, trying to show how in each of them there have emerged contradictions between two views of socialism, which we will refer to here as the orthodox Marxist-Leninist and the historical Mozambican experience. The three we will discuss are political organization, economic development and social services.

1. Political Organization

The components of the overall political system in Mozambique include the party, the dynamizing groups, the mass organizations, the state bureaucracy, people's assemblies and the *aldeias communais,* or communal villages. The keystone was, of course, Frelimo, first the liberation movement leading the country to independence and then the vanguard party leading it to socialism. One of the most remarkable characteristics of Frelimo, particularly in comparison to other African parties, was that it came close to being in practice what it was supposed to be in theory: a tightly structured, hierarchical organization actually running the country. The strength of the party depended to a large extent on the tradition of collective leadership and discipline established during the war years and on the fact that it managed to maintain a high degree of unity both before and after independence. This meant that decisions were made by the Frelimo Central Committee and not by Machel alone, and that the disagreements which doubtlessly existed over policy were contained within the organization and dealt with through it. This is not to say that Frelimo had no problems; it did, notably in organizing at the lower levels. But these problems could be dealt with from within an essentially unified structure.

A second and initially very important component of the Mozambican political system were the dynamizing groups. These organs were for a time, together with the communal villages, the symbols of the democratic and highly participatory Mozambican approach to socialism. Yet the existence and role of these semiautonomous groups became later somewhat problematic. After independence, hundreds of dynamizing groups were formed at the instigation of Frelimo, which saw them as useful tools for spreading its ideology and rallying support. Things did not always work out as expected, however: the party did not always succeed in preventing the groups from being infiltrated by anti-Frelimo elements or simply opportunists seeking a measure of power for themselves. This remained a relatively minor problem, and the dynamizing groups certainly never became part of an overall opposition movement, as happened in the case of the *poder popular* committees in Angola. Nevertheless, there was a certain amount of distrust of the dynamizing groups by the Party, since their allegiance was not always clear nor their activities authorized. This mistrust was particularly prominent in government offices. In late 1977, a high Frelimo official publicly decried the fact that the dynamizing groups there had degenerated into little more than personnel and grievance committees. The reason, he explained, was the suspicion with which Frelimo officials regarded all government employees, considering them to be "petty bourgeois" by definition and moreover often compromised because they had worked for the Portuguese before independence. As a result, Frelimo had deliberately discouraged political debate by these groups in government offices.[37]

When the Third Congress approved the new statutes of Frelimo, proclaiming it to be a Marxist-Leninist vanguard party, nothing was said about the fate of the dynamizing groups. Yet, the very logic of the vanguard party appeared such as to doom them to disappear, or at least change completely in character. Basically, their decentralized and semiautonomous nature implied a concept of direct democracy and mass participation which contradicted that of the vanguard party. According to the new Frelimo statutes, one of the principal duties of party members was to "explain the party's political line to the masses, unite them around the Party, mobilize and organize them to undertake tasks defined by the Party."[38] Since the dynamizing groups had performed these tasks until that time, they clearly were going to be forced to narrow the scope of their activity. By 1979, a consensus seemed to have emerged that the groups would disappear in the rural areas as soon as a Frelimo cell was implanted but would continue to exist in urban areas as neighborhood committees, dealing primarily with concrete problems and not with general political issues.

With the decrease in the importance of the dynamizing groups, the major avenue for political participation open to the overwhelming majority of the population which did not belong to the Party was the mass organizations. As in all communist systems, the mass organizations were subordinated to and controlled by the Party. The most important of them was the Organization of Mozambican Women (OMM), first established in 1972 and thus fairly well implanted. The OMM's major task was that of promoting equality between man and women, both by organizing women to accomplish economic tasks so as to give concrete proof that they were the equal of men, and by directly denouncing men, and particularly male party and government officials, still tainted by traditional attitudes. The other organizations were not as important. The youth movement was only launched after the party congress, and the labor union had to be reorganized completely to eradicate its past, fascist corporate biases. By and large these groups all saw their task as that of mobilizing their respective constituencies to help implement party policies, thus contributing to the political education of Mozambicans as well as Frelimo's overall effectiveness.

While the congress initiated a process of party reconversion promising in the long run to regulate political participation closely, it also started a major overhaul of the old Portuguese administration making the new state far more democratic. Between September and December 1977, all adult Mozambicans for the first time in their lives took part in elections establishing "people's assemblies" at the local, district, municipal, provincial, and national levels. The elections for the 894 local assemblies were a particularly striking example of grassroots democracy at work.[39] Candidates were nominated by the dynamizing groups, and the names were then submitted to public scrutiny at open meetings where villagers were invited to speak up and comment on the qualifications of the candidates. Ten percent of the proposed deputies were rejected at these meetings. Many of the rejectees were traditional chiefs, others former collaborators, and some people whose personal conduct was considered objectionable. The higher level assemblies were elected indirectly. Members of the local bodies were called upon to choose from among themselves deputies to sit in the district assemblies. The municipal elections for the largest towns were held in stages, with neighborhood groups nominating representatives who in turn elected the members of the assemblies. Within each province, district and municipal representatives elected a provincial assembly. In all these elections there was a significant number of rejections, showing that the process was not simply one of rubber-stamping nominations. The 226 members of the National People's Assembly, however, were simply chosen by Frelimo's Central Committee and the list submitted to the provincial bodies for *pro forma* ratification. Whether such direct local control over the selection of candidates would continue once Frelimo was organized as a vanguard party and in control at all levels remained to be seen. The normal procedure in a Marxist-Leninist state would be for the party to dominate in the selection process, with the people simply called upon to ratify its choices.

Aside from the creation of these elected assemblies, reform of the old colonial administration made slow progress. The shortage of cadres was one of the main obstacles. While old agencies could be eliminated and new ones set up, the personnel staffing them remained largely the same. Frelimo believed that "the old kind of bureaucracy is politically, professionally, morally, and ideologically incapable of carrying out the tasks set by the construction of a people's democracy."[40] But since a wholesale purge would have decimated the ranks of the existing civil service, it decided instead to "win them (the civil servants) over to the correct political line, to reintegrate them into the heart of the broad masses, to transform them into true workers of public administration in the service of the People."[41] What this meant in practice was two things: first, the holding of endless rounds of discussion and self-criticism sessions in government offices, and second, the public denunciation of all those considered "compromised" by their past association with the Portuguese. Pictures of these *comprometidos* were posted at the entrance to ministries and other public offices for all to see, and they were called upon to discuss their activities and behavior with their colleagues. It was assumed that after a year of such public scrutiny and reeducation, the *comprometidos* would be reformed.

Other problems involved in reforming the state apparatus had not yet been tackled as of the time of this writing. Most important among these was that of the formation of a privileged elite based in the government bureaucracy. Frelimo was officially at war with the bureaucratic bourgeoisie. In practice, however, it took few steps to curtail its privileges. Government officials continued, as under the Portuguese, to be very well paid compared to the rest of the population, and even the wage gap within the civil service hierarchy remained wide. In state industry, the lowest salaries were under 2,000 escudos a month ($1.00 equals 33 escudos). In the civil service, salaries ranged from 3,000 to 4,000 escudos. At the other end of the scale, a minister was paid 40,000 to 45,000 escudos a month. This roughly 20:1 ratio was double that prevailing in Tanzania. In late 1979, the issue of a reform of the public wage scale was being discussed, but the debate seemed to be centered on the necessity for linking industrial wages to productivity while little was being said about the relatively high level of civil service salaries.[42]

Another important issue when considering the new political organization of Mozambique is the relationship between party and state. In the preindependence and immediate postindependence period, the line between the two was somewhat blurred, in the same way as the line between party members and the rest of the population was softened by the existence of the dynamizing groups. Frelimo cadres in the liberated zones had represented party and government, supplemented in their efforts by sympathizers among the local population. After the congress, the notion came to prevail that party and state should be clearly divided. As Machel explained:

> ... there must be no confusion between the functions of the party and those of the state, they are quite distinct. It is true that in the past some party structures took it upon themselves to solve social problems, juridical problems, problems concerning marriages.... There was a phase during which it was the party and the dynamizing groups which performed those functions.... Why? Because we were not structured, the state apparatus was not structured. It was still the colonial state apparatus. The population started immediately to turn away from it and to Frelimo. Today, the functions are quite distinct. The function of the party is that of establishing the broad lines of our development. The party gives an overall direction to the society, sets priorities, issues statements concerning the main tasks. The state exercises sovereignty and authority.... The state exercises above all the political and administrative power....[43]

The separation of party and state was hampered in practice by the weaknesses in organization of both. Those of the state apparatus we have already discussed. But the reorganization of Frelimo as a vanguard party also proved a slow, arduous task. Nearly one year after the Third Congress, one

Frelimo official complained that the recruitment of new members was "insufficient, marginal, and only taking place in a few areas."[44] What was called "the national campaign for structuring the party" continued throughout most of 1978, with the deadline postponed from September to November to complete the process. Figures on the size of the new party membership had not been released as of the time of this writing. Machel and other Frelimo officials would only say that there were "thousands" of militants and that the percent of the total population enrolled would eventually be the highest of any socialist country. Procedures were used to screen candidates to assure that only individuals acceptable both to Frelimo and their coworkers or neighbors would be allowed in. Every aspiring member was submitted first to the scrutiny of a Frelimo committee and then to the criticism of community residents or workers assembled in a general meeting. Subsequently, those who passed these tests had to have their names approved by the party provincial committees. The party statutes also specified that candidates other than proven wartime Frelimo militants had to wait at least one year before being admitted to full membership in order to prove their dedication, moral rectitude, and ideological purity. A party school was set up at Matola near the capital with East German assistance to help provide for the latter.

A visit by the authors to Mozambique in mid-1979 suggested that both the Party and state still have some way to go before either would be well enough implanted to make a clear division of functions possible. Very often an official present in a given locality appeared to be doing all jobs irrespective of whether he was formally a party or state representative. For example, the authors found that in Gaza Province local Frelimo cadres had approved detailed production plans, down to the acreage of tomatoes and onions, for the peasant cooperatives. Such a task hardly conformed to the definition of the Party's functions as that of "establishing the broad lines of our development." While there was no indication that Frelimo was intending to become another "party-state" like the PDG in Guinea, it was clearly running up against the general African problem of having enough qualified personnel to afford a clear separation of party and state, particularly at the local level. In fact, in March 1980 a new effort was undertaken to delineate the functions of the two more sharply, making the party into the one and only policymaking body. Two of Frelimo's most prominent members and principal ideologues, Marcelino dos Santos and Jorge Rebelo, were taken out of the cabinet and assigned to full-time work in the party secretariat respectively as chief economic strategist and ideologue. They were replaced in their former ministeral posts by technocrats, a choice further empahsizing Frelimo's thesis that the state should simply be the executing arms of the party. Frelimo made it very clear that the move was not a demotion of dos Santos and Rebelo by stressing that the party was far more important than the state. Lending credibility to this explanation was the fact that their transfer came as part of an overall campaign to curb the power of the state bureaucracy and to reaffirm the primacy of the party.

2. The Communal Village Controversy

The *aldeias communais* evoked enormous emotion among Mozambicans for reasons that went back to Frelimo's struggle against the Portuguese and its wartime experience in the liberated zones. More than any other institution, the villages were the symbol of what the party regarded as its own original contribution to socialism and as the wellspring of its revolution. Less than a year after independence, in February 1976, the communal villages were the object of a lengthy Central Committee resolution defining their overall importance to the country. "The communal villages are the spine of the development . . . in the countryside. It is in the communal villages that we focus the collective productive efforts of the peasant masses, and that, thanks to collective life, the organized population frees its enormous collective energy."[45] The villages were to develop the political consciousness of the peasantry, promote a collective life style, improve the material standard of living in the rural areas and boost production through collectivization to the point where a sizeable surplus would become available to feed the cities. They would also make it possible to provide the peasantry with education, health care, and other social services so totally lacking under Portuguese rule. Frelimo's commitment to the *aldeias communais* was totally reaffirmed at the Third Congress. Yet by 1980, no law had been issued giving a legal basis to the villages or specifying their political and economic role in the overall system. They had received very little government assistance and had been generally neglected in comparison to the new state farms. The position the *aldeias communais* occupied in reality was simply not commensurate to that that they occupied in the Frelimo rhetoric.

There are two principal explanations for this discrepancy: Frelimo's commitment to Marxism-Leninism and thus to central economic planning, and the concrete economic conditions the country faced at independence. The concept of a planned economy came into direct conflict with that of the communal villages. The *aldeias* were small, decentralized, and largely autonomous and most cultivation was still individual. They hardly lent themselves to being integrated into an overall planned economy to meet the scientifically established food and raw material requirements of the country. The economic problems immediately facing the government also played against the communal villages. The collapse of the agricultural sector stemming from the flight of Portuguese farmers and a disastrous combination of poor rainfall in the northern regions and floods in the Zambezi and Limpopo valleys had reduced the index of per capita food production from 100 in the period 1960 to 1971 to 85 in 1977.[46] Scarce foreign exchange was being consumed by the massive import of staple foods from abroad, amounting to 350,000 tons in 1978 and 1979.[47] Increased production was thus a vital national need. Notwithstanding numerous declarations of total commitment to the communal villages, Frelimo concentrated its efforts on reactivating the abandoned Portuguese farms as state farms, which seemed to hold the promise of a quicker solution to the food shortages. There was a seemingly sound economic rationale for this decision. The Portuguese farms were located in the most fertile and developed lands, were linked to the cities already by roads, and the government could itself control the marketing of their produce. The communal villages, by contrast, were located mostly in the subsistence sector and were often geographically isolated. Whatever the rationale, the policy had long-term economic and political implications. The state farms would continue making demands on the government for funds, management personnel, and supporting services, reducing what little of these were available for the communal villages. The inevitable result would be an economic and financial commitment to the state farms and the strengthening of the trend toward centralization.

The few available figures on government spending in agriculture tend to confirm the priority given to the state farms. For example, in the period 1978 to 1979 the government budgeted $38.5 million for agricultural development, of which fully $25 million was earmarked just for importing agricultural equipment almost exclusively destined for the state farms.[48] But the clearest indication that the government had in fact devoted most of its funds and efforts to the state farm sector was the sudden dismissal of Minister of Agriculture Joaquim de Carvalho in August 1978. The list of his failings was long and varied. He was accused of demonstrating an antiparty attitude, of having encouraged "liberalism and indiscipline" within the Ministry of Agriculture by discussing problems outside the proper channels, of displaying wrong ideas on the subject of the emancipation of women. But above all, he was accused of having disregarded the "popular line" which called for stimulating the organization of communal villages. According to the communique announcing his dismissal:

> In particular, he (Carvalho) sought to block the process of creating communal villages, thus jeopardizing one of our decisive development choices. Systematically giving priority to technology, he scorned the people's initiative and contribution. The sector of family production, our country's main source of agricultural produce, was disregarded.[49]

The dismissal of Carvalho, naturally enough, was interpreted at the time as the triumph of the supporters of the more democratic and decentralized concept of the communal villages against those favoring the more centralized and bureaucratic solution of state farms; or, as some put it, the victory of the "independent" Mozambican Marxists against the Soviet-oriented, orthodox ones.

In retrospect, such an interpretation was overly hasty, since the dismissal of Carvalho was not followed by any significant change in policy. No funds were reported shifted from the state farms to the *aldeias*. The National Commission for the Communal Villages had no budget of its own, and the empty offices and bare desks at its headquarters when visited in mid-1979 strongly suggested a lack of activity. A nationwide debate on the future of the villages, leading to the promulgation of a charter, had been scheduled for the latter half of that year but was postponed until March 1980. There was no rural bank to provide loans to the villages on a systematic basis, although *ad hoc* financing was made available to the cooperatives. Nor was an agricultural extension service being established to support them, either. The pattern of foreign assistance further confirmed the absence of any fundamental shift in the government and party bias toward state farms. The vast majority of Cuban, Bulgarian, East German and other Eastern block agronomists working in Mozambique continued to serve as advisers and managers to the state farms. As for the Nordic aid consortium of Scandinavian countries, providing the largest amount of foreign assistance to the agricultural sector, its representative in Maputo reported in 1979 that only two of the 33 new projects they were discussing for the 1980 through 1983 period were directed toward helping the communal villages.[50]

The state farm sector, for its part, was becoming extremely centralized. The Mozambican government favored the creation of huge mechanized units regrouping numerous Portuguese farms. While the shortage of managerial personnel in part accounted for such a trend, this does not appear to be the only explanation. Size and centralization in general were equated with modernity and efficiency. Thus, the Ministry of Agriculture in late 1979 was setting up an office to control the allocation and repair of farm machinery on a nationwide scale, justifying the endeavor on the ground that "we must develop a mentality of efficiency to overcome the artisanal mentality."[51] Some of the new state farms were huge for a developing country of Mozambique's capabilities. The Limpopo Agro-Industrial Complex, which had been a small holder scheme grouping 1500 Portuguese families, was aggregated into one large production unit with a permanent work force of 2,500 and a seasonal one of 8,000 to 20,000 cultivating 15,000 hectares of rice and some vegetables with the help of 240 tractors and 150 combine-harvesters. The state director told the authors that the ultimate objective was to increase the size of the farm by stages to include 90,000 hectares of rice-growing land. Another state enterprise, a ranch near Beira in central Mozambique, had 140,000 hectares with 22,000 head of cattle. These were probably the most extreme examples of vast state-run schemes, but the same tendency toward centralization was evident among all the existing 200 state farms.

It is not clear how, in the long run, Mozambique can reconcile this emphasis on state farms with its professed commitment to communal villages. One approach favored by some Frelimo officials consists of literally defining the problem out of existence by altering the basic concept of the communal village and its purpose. The director of the National Commission for the Communal Villages, Job Chambal, said in an interview that it was a mistake to view the communal villages and state farms as conflicting or contradictory forms of organization.[52] The *aldeias* were political and social units, while cooperatives and state farms were economic ones. A well-developed communal village had to have either a cooperative or a state farm as its economic base. The latter, he said, was the higher form of economic organization and thus the more desireable one ultimately. The commission's position at that time was that the state farms both warranted and needed more economic assistance than the communal villages, which were expected to rely primarily on their own efforts and resources to get going. That the commission set up to defend the interests of the communal villages was thinking in these terms illustrated how pervasive the statist approach was becoming in Mozambique by mid-1979.

At present, the *aldeias* are neither mere extensions of state farms nor really collectives. In fact, they fall into all sorts of categories, the most numerous being those where private cultivation still prevails. Despite assertions by Mozambican officials that the *aldeias* are very different from the Tanzanian *ujamaa* villages, in practice the vast majority of them were not, at least as of mid-1979. At that point, there were about 1,000 "communal villages" officially, grouping 1.6 million peasants, or roughly 15 percent of the total population.[53] They differed greatly from each other both in terms of their origins and degree of collectivization. One category consisted of the villages formed in the old liberated zones during the war, concentrated in the northern part of the country. Interestingly enough, while being the oldest, they were not necessarily the most collectivized. It appears that independence had brought a setback in this respect, since party officials in these areas complained of the difficulty encountered in convincing the peasants to cultivate collectively, or at least to cultivate individual fields side by side in "block farms," to facilitate their eventual collectivization.[54] Other villages had been Portuguese *aldeiamentos,* similar to the "strategic hamlets" in Vietnam, into which the population had been forced during the war in an attempt to deprive the guerrillas of their base of support. A third group consisted of villages created in 1977 to 1978 to relocate the refugees from the floods in the Zambezi and Limpopo valleys. Even government officials admitted readily that these hastily assembled villages were mostly a conglomeration of huts without a real collective economic organization, and that much work remained to be done. Finally, there were the best communal villages, those formed after adequate political preparation and having a high degree of collective production, but they constituted by far the smallest group.

Only a minority of the communal villages had a cooperative as their main production unit. Even fewer were linked to a state farm. One of the most interesting examples of both was afforded by the Limpopo Agro-Industrial Complex. This gigantic state farm was officially considered the productive unit of a number of villages which housed its 2,500 full-time workers. To talk of these villages as "communal" meant departing completely from the wartime definition of the term. While the workers were organized into production brigades, each electing its own leaders, the management of the gigantic complex was a highly complex matter in the hands of a state appointed director and of a number of agronomists and engineers from Eastern bloc countries. Moreover, there were many villages on the farm, but the farm was run as a single unit. The villages simply had no control over their so-called productive units.

The same complex also contained some villages organized into cooperatives. A small part of the irrigated land was turned over to nearby communal villages, rather than being fully integrated into the state farm. The production units of these villages were cooperatives, which could recruit members from more than one village. One of their most striking characteristics was their size, with hundreds of members and hundreds of hectares of land. The members drew a regular salary as an "advance" on their share of the cooperative's profits, the amount being roughly equivalent to the wage received by the state farm workers. The cooperatives were so large and complicated that their management was somewhat beyond the competence of the villagers. As a result, they received their production plans from Bulgarian agronomists based in the provincial capital and having only periodic contact with the cooperatives. The plans were also approved by the party before being sent back to the villagers for implementation. Even these cooperatives thus tended to be managed in a bureaucratic and centralized manner. To be sure, these Limpopo Valley villages were not typical. They were much more adjuncts of the state-run complex, and while they were privileged from an economic viewpoint, they were also much more closely controlled than most others. Though they were not typical, it seems very significant that they were regarded as more advanced and a model to be imitated by the others eventually.

2. Economic Policies

The economic policies followed by Frelimo since the Third Congress are difficult to summarize succintly. First of all, the government has regarded the period up until 1980 as one of recovery rather than of new growth, setting as its main goal the attainment of preindependence levels of production by that time. The patchy statistics available suggest that this target was not reached, although there had been significant recovery in some sectors. The few published figures indicated increases of between 15 and 50 percent for many agricultural products during the 1979 season as well as for key export commodities like cotton, citrus fruits, sugar, shrimp, and coal. The country was still far from meeting its own food needs, however, as was indicated in its projected imports for the same year: 120,000 tons of wheat; 155,000 tons of maize (corn) and 65,000 tons of rice.[55] Secondly, the government has not been able to prepare a proper plan of development and has even been slow in establishing a legal framework for its new socialist system. The result has been a mixture of policies, some clearly inspired by ideology and others quite pragmatic. But no economic measures have really violated the commitment to Marxism-Leninism and most have been aimed at preparing the country for the day when an integrated overall approach to socialist development will be technically possible.

The major pieces of economic legislation promulgated by 1980 concerned private investment in the country and the status of land. Decree-Law 18/77 stated that private investment would be permitted if it contributed to national reconstruction and helped to meet "the basic needs of the people."[56] The measure guaranteed repatriation of profits and compensation in case of nationalization, but made clear that all private investors would have to work closely with the government and establish mutually acceptable goals. "The state must discipline the private sector," the decree stated. The government has increasingly shown interest in attracting foreign capital. President Machel met personally with a number of American company executives during his visit to the United Nations in the fall of 1978 and Business International organized a seminar for interested Western investors in Maputo in March 1980. Whether Mozambique would succeed in linking up with Western investors to promote its stated policy of industrialization was too early to determine as of the time of this writing. So far, the only new plant to open in Mozambique since independence has been a General Tire Factory, a project which had been launched in the colonial period. While the government has shown great interest in entering joint ventures with foreign companies, it has pursued slowly but steadily a policy of squeezing out the existing major private industries, particularly those belonging to the Portuguese or regarded as having failed to keep up production without good cause. The result has been the sporadic nationalization of factories, plants, and agro-businesses to the point where the state now controls most of the industrial sector.

In September 1979, the government nationalized all land. By then, the move was hardly revolutionary.[57] Most of the Portuguese plantations had already been nationalized *de facto*, and the peasants had never really owned the land in the modern sense of the term, although they had the right to cultivate it. Their rights to the use of the land continued to be recognized by the new decree, which stipulated that peasants employing no outside labor would not pay rent and could pass their farms onto their children. Collective farms and cooperatives also paid no rent. Only those operating with paid labor, even if only a single individual was hired, were subject to rent. The legislation made clear the government intended to discourage any private commercial farming, even on a small scale, favoring instead various forms of collective agriculture.

Government policy regarding the internal organization of the industrial sector has been one of promoting worker participation, although on an increasingly restricted and carefully defined basis. Initially, the activities of the workers went almost unchecked in both private and state-run enterprises, resulting in wildcat strikes and unrealistic demands for an immediate improvement in wages and conditions. Such labor agitation bordered at times on chaos and almost paralyzed the economy. In October 1976, the government sought to regulate more closely participation and the system of management within the industrial sector: it recognized the dynamizing groups and their basically political functions; it established "production councils" to assure that the workers "will participate in an active, collective, and conscious manner in the discussion and solution of problems and will plan and control production";[58] and it institutionalized the already existing administrative commissions consisting of both a state-appointed director and worker representatives in the public sector and of the owner or manager plus worker representatives in the private sector. While on paper the functions of the three organs were distinct, in practice the situation remained very confused. The dynamizing groups in most cases preexisted the other institutions and had been responsible for most tasks, from preventing sabotage to encouraging productivity and trying to keep the plants operating. They should have reverted to strictly political tasks after the organizing of the other committees, but this did not always happen. The crucial question, and one difficult to answer in general, was whether the production councils were effective in counterbalancing the power of the state-appointed director or whether the latter was really running the enterprise on his own.[59]

Two aspects of the economy badly affected by the crisis of independence were retail trade and transport. With the departure of the Portuguese, most stores closed down, leaving an enormous problem not only concerning the distribution of essential consumer goods but also the purchase of cash crops which had been done previously by the Portuguese shopkeepers. Two solutions were adopted: cooperative shops and state-run "people's stores." While these measures brought about some improvement, consumer goods were scarce everywhere, in part because of insufficient production or imports. In the cities, there were often long lines of people waiting outside the shops. In rural areas, the peasants complained that even essential commodities such as salt, soap, and cloth were often not available, and that when they finally arrived they were too expensive. While prices were lower in the state or cooperative stores than in private ones,[60] the peasants received little for their produce, a situation which both created discontent and served as a disincentive to produce more, or at least to sell more.[61]

In the transport sector, investment has been high, but it would be difficult to base any conclusions about the economic policies of Mozambique on this. In 1978 to 1979, for example, the government devoted to transport $192 million, or over one third of its total investment budget of $460 million.[62] But it could hardly have been otherwise, no matter what the government's orientation, given the almost total destruction of the country's transport system through the export of most trucks at the time of independence.

While the economic policies of Mozambique were guided by ideological considerations, Frelimo also showed itself capable of recognizing situations it could not immediately control and of dealing with them pragmatically.

Nowhere was this pragmatism more easily discernible than in its relationship with South Africa, which ideologically and politically was one of Mozambique's major enemies but in practice remained a major economic partner. Like all countries in southern Africa, Mozambique was in a sense colonized not only by a European power, but by the Republic of South Africa as well. As the major economic force in the region, the Republic was a source of investment funds, personnel, and machinery for all its neighbors. Like the other countries, Mozambique found it very hard to disentangle its economy from South Africa's and made major accommodations to this reality. The Republic was historically a major source of foreign exchange for Mozambique, providing probably close to $200 million annually, a figure representing well over half the value of all its exports. Two items were particularly important: remittances from Mozambicans recruited to work in the South African mines and payment for the shipment of South African exports through Mozambican ports and railroads. While the importance of workers' remittances decreased sharply after independence, the South African use of ports and railroads increased following the ratification of a new agreement between the two countries.

At its peak in the colonial period, the number of Mozambican workers in the Transvaal mines was over 100,000. An agreement between the two countries stipulated that 60 percent of the workers' salary should be paid directly to Mozambique and in gold, with the amount being calculated at the initial fixed price of $36 an ounce. As the world market price increased well above that level, the colonial administration was able to resell the gold at a sizeable profit. The workers for their part received the remainder of their pay in escudos upon their return home. In the last year prior to independence, Mozambique earned in this manner nearly $150 million, making exported labor the largest single source of foreign exchange. After independence, the Mozambican government sought to decrease the flow of workers to South Africa, which in turn was anxious at that time to reduce the number of foreigners in order to given precedence in employment to its own black population. The number of Mozambican workers in the Republic dropped to 35,000 by 1978, and in the same year the South African government abrogated the old gold sales agreement. Altogether, Mozambique's earnings from this source was probably reduced to about one third of the preindependence amount. But economic relations between the two countries still remained very important as illustrated by the signing in February 1979 of a five-year agreement strengthening their trade and transportation links. According to its terms, South Africa committed itself to doubling the amount of cargo it shipped through Maputo from six million tons to twelve million tons a year. As part of the deal, the South African government extended to Mozambique a $120 million line of credit, to be used partly to improve the railroad line and the facilities at the port of Maputo, and partly to import commodities from the Republic.[63]

Mozambique's willingness to enter into such an agreement, all the more paradoxical politically since South African exports from Maputo included coal destined for Israel, can be best understood against its growing trade deficit, amounting to $353 million in 1978 and expected to be $419 million the following year.[64] Invisible earnings, most notably those from worker remittances and South African transit trade, lowered the overall balance-of-payment deficit to $239 million in 1978.[65] Since its imports, consisting largely of food, spare parts and machinery, were difficult to reduce and its export earnings were growing slowly, Mozambique remained extremely dependent on these earnings.

Despite the seriousness of the economic situation, Mozambique was not willing to compromise in a similar manner with Rhodesia, which also used to provide a substantial amount of income from transit traffic and tourism. After independence, the Mozambican government abided by the UN sanctions resolution against that white-ruled nation, closing its borders in March 1976 to all Rhodesian trade and traffic. This action was estimated to have cost the Mozambican economy between $110 million and $135 million annually.[66] The end to the Rhodesian conflict in early 1980 led to the reopening of the border and was expected to alleviate somewhat the balance-of-payment deficit, without however totally resolving it.

A serious obstacle to both economic recovery and development has been the shortage of technicians and administrators at all levels, a legacy of Portuguese colonialism. This shortage has had two major consequences: the reliance on a very motley array of foreign *cooperantes,* or technical assistants, and the reinforcement of the tendency toward centralization which was to some extent already implicit in the ideology. The *cooperantes* came from around the world, mostly on government-to-government contracts, but some as the result of direct hire. The bulk of the *cooperantes* were Portuguese. In June 1979, there were 15,000 of them in the country, but about 7,000 would complete their contracts by the end of the year, and it was still not clear whether they would all be replaced. Another important contingent, but much smaller than the Portuguese, came from Cuba, which provided probably around 400 civilian personnel. The Cubans were reported to enjoy the closest relations with the Mozambicans, partly because of their language facility and partly because their style of life—they were housed and fed in barrack-like hostels, and only received pocket money—was closer to that of the Mozambicans themselves. East Germans, Bulgarians, and Soviet technicians were also working in the country as was a small group of Chinese. In addition, a number of European and Latin American *cooperantes,* most of them ideologically committed to some form of socialism, also lent their services to Mozambique. The presence of such a mixture of foreign nationals posed a problem of communications—a hospital might be staffed by doctors and nurses from five or six different countries, having difficulty speaking Portuguese let alone any of the African languages. More serious were the conflicting biases the *cooperantes* brought to their jobs. For example, East German and Bulgarian agronomists experienced in the management of mechanized state farms thought about the organization of agriculture in those terms only. The Scandinavians, on the other hand, favored small scale cooperatives and the creation of an extension service to aid the communal villages. Many Western radicals saw socialism as direct workers' management. It is difficult to know, however, how much influence these various views really had on policy decisions. Westerners reported that they were not allowed to sit in on policy discussions but claimed the *cooperantes* from socialist countries, particularly from Cuba, sometimes did. The trend toward statist farm management and the emphasis on industrialization, at least in theory, could be the result of the advice from Eastern bloc experts. It could equally well be the result, however, of the Mozambicans' own interpretation of what Marxism-Leninism implies and of the specific conditions facing the government.

3. Social Services

The Third Congress had proclaimed that the country's main preoccupation should be to "raise material production and productivity in work, the indispensable preconditions for the improvement of living conditions" and that "our basic resources and efforts will thus be mainly applied to the economic sector." In reality, Mozambique has devoted a large share of the budget to the delivery of social services. In 1978, for instance, the regular government budget totalled $415 million, of which fully $109 million went for social services and only $85 million to the economic sector.[67] The following year, the social sector received $125 million compared to $92 million for the economic sector.[68] These figures raised the very serious question of whether Mozambique was not embarking on a path leading to the Tanzanian plight of "development without growth."

Progress in the field of social services has been remarkable. The number of children attending primary schools almost doubled to 1.3 million in the first three years of independence, while that in secondary schools tripled to 60,000.[69] To be sure, the absolute numbers are still relatively small, but the increase has nonetheless been impressive. Enrollment at the university has grown very slowly, on the other hand, because of the small number of high school graduates at independence. Within a few years, there will certainly be an explosion of enrollment at the university level as well as more and more students come through the secondary schools. Much of this expansion in education has been achieved through emergency solutions such as the use of untrained teachers often holding class in the open air and without textbooks or other materials. The quality of such education is probably not very high, an unavoidable result facing any country intent upon increasing enrollment rapidly in an effort to make up for lost time. Despite its desire to expand education, the government has closed down missionary and other private schools in keeping with its belief that this task must be reserved for the state so that the new generation will be brought up imbued with the principles of Marxism-Leninism. This concern for a correct socialist upbringing also explains the Mozambican decision to send some 2,000 children to Cuba for their entire primary and secondary education.

In the field of health, too, the Mozambican government has begun a highly ambitious, sweeping reform of the old system. It envisages a whole new basic health program covering the entire country, though the services presently offered are still quite rudimentary. Private practice was banned immediately after independence, preventive medicine stressed and medical care immediately made available to the rural areas. The long-term plan is to have part-time paramedics present at the village and neighborhood level and supported by a network of some 280 "sanitary posts" and 190 mother-and-child care clinics. This system will be supplemented by about 90 health centers, staffed by at least one nurse, and by 25 rural hospitals having a minimum of one part-time doctor.[70] Finally, a few district hospitals will offer a wide array of services for the most serious cases. For a country with a population of better than eleven million, these figures may seem low. Considering the fact that in 1975 Mozambique had only 80 doctors (mostly foreigners) compared to the 425 present even in Tanzania at independence, the implementation of this plan would represent a major step forward in providing basic health services for the entire population.[71] That the peasantry has been foremost in the minds of Mozambican health planners is also evident from the first ever national vaccination campaign, begun in June 1976 and lasting nearly three years. Approximately 96 percent of the entire population was vaccinated against smallpox, measles, tuberculosis, and tetanus.[72]

The dilemma of development in a country like Mozambique was vividly illustrated by the problems of education and health care. There could be no doubt that the government was trying to provide basic services which had previously been totally neglected and were desperately needed. It was certainly not being extravagant in its approach. Even these basic services provided in a very rudimentary form, however, were putting an enormous burden on the country's budget and impairing the government's capacity to promote economic growth more rapidly. There was no doubt that Mozambique needed both "growth" and "development," but there was also reason to question whether it could afford both simultaneously.

Conclusions

The transition in Mozambique from war of national liberation to Marxism-Leninism has been a remarkably smooth one. The complete absence of overt factional fighting among Frelimo leaders, or of deep ideological dissension, has provided the Mozambican experience with a degree of continuity unique among radical African countries. While the commitment to Marxism-Leninism appears firmly rooted, there has nonetheless arisen an underlying conflict between the policies perceived as dictated by this ideology and those inspired by "the revolutionary experience of the Mozambican people." The proposed "synthesis" between the two has turned out to be much more problematical than Frelimo leaders supposed. Indeed, it would not be surprising if Frelimo underwent at some point soon a third crisis of "criticism" in which the outstanding issue of how precisely to carry out this synthesis will have to be resolved or the attempt simply abandoned.

The most obvious manifestation of this growing malaise is the controversy surrounding the organization of the agricultural sector and whether priority will be given to the *aldeias communais* or the state farms. The choice is fraught with theoretical and practical questions and has far-reaching consequences for the entire political and economic system. For example, can the communal villages really create the structural conditions for the emergence of a collective consciousness or do they risk instead spurring the growth of individualism? Is it possible anyway to integrate thousands of semiautonomous villages into a centrally planned economy or can the goal of "scientific planning" best be achieved through the development of state farms? Can production in the *aldeias* readily be transformed to reflect a "mentality of efficiency" rather than an "artisanal mentality"? A decision to opt for a development strategy based on the villages is very likely to give rise to a large degree of uncontrollable decentralization and rural democracy, while one relying upon state farms would fit much more naturally into a centralized planned economy and a polity whose basic principle of political organization is democratic centralism. In other words, the state farms comply far more readily with the dictates of orthodox Marxism-Leninism than do the communal villages. But the *aldeias* have enormous appeal and emotional significance as the very symbol of the Mozambican wartime experience.

While the lack of agreement concerning the communal villages has come out into the open because of the firing of Carvalho, a similar controversy surrounding other related issues has remained much more covert. The clearest indication of its existence has been an indirect one, namely the failure of the Mozambican government, after five years of independence, to enact precise legislation for a number of crucial institutions. As we have already pointed out, the communal villages still had no statutes as of early 1980. Nor had the relationship between the *aldeias,* the state farms and cooperatives been spelled out in any document. Similarly, the form and scope of workers' participation in the state sector was still not clearly regulated, nor had the fate of the dynamizing groups in a political system dominated by a vanguard party been settled. In other words, a large number of fundamental decisions had not been reached. We do not believe that lack of time was the principal factor here. Facing a much more difficult internal political situation and a high level of conflict, Ethiopia and even Angola were quicker in issuing legislation spelling out the details of their social and economic organization. This suggests that Mozambique deliberately avoided taking certain decisions because of fear of a fundamental disagreement.

It is difficult as a result to reach any clear-cut conclusions yet about the precise meaning of Marxism-Leninism in Mozambique with regard to the overall shape of the political and economic system and above all the nature of political participation. There has certainly been a trend since independence away from unbridled participation, but since the initial situation bordered at times on anarchy, this was neither surprising nor clearly indicative of the future. At first, workers tried to take over the factories and impose their will, dynamizing groups ruled neighborhoods and villages, and committees of all kinds engaged in endless discussions in government offices, plants, and farms on everything from work attitudes and grievances to the meaning of true socialism. The entire country appeared at times to be undergoing "group therapy." Inevitably, such a high pitch of revolutionary enthusiasm and participatory zeal could not be sustained, and just as predictably Frelimo sought to channel and control participation, bringing it within limits compatible with the principles of a vanguard party. But the system is still not completely run from the top down in a highly centralized and authoritarian manner; the country is too underdeveloped and the party too much of a skeleton organization to make this possible. Furthermore, there are local institutions acting as a countervailing force to such a centralization, namely the people's assemblies in each and every village, the workers' production councils in the factories, and the dynamizing groups in the neighborhoods. The political system is still very much in a state of flux but the dangers of over-centralization and authoritarianism remain very real as they are in other countries where Marxism-Leninism is taken seriously and "democratic centralism" is the guiding principle.

Chapter V
Angola

The Wartime Heritage

The origins of Marxism-Leninism in Angola go all the way back to the year the *Movimento Popular de Libertação de Angola* (MPLA) was founded in 1956. But the history of the Angolan nationalist struggle was so beclouded by other issues of race, ethnicity, regionalism, factionalism, and personal feuding that the already clear ideological orientation of the MPLA was often overlooked. In order to understand the interplay between ideology and other forces at work in Angola, it is necessary to review briefly the wartime struggle and above all the tortuous evolution of the MPLA, the party responsible for introducing Marxism-Leninism into Angola after independence.

The history of the Angolan nationalist movement was one of repeated unreconcilable rifts leading eventually to civil war. Three rival movements participated in the liberation struggle. The MPLA itself was riven by factionalism, "autonomism," and a power struggle among the top leaders, all of which stemmed from the difficulties of prosecuting a war on many fronts that were disconnected from each other and even from an effective overall command. Like the FLN in Algeria almost fifteen years earlier, the MPLA was wracked by conflicts between the "internal" military leadership and the "external" political one and among a number of semiautonomous guerrilla leaders with their own following. Both the FLN and the MPLA had a clandestine underground in the urban areas with its own leadership, and both saw a number of their top leaders arrested and condemned to spend some of the war years in prison, only to emerge at independence with their own ambitions. In Algeria, this general problem of rival factions and wartime leaders vying for power was known as *wilayism,* a *wilaya* being one of the subdivisions of the FLN's political-military organization inside Algeria. The MPLA called the same phenomenon simply "fractionalism." It is essential to understand how and why this came about during the anticolonial struggle in Angola, for fractionalism both within the national liberation movement generally and the MPLA particularly was destined to have an enormous impact on later developments.

The MPLA was founded in 1956 while Agostinho Neto, who became its president six years later, was serving one of his many stints in a Portuguese jail. It seems that Marxism was already the prism through which many

Angolan nationalists were looking at their struggle. One of the movement's immediate predecessors was the Angolan Communist Party, which had been established a year earlier and which apparently dissolved soon after the MPLA came into existence. The MPLA's chief theoretician, Lucio Lara, described this organization as "much more an ideological study center" than a proper party.[1] Neto himself said that he did not approve of this "initiative"; above all he rejected the communists' central tenet, namely that it was necessary to develop "antagonistic social classes" by passing through a phase of capitalism in order to prepare the way both for the anticolonial struggle and for socialism.[2] Yet it is interesting to note that this idea, according to Neto himself, was discussed "at great length in numerous meetings" among the Angolan nationalists, one clear indication of the Marxist influence at work from the very beginning. "The line we followed," Neto said in his memoirs, "was dictated to us by the conviction that nothing proved—in fact the very contrary was true—that our postcolonial society had to pass through a capitalist phase to arrive at socialism."[3] While studying in Portugal Neto and other future MPLA leaders were also in contact with "revolutionaries" from that country, presumably communists and socialists who were waging their own struggle against the Salazar regime.[4] The MPLA was finally formed by bringing together several noncommunist groups which had been organizing clandestinely in the *musseques,* or slums, of the Angolan capital of Luanda.

It was five years before any fighting took place against the Portuguese after the MPLA was established. The Movement itself dates the outbreak of its struggle from a daring but poorly organized assault by 3,000 supporters on the central prison and other strategic points in Luanda on February 4, 1961. The aim of the attack was to free a number of political prisoners being held there. It was an abortive affair that resulted in bloody reprisals by the Portuguese against the African population living in the *musseques* with hundreds, and possibly thousands, killed. Five weeks later, another uprising organized by a movement led by Holden Roberto, later known as the *Frente Nacional de Libertação de Angola* (FNLA), took place in the north among the Bakongo people. It resulted in the widely publicized death of some 300 Europeans and the less known slaughter of scores of *mestiços* (mulattoes) as well as *assimilados* (Africans deemed to have assimilated sufficient Portuguese culture to be treated almost as equals). Other smaller attacks by MPLA and FNLA followers took place all across northern Angola in the following months, but by October the Portuguese had succeeded in crushing the uprising after the official death toll reached 2,000 Europeans and 50,000 Africans.[5]

The two nationalist groups launching the anticolonial struggle were extremely different from each other right from the beginning. The MPLA was an urban-oriented and urban-based organization, which drew its support above all from the Mbundu people heavily represented in Luanda and was led mostly by *assimilados* and *mestiços*. The MPLA even felt obliged to justify the special nature of its leadership and to defend those who spoke only Portuguese as the "driving force behind the awakening of political consciousness."[6] These characteristics of the MPLA help explain why Marxism held a special appeal for its leaders. By stressing class conflict over all others, it provided the urban *mestiços* and *assimilados* with an ideology that transcended race and allowed cooperation between them and the black workers and lumpenproletariat of the *musseques*. The FLNA was very different. Its stronghold was in the rural north of Angola, its support came mostly from the Bakongo population, and the leadership was not only entirely black, but overtly racist as well, denigrating not only the Portuguese settlers but also the *mestiços* and *assimilados* they had created. The killings of members of these two groups in the initial FNLA insurgency was only the beginning of a lasting problem.

Between 1961 and 1966, the MPLA underwent extremely trying times. It did little fighting against the Portuguese, opening a front in the tiny enclave of Cabinda north of the Congo River but failing to take the struggle into the heartland of Angola. Furthermore, it was rent apart by the first of many power struggles. Neto was released from prison and made president in December 1962, but an ultraleftist faction led by party Secretary-General Veriato da Cruz refused to accept his leadership and tried to set up a splinter MPLA. In Angola and abroad, the MPLA began to be perceived as an unreliable and ineffective movement. Some of its guerrillas defected to the FNLA, and the Organization of African Unity decided to recognize the latter liberation movement as the only one worthy of support. The Zairian government used this decision as a pretext for expelling the MPLA from Kinshasa, forcing Neto's followers to move their headquarters to Brazzaville. The Movement's fortunes had reached such a low ebb by the end of 1963 that one of its staunchest outside supporters, British scholar Basil Davidson, wrote at the time that Neto was finished as a leader and the MPLA had "fractured, split, and reduced itself to a nullity."[7] Yet like the fabled phoenix, the Movement managed to rise again from its own ashes, thanks to a reconsolidation of the organization under Neto's leadership, Cuban assistance, and a reversal in the OAU attitude toward it.

When Cuban leader Ché Guevara met Neto in Brazzaville in early 1964, the MPLA leader was embarrassed, as he later wrote, by "not having anything much to show" him regarding the Movement's military acivities.[8] But Guevara was sufficiently impressed with Neto himself to provide Cuban instructors for the MPLA and to promise Cuban diplomatic and political support. With Cuban backing, and renewed OAU aid, the MPLA's fortunes began to pick up on both the diplomatic and guerrilla fronts. The year 1966 was a watershed. After multiple abortive attempts, the MPLA finally managed to get a "relief column" of guerrillas past Portuguese and FNLA patrols to its isolated partisans still holding out in the Dembos forests north of the capital. The same year, it opened its third front (Dembos and Cabinda were regarded officially as the first and second ones) in eastern Angola after securing permission from the Zambian government to operate from its territory. This "eastern front" became the main staging area for extending the struggle deeper into south-central and northeastern Angola, where a fourth and fifth military region were formally constituted in 1968. In many ways, the years 1966 to 1970 marked the high points of the MPLA guerrilla struggle. After this, multiple and increasingly successful Portuguese counter-offensives against the eastern front, plus renewed internal feuding, combined to have a devastating effect on the Movement.

Despite these seemingly perpetual difficulties in trying to wage an effective war against the Portuguese, the MPLA did manage to develop a fairly consistent ideological line reflecting Marxist-Leninist thinking and even to set up a number of institutions in its "semiliberated zones" within Angola that were to serve as an inspiration for future policies. The first platform, published in 1956, already looked beyond the attainment of independence, and called for planned economic development, the establishment of producers' cooperatives, state control over all foreign trade, and an agrarian reform "to liquidate private monopoly" as well as to redistribute land to the poorest peasants.[9] By 1968, the leadership had decided it would eventually have to create a vanguard party to lead the coalition of groups within the Movement. As a first step, the MPLA would have to start forming cadres and developing a clear ideological line. One member of the five-man Political-Military Coordinating Committee, Daniel Chipenda, stressed that such a line should be neither pro-Soviet nor pro-Chinese but simply socialist and based on the specific Angolan experience.[10] Another Coordinating Committee member, Spartacus Monimambu, was far more explicit:

> Political education is first of all nationalist.... But we know that tomorrow there will be many problems in Angola; solving them requires that we educate people in the ideological sphere. Our ideology is scientific socialism. We are going to be a socialist country tomorrow. There is no other way.[11]

The clearest professions of socialism and above all Marxism-Leninism, however, were confined to interviews with leftist foreign supporters. Official propaganda was far less explicit. The reason for this coyness was a Portuguese and FNLA campaign to discredit the Movement in Europe and the United States by portraying it as a communist party. This campaign even prompted the MPLA to put out a statement in 1971 denying this "false propaganda" and asserting it was "not a Communist movement."[12] But this reputation remained with it until the end of the anti-Portuguese struggle. The MPLA's professed sympathies for the socialist bloc and the aid and praise it received from the Soviet Union and Cuba both served the purpose of its detractors only too well. Furthermore, the MPLA regularly attended conferences of the Soviet-sponsored Afro-Asian People's Solidarity Organization and was a member of the Havana-based Tricontinental's directing body.

As early as 1966, the MPLA dispatched its first guerrilla recruits to Cuba for training. It also obtained an estimated 70 to 80 percent of all its arms from the Soviet Union.[13] Despite all this evidence of Eastern bloc ties and markedly Marxist inclinations, it was probably correct that the MPLA was not a communist movement during the war years; rather it was a coalition of various socialist and nationalist factions strongly influenced by Marxists who would only consolidate their leadership during the civil war of 1975 through 1976.

Some of the institutions reflecting the MPLA's Marxist-Leninist orientation began functioning during the anticolonial struggle. The *Escola de Quadros*, or party school, began operating in Kinshasa in early 1963 under Lara with the objective of assuring the supremacy of political over military leaders and "ideological over armed struggle."[14] Later, the school had to be moved to the Congo, but it managed to prosper and reportedly turned out 2,000 cadres by 1967.[15] The school spawned a number of smaller Revolutionary Instruction Centers inside the MPLA semiliberated zones. According to Davidson, 10 such Centers were operating inside the country by 1970.[16] Some of these cadres were assigned to the various war zones as political commissars in an attempt to check the power of the guerrilla commanders and to make sure the latter would follow the MPLA political line. But the attempt to curb warlordism essentially failed and in 1968 the MPLA was forced to recognize the guerrilla commanders as the chief political commissar in their zones. As Davidson noted, there was an inherent difficulty "of preventing the guerrilla war from degenerating into a military adventure."[17]

The MPLA also started organizing the population of the semiliberated zones into a fairly sophisticated politico-military system, setting up institutions it would later consider the pillars of its socialist revolution. The peasants were grouped into small villages of no more than 100 persons each to avoid the risk of exposing large numbers to a sudden Portuguese attack. Each village had its own elected "action committee"; a militia, albeit poorly armed; a "people's plantation"; and a "people's shop," generally serving a cluster of units. There were also the rudiments of a "labor union" charged with stimulating production, and organizations for women and even children, embryonic bodies that would later turn into the MPLA's mass organizations. The villages were grouped into sectors led by a "revolutionary action committee," and each five or six sectors formed a zone. The entire eastern region consisted of five such zones, each led by a political-military commander. Just how many people the MPLA actually brought under its administration before independence remains unclear, but it was certainly far fewer than the 800,000 Frelimo had under its control in Mozambique. According to one eastern front commander, there were about 30,000 peasants in MPLA zones by 1968 and the total may have risen to around 150,000 at its peak.[18] The number dwindled in any case as the Portuguese began to mount counter-offensives in 1972, inflicting considerable damage on the MPLA in eastern Angola. Nonetheless, the experience of the semiliberated zones was enormously important to the subsequent development of MPLA's concept of socialist institutions. Undoubtedly the most important of these was the "action committee," which later became the basis of the *poder popular* movement, regarded by the MPLA and its foreign supporters as the very essence of popular participation in the revolutionary process. Davidson, for example, hailed *poder popular*, or people's power, as the main instrument for achieving "major socio-political transformation,"[19] while the American Liberation Support Movement described it as "the force that will enable the Angolan people and the MPLA to build socialism."[20] Precisely how effective the action committees were as agents furthering social transformation in the semiliberated zones remains unclear to the authors. Traditional village leaders apparently often headed these bodies, suggesting that the amount of significant social change remained quite limited.[21] Furthermore, not all of the MPLA guerrilla commanders saw the committees as institutions for promoting grassroots democracy. Commander Monimambu, for instance, was quite explicit in one interview that he viewed them as little more than the last cog in the chain of command set up to execute MPLA Central Committee directives coming from outside the country.[22] Other accounts of their operations, however, suggest the action committees were really quite autonomous and democratic, effectively putting power into the hands of the people.[23] Given the difficult circumstances of war, it seems likely that the 150 committees reported existing as of 1970 differed greatly in their degree of autonomy and mode of operation.[24] It also seems apparent that already at this early stage, MPLA leaders held conflicting views regarding the meaning of *poder popular.*

Most civilian institutions created by the MPLA during the war in the semiliberated zones are more important for what they reveal about the political and ideological orientation of the Movement's leadership than for what they accomplished in practice. By and large, the system envisaged was not only definitely socialist but also quite elaborate. One example is that of the "people's plantations." Despite the somewhat grandiose title, these plantations were simply collective fields supplementing the family plots. Under the highly structured arrangements, peasants were expected to work two days on the plantations and two days on their own fields, and to spend the rest of the week on other tasks such as adult literacy or political education.[25] But commanders agreed that it was difficult to convince people to accept the system, although by 1970 some peasants were apparently "coming to learn that collective farms are better, or at least necessary."[26] The produce from these collective fields was handed over to the "people's stores" run by the action committees and traded there for whatever goods the MPLA managed to bring in from the outside. In this manner, a kind of small-scale barter trade was established between the interior and the exterior.

From what one can glean from various accounts of life in the semiliberated zones, it seems that the MPLA by 1970 had developed a fairly sophisticated politico-military infrastructure and established the rudiments of new institutions. In the following years, however, the Movement suffered serious setbacks, which produced a considerable hiatus in the burgeoning social and economic revolution. First, Portuguese counteroffensives in 1972 and 1973 weakened the MPLA institutions in the semi-liberated zones. Second, yet another nationalist movement, UNITA, was formed. And finally, a new wave of factional infighting once again almost led to the disintegration of the MPLA. The new nationalist group, the *Union Nacional para a Independencia Total de Angola* (UNITA), led by Jonas Savimbi, broke off from the FLNA and set up its own *maquis* in eastern Angola in March 1966. By the early 1970s UNITA was not only competing with the MPLA for the allegiance of the Ovimbundu people of south central Angola, but also actively fighting MPLA guerrilas, just as the FLNA had long done in the north. The Movement was thus battling against three external enemies at once when it was hit by its worst internal crisis yet. The central issue did not revolve around different ideological viewpoints, how the struggle should be waged or the country's future socialist course. Instead, it was basically a power struggle to determine which of a number of contending factions and individuals would emerge as the dominant force. That the crisis was serious and deeply troubling to the MPLA's foreign supporters became clear when the Soviets in 1973 suspended their support for the Movement in general and for Neto in particular, and Tanzanian president Julius Nyerere urged the Chinese to arm the FNLA in order to keep the Angolan struggle alive. (The Soviets subsequently renewed their backing for Neto but not until well after the April 1974 military coup in Lisbon.)

In mid-1973, Neto accused another member of the MPLA directing committee, Daniel Chipenda, of plotting to "physically eliminate" him and take over as president with the backing of the Movement's Ovimbundu supporters.[27] Chipenda, in turn, accused Neto of "presidentialism" and blamed him for all kinds of unresolved problems within the eastern front's jurisdiction, resulting in "massive defections of guerrillas and other leaders."[28] Chipenda also accused the MPLA generally of being "too arrogant" toward the people and of "imposing its methods without taking into account the wishes of the militant masses."[29] By mid-1974, the Movement was divided three ways between Chipenda's so-called "Eastern Revolt"; the "Active Revolt" led by Mario de Andrade, a former MPLA acting president and foreign minister, and by Commander Monimambu; and Neto's own centralist or "authoritarian" group, as its opponents called it. A final attempt to reunite the three at a party congress held in Lusaka in August of that year aborted when Neto walked out with his supporters in an overall minority and Chipenda was elected as president by a rump of his followers. At that point, the Neto faction had no more than 2,000 loyal troops and possibly as few as the 800 he had called back from the eastern front war zone to Brazzaville.

Altogether, the "Netoists" were in an extremely weak position going into the civil war that got under way in deadly ernest in early 1975. They were vying for control of the MPLA with two other factions and struggling to gain dominance over the entire country against both the FNLA and UNITA. the FNLA had by far the largest military force, and even Chipenda's Eastern Revolt could count on more guerrillas than the Netoists. But in this bewildering constellation of warring factions, the Netoists, though numerically weak, had some advantages. They had achieved a degree of ideological coherence and a temporary political unity among themselves that was lacking among their very diverse and numerous opponents. The adoption of Marxism-Leninism as a guideline for independent Angola was a foregone conclusion and not an issue likely to divide them further after independence. They had also reached a basic agreement on the need for the MPLA to become a vanguard party to lead the country. Furthermore, the struggle for independence had produced some concrete experience with the kind of new institutions they wanted to create for Angola: they all upheld the concept of *poder popular* and its system of local action committees developed in the semiliberated zones. Only later, after the Neto faction had secured power, did people's power become a controversial issue at the center of yet another internal MPLA factional struggle. As the civil war approached, however, *poder popular* was a powerful rallying cry and an instrument for mobilizing supporters that would give the Netoists a leading edge over the over less cohesive nationalist factions.

The Civil War

It is impossible in this limited space to trace in detail the struggle for power that consumed Angola from the April 1974 coup in Lisbon until the final triumph of the MPLA in March 1976. What we shall do here is simply concentrate on certain aspects of the civil war that will help to explain later problems affecting the revolution.

From the very beginning, the aim of the struggle was not really to gain control immediately over the whole country—none of the factions could possibly hope to achieve this—but to establish control over the key cities, most notably the capital, and of the country's principal resources, above all the oil fields of the Cabinda enclave. Looked at from this perspective, the MPLA was uniquely positioned to win, despite its military weakness. First, the Movement had germinated in the *musseques* of the capital and was well implanted among the Mbundu people constituting the majority of its population. Second, its influence also spread eastward along the Luanda-Malange corridor to the diamond fields of eastern Angola. Third, the military forces still loyal to the Netoists, however small they may have been, were strategically located in Congo-Brazzaville bordering on Cabinda. Once in control of the capital, a few other urban centers, and Cabinda, the MPLA could reasonably assume it would obtain some diplomatic recognition, call "legally" for outside help, and then outlast its opponents if not altogether defeat them militarily. The first group to try seizing the capital was not the MPLA but the FNLA, which had a far larger military force than any of its rivals. But the "battle for Luanda" was won by the MPLA. It has generally been forgotten in the hue and cry over Soviet and Cuban intervention in Angola that even before Cuban combat troops arrived and while upwards of 1400 Zairian regulars were aiding the FNLA in the north, the MPLA had not only secured the capital but also seized control of Cabinda with its own forces and established at least a tenuous hold over 12 of the 16 provincial capitals, including the ports of Lobito and Benguela in the south.

Key to the MPLA's success was *poder popular,* the network of action committees and militia groups organized in the *musseques* of the capital and many other cities and towns immediately after the coup in Lisbon. The real leader of the movement in the urban areas was not Neto himself but Nito Alves, the military commander of the isolated Dembos Forest *maquis* north of the capital and the man Neto entrusted with the task of organizing MPLA supporters in Luanda. It was a strange choice, because Alves was a typical example of the "autonomism" which plagued the MPLA, the leader of a war zone cut off from the exterior who had developed his own military and political power base. In setting up the urban action committees, Alves was aided by various fringe groups consisting of Maoists, Trotskyites, and other ultraleftists—some Angolans but many others Portuguese whites who flocked to Luanda in the wake of the Lisbon coup. These leftist groups were pursuing to a large extent their own dream of revolution. They set up "Amilcar Cabral Committees," "Henda Committees," and "Unity Committees" in the *musseques* as well as in factories and other workplaces to organize and promote the direct involvement of the working class in the revolution.[30] They published journals like *People's Revolution* and *Socialist Revolution* urging the mobilization of the urban workers to seize power and establish immediately a "people's democracy." There can be no doubt that these leftists had objectives that were not identical to those of the Netoists. But an MPLA victory suited their purposes, and thus they supported it wholeheartedly in the battle for Luanda in the spring and summer of 1975. The neighborhood committee militias, armed with Soviet AK-47s and RPG grenade launchers, helped MPLA guerrillas to drive both the FNLA and UNITA out of the capital by early August. They also pushed out most of the Bakongo and Ovimbundu peoples who were supporting these nationalist groups. In addition to controlling Luanda, the committees played a major role in securing for the MPLA the ports of Lobito and Benguela in the south, Melange and Luso in the east and Nova Lisboa (Huambo) in the south-central part of the country. Only in the north was the MPLA unable to take over the main urban centers from the FNLA. The same network of committees became the recruiting grounds for the new MPLA army, the *Forcas Armadas Populares para Libertação de Angola* (FAPLA) which the Netoists began organizing only in August 1974. The committee militas probably had altogether over 10,000 armed members throughout the country by mid-1975, while FAPLA consisted at that time of only slightly more than 2,000 battle-ready troops and another 5,000 to 6,000 undergoing training.[31] FAPLA drew from this militia the best and most zealous youths to begin forming quickly an army that would soon number some 30,000 troops.

Several other factors contributed to the victory of the MPLA: its superior sense of tactics and the massive assistance provided by the Cubans being the most important. The Netoists maneuvered toward victory with great ability. Despite opposition from within its own ranks, the MPLA joined the transitional government established by the Portuguese in January 1975 which gave equal representation to the three rival national factions. It then manipulated the situation from within this shaky government to its own advantage, discrediting its rivals and exploiting the presence of sympathetic leftist Portuguese army officers to bolster its own position. Evidence of the MPLA's tactical skills was seen once again in its early seizure of the strategic coastal towns of Lobito, Benguela, and Novo Redondo, which later became the landing points for Soviet arms and Cuban troops. It was also illustrated by its alliance of convenience with the ex-Katangese troops serving in the Portuguese army and hostile to Zairian President Mobutu Sese Seko and the FNLA. This provided the MPLA with 4,000 to 6,000 trained troops and helped it to gain control of northeastern Angola where the diamond mines were located.[32]

The issue of the Cuban role in the victory of the MPLA—"proletarian internationalism" to the Angolans, and foreign intervention to the West—is very controversial, and some facts have been obscured in the partisan debate. Most important, it has too often been overlooked that the MPLA had managed to seize control of Luanda, most of the main towns and cities of eastern and southern Angola, and of Cabinda on its own. Also forgotten is that foreign intervention in the civil war did not start with the Cubans. Regular Zairian combat troops were fighting with the FNLA in northern Angola and South African soldiers were sent across the Namibian border into southern Angola to help UNITA at a time when only Cuban advisers were aiding the MPLA. But in the end Cuban assistance was crucial, for the Movement could not have routed the FNLA as it did and contained UNITA on its own. Neto frankly admitted later that Soviet arms and the 15,000 to 20,000 Cuban combat troops were the "principal force" which stopped the South African offensive begun in early October 1975.[33] Without Cuban intervention, Angola would probably have been partitioned into three areas, each controlled by one of the nationalist factions.

Despite its victory, the MPLA was beset with internal problems at independence. The *poder popular* committees were an unreliable base of support. Alves immediately proved to have his own ambitions and to be intent upon using the committees to promote them. The ultraleftists who often were in control of them were principally interested in provoking a revolution, while the Netoists wanted first to consolidate their control of the country. Making matters worse, there was an enormous amount of general indiscipline among the committees' untrained youthful members, who indulged in robbery, rape, and all sorts of exactions. Finally, the entire MPLA was still an uneasy coalition of groups and individuals. After the three-way split during the summer of 1974, Neto had rebuilt the Movement around a small nucleus of loyal supporters consisting principally of Lara, the head of the party school; his chief assistant, Carlos Rocha "Dilolwa"; Jose Eduardo dos Santos, the MPLA bureau head in Brazzaville; and Henrique Tiles "Ike" Carreira, the overall guerrilla commander. By and large, these men represented the "external" MPLA during the anticolonial struggle. Alves, the Dembos guerrilla leader, brought into the coalition the "internal" guerrilla fighters and later the urban workers. Lopo do Nascimento represented the internal political underground and the large number of MPLA supporters who, like himself, had spent long years in Portuguese jails inside Angola. Like the FLN in Algeria, the MPLA counted among its leaders at independence a fairly large number of strong individuals with their own wartime followers. Yet, they scarcely represented the entire country. One keen American analyst of the MPLA was struck by the narrow ethnic base of the 10-man Political Bureau and 35-man Central Committee elected in September 1974: "As in the past, the leadership was preponderantly *mestiço/ assimilado/* Mbundu," noted John Marcum.[34]

Angola at Independence

By the time of independence, Angola was in the midst of enormous social and economic change spurred on by a belated Portuguese attempt to win the hearts and minds of the African population away from the nationalist cause by developing the country. Portuguese colonies were generally far poorer and underdeveloped than the British and French African ones, because Portugal itself was so poor. Not until the launching of the liberation war did Lisbon change its policy of preventing other Western countries from investing in its colonies and invite British, Belgian, American, and French companies to come in. Angola attracted the most investment because of its natural resources, including oil, iron ore, and diamonds. As a result, the country underwent a veritable boom in development during the last decade before its independence. Simultaneously, the war and Portuguese counterinsurgency tactics led to the uprooting of at least one third of the rural population. The combined effect of all these various forces was to spur change of all kinds, both negative and positive.

A first glance at the socioeconomic indicators for Angola suggest a very underdeveloped African country. The literacy rate among Africans, for instance, was less than 10 percent even after a big push in public education in the last years of Portuguese rule.[35] Eighty-five percent of the population was rural and the life expectancy was only 38 years.[36] The Physical Quality of Life Index developed by the Organization of Economic Cooperation and Development, integrating various social indicators such as infant mortality and literacy, gave Angola a score of only 15 on a scale of one to 100.[37] (This was even worse than Zaire.) The main exports were raw materials and minerals—traditionally coffee, cotton, bananas, iron ore, and diamonds.

The discovery of a major oil deposit in Cabinda in the mid-1960s radically modified this picture. Though production was low by the standards of the Middle East or even Nigeria—roughly 140,000 barrels a day by 1975—it provided the government with between $400 million and $500 million a year in earnings[38] and drove the per capita GNP up to $474, the second highest in all of sub-Saharan Africa.[39] Oil quickly displaced coffee as the leading export. With the help of this bonanza and Western investment, the Portuguese government was able to launch a sizeable industrial development program. Half a billion dollars was invested in mining and manufacturing alone during the Third Development Plan of 1968 through 1973.[40] The growth in manufacturing in the decade after 1962 averaged 19 percent annually, reaching a high of 26.5 percent in 1973, the last normal year before independence.[41] By that time, the secondary sector of the economy accounted for between 18 and 20 percent of the GDP, a high proportion for an African colony, and Angola had a wide range of industries, including 500 classified as "heavy."[42] One effect of this rapid industrial growth was the spawning of an African wage-earning population. In the early 1970s, there were 100,000 African workers in industry; 35,000 in mining; 5,000 to 10,000 in fishing; 20,000 to 40,000 in construction, 55,000 in transportation; and upwards of 70,000 in the service sector.[43]

The agricultural sector had also been changing. The bulk of the Angolan peasantry still consisted of 1.2 million farm families having two hectares or less of land and growing food almost exclusively for their own consumption.[44] But by the time of independence, an estimated 150,000 Africans were raising crops for the internal market or for export.[45] While they accounted for only 14 percent of the total value of farm exports in 1971,[46] some 8,000 Portuguese settlers providing the remainder, a class of African commercial farmers was clearly in the making. Moreover, the coffee plantations located primarily in the north spawned a small rural proletariat of mostly Ovimbundu migrant laborers, numbering 140,000 before independence.[47]

This period of economic growth was accompanied by a high rate of Portuguese immigration into Angola, with the number of settlers increasing from 172,000 in 1960 to 335,000 in 1974.[48] The new immigrants were by and large "white trash" as their level of education, among other characteristics, so clearly revealed—less than 6 percent of the 100,000 new arrivals between 1950 and 1964 aged seven years and over had gone beyond fourth grade.[49] They took over most of the menial jobs which in other French and British colonies had always been held by Africans. Taxi and truck drivers, fishermen, hotel maids, newspaper vendors, and small corner shopkeepers, even in the *musseques,* were overwhelmingly Portuguese whites. This situation severely limited opportunities for African to gain experience. Thus when the Portuguese fled *en masse,* they left a vacuum not only in the top managerial and technical positions but also in the lowest levels of the occupational scale.

The change brought about in Angola by this spurt of growth was nothing compared to the dislocation produced by the anticolonial struggle and then the civil war. One American scholar, Gerald Bender, reckons the Portuguese moved one million Angolans—a sixth of the African population—into resettlement camps in an attempt to isolate the guerrillas from their natural source of support and food.[50] This resulted in both "serious breakdowns in the social and psychological security" of the peasantry and "a marked decline in economic productivity and food supplies."[51] Another 500,000 to one million people fled Angola to the neighboring countries of Zaire and Zambia.[52] Hundreds of thousands of Angolans went to the cities, primarily Luanda, seeking jobs and security. The capital, which had already doubled in population between 1950 and 1960 to 250,000 doubled again in the next decade to half a million, three-fifths of this number Africans.[53] Altogether, 15 to 18 percent of the total African population was living in urban areas by the time of independence.[54]

The worst shock to Angolan society came at the time of independence, however. Angola's Portuguese-dominated society collapsed as over 300,000 Portuguese hurriedly departed from the country within the space of less than a year, leaving behind their homes, apartments, factories, and farms, but taking with them everything movable, including cars and trucks. It was the biggest mass exodus of whites from Africa since one million Europeans streamed out of Algeria in 1962. Almost all of Angola's technicians and managers, skilled workers, civil servants, farm and factory owners, and even taxi drivers and shop keepers left, virtually paralyzing the economy. The internal migration among Africans was probably just as massive. The 100,000 Ovimbundus working on the northern coffee plantations were driven out by the FNLA and trekked back to their villages in the south. The Ovimbundu and Bakongo people living in the capital, numbering another 30,000 to 40,000, were forced out by the MPLA and its supporters during the battle for Luanda. Tens of thousands more simply fled into the bush to escape the fighting.

The economic consequences of the civil war and Portuguese flight were dramatic. While the Gross National Product supposedly declined by only 20 percent, down to $1.8 billion by 1976,[55] production actually dropped much more in most fields with only the increase in the value of oil exports keeping the GNP figure so high. Industrial production, for instance, declined by about 75 percent in the period 1975 to 1976, while coffee exports plummeted from their preindependence level of 200,000 to 72,000 tons.[56] Only existing stocks kept coffee sales even at this level, for virtually no new coffee was collected during the 1975 through 1976 harvest. Mining of iron ore at Cassinga in Southern Angola came to a complete stop.[57] Diamond production dropped by two-thirds.[58] The livestock industry was virtually destroyed, and so was the fishing industry as two-thirds of the country's 800 vessels were either destroyed or taken away.[59] Only oil exports revived quickly after an initial decline, providing the government with its only reliable source of income and foreign exchange.

The collapse could be measured in other ways even more dramatically. The entire internal transportation system was virtually wiped out as fleeing Portuguese took with them two-thirds of the 28,000 trucks in the country.[60] Destruction of bridges and roads caused by the civil war made it nearly impossible for the remaining trucks to circulate, and the towns and cities were cut off from the countryside. Obtaining food in the capital became a full-time occupation for its denizens. Whereas Angola had imported only 10 percent of its food requirements prior to independence, imports accounted for one-half of all marketed staples in the years immediately afterwards.[61] It was not just the disruption of the marketing system; food production declined enormously, too, with 6,250 commercial farms abandoned by their Portuguese owners.[62] This affected not only export crops, like coffee and bananas, but food crops, like rice and maize, as well as sugar, meat, and fish. Everything was suddenly in extremely short supply or no longer available at all.

As a result of the Portuguese mass exodus and the civil war the country's economy had almost totally collapsed, while large portions of the countryside still escaped the central MPLA government's control. This was particularly true in the south central highlands, the breadbasket of Angola, where UNITA guerrillas remained extremely active, severely disrupting the economy. It was in these unenviable circumstances that the MPLA took power and sought to develop a set of policies to right the economy and give it a socialist character. In so doing, it was certainly influenced by Marxist ideology. But the Movement was also severely limited in what it could do by the calamitous conditions facing the country. As if these were not enough to confound its efforts, the MPLA's reemerging internal divisions provoked yet another major political upheaval and a new discontinuity in its history.

Ideology

Probably the most consistent thread in the MPLA's often tangled and tortuous history has been its ideology, which started as a commitment to a fundamental restructuring of the Angolan economy and society and grew into an explicit allegiance to Marxism-Leninism. The basic tenets of the Movement's postindependence program were already evident in the statutes establishing the organs of *poder popular*, issued even before the end of the civil war. Within seven months of independence, the MPLA had officially declared its adherence to Marxism-Leninism, its intention to establish a vanguard party, and its faith in a centralized, planned, state-dominated economy. At the same time, the Angolan leadership also attempted to reconcile its orthodox Marxist views with the concept and institutions of *poder popular*, which had been so central to its wartime experience in the semiliberated zones and were widely regarded as the essence of what the MPLA meant by revolution. But the effort to synthesize the two ended as an ideological and political confrontation between two factions vying for power within the Movement's top leadership.

The first official document spelling out the MPLA's concept of socialism was the Law on People's Power, published on February 5, 1976. The Law very explicitly interpreted socialism to mean mass participation, direct democracy, and mobilization in the name of revolution. Its preamble explained how people's power had been born of a "popular war of long duration" and as the result of a "popular insurrection" against the dominant colonial bourgeois class.[63] It was, the Law said, an integral part of the class struggle and the foundation stone for the establishment of a "people's democracy."[64] The national liberation struggle "already guarantees the conditions for the development and consolidation of people's power throughout the country," it declared, while the MPLA constitution embodied the principle of "popular mass participation in the exercise of political power."[65] The Law went on to outline the various organs of the people's power system from the neighborhood and village to the national level. Each unit would have a "people's assembly" of all adult residents and an elected "people's commission" consisting of between eight and fifteen members. At the local level, the commissions' chief task was described as "mobilizing and organizing the masses to discuss and resolve their own most pressing and immediate problems" and to provide vigilance and defense.[66] They were also meant to promote "collective forms of production" and to operate on the basis of democratic centralism—free discussion, subordination of the minority to the majority and of lower organs to higher ones.[67] To all appearances, the links between the assemblies and the MPLA were particularly tenuous. Candidates for the various people's assemblies were to be selected by an electoral commission consisting of representatives from the MPLA and various other national organizations. Discussions and decisions within the commissions were to be "inspired" by the "just political line" of the Movement.[68] There was also an MPLA voice in the selection of the "commissars" or state representatives at the village, municipal, and provincial levels: But the real superior authority for the system of people's assemblies and commissions was the Ministry of Internal Administration, creating in effect an organization parallel to the MPLA, rather than under its control.

A few months after the formal institutionalization of people's power, the MPLA started defining more clearly its ideological platform, and in so doing it spelled out a concept of power and organization antithetical to *poder popular*. Once again, we are dealing with a phenomenon similar to the one we have already discussed in the case of Mozambique, where the party platform conflicted with past wartime traditions. A meeting of the MPLA Central Committee in October 1976 adopted "the doctrine of scientific socialism—Marxism-Leninism" as well as the goal of establishing a "people's democracy."⁶⁹ The final resolutions described the workers as the "leading force" of the revolution and the peasants as the "principal force" and appealed for a "worker-peasant alliance." "Socialism," it emphasized, "cannot be built without the leadership of the working class party."⁷⁰ The revolution was said to be entering a new phase of national reconstruction, having as its main objective the attainment of 1973 production levels "in the shortest possible time."⁷¹ While the resolutions gave great attention to *poder popular,* they also put enormous emphasis on "planned economic development" as a "necessary condition for building a socialist society."⁷² Centralized planning was to be the rule "in all sectors of political, economic, and social life" using Marxism-Leninism as the ideological base and as a guide to action."⁷³ The MPLA was called upon to "ensure the drawing up of a single, integrated, and indivisible plan with the status of a law" in which agriculture was to be the "base" for development and industry the "decisive factor."⁷⁴ A National Planning Commission having a cabinet-level ranking and with a bureau in every ministry (planning cabinet) was put in charge of drawing up a National Plan.

The inherent conflict between an economic and political system based on people's power, by its very nature highly participatory and decentralized, and one run under a national plan, by its very nature centralized and restrictive in the degree of participation, was not addressed or even acknowledged by the Central Committee resolutions. What they did address at length was an issue of immediate political importance, namely the possibility of a conflict between the party and state. The problem had two aspects: one, typical of all socialist countries, was the inherent tendency toward statism. On this point, the resolutions noted that a lack of party cadres and "underestimation of the leading role of the MPLA" was twisting the whole party-state relationship "in favor of the state apparatus."⁷⁵ This was found particularly disturbing because the state had inherited "structures and vices" from the colonial era. "The lack of trained cadres necessitates the use of civil servants who were least compromised with colonial policies and an attempt to 'decolonize' their mentality and bureaucratic habits," it said. But the old state apparatus was still afflicted by "bureaucratism."⁷⁶ The second aspect of the troubling party-state conflict, and the one of most political import, was more peculiar to Angola: the state had more control over the people's power commissions than did the party, and thus could turn them against the MPLA. The resolutions expressed great concern for reasserting the party's authority over the organs of *poder popular.* "Elections (for commissions)," they said, "are only to be held when MPLA structures are sufficiently strong, organizationally stable, and mature from the political and ideologial point of view."⁷⁷ The establishment of people's power commissions "is a function of the revolutionary vanguard and not merely of the state."⁷⁸

The Central Committee resolutions were filled with ominous hints as to the problems the MPLA was facing not only in regard to the people's power movement but also to political divisions within the ranks. It spoke of the "pernicious activity" of elements linked to the internal and external reaction and of "ultraleft groups, who by feeding destructive tendencies and using leaders' names, seek to provoke ideological confusion, to disturb the cohesion of MPLA structures, and to divide the militants."[79] It urged the latter to fight against "divisiveness, sectarianism, and opportunism" and said it would take firm measures against those spreading rumors that "threaten the internal unity of the MPLA."[80] What it did not say, although every one knew, was that those implicitly accused of factionalism were the prime promoters of the *poder popular* movement, using it to build a separate power base from which to challenge Neto's leadership.

The Crisis

The brewing crisis finally came to a head in late May 1977 when Alves, initially the interior minister in charge of the people's power organs, and Jose van Dunem, deputy FAPLA political commissar, made a bid to overthrow Neto and his supporters. On May 21, the two were expelled from the Central Committee and accused of heading a "black racist" faction, of promoting "splittism" within the party and of spreading racism and populism."[81] They were also said to have been working to undermine the friendship between Angola and the Soviet Union by circulating rumors that the MPLA leadership was anti-Soviet and Maoist. The two ostracized leaders then put into action a plan that had obviously been long in the making and had the support of elements in virtually every national mass organization, including the FAPLA. Alves was also counting heavily on the Luanda neighborhood commissions to rally public support for the coup. At least five provincial commissars, the trade minister, the acting commanding officer of the 9th Brigade stationed in Luanda, the FAPLA deputy chief of staff and top political commissar, and two members of the Political Bureau, Alves and Jacob Caetano João, were involved in the takeover attempt. The conspirators went into action early May 27 and came very close to succeeding. What saved the Neto faction was the lack of any show of support for the coup by the Luanda population and the prompt intervention of Cuban tanks.[82] The entire episode was over in only ten hours, but in this short time Alves and his partisans killed several hundred people, including seven Central Committee members.

Many explanations have been given for the Alves coup attempt. The most prevalent one characterized him as a black nationalist acting to eliminate the whites and *mestiços* so prominent in the MPLA's top ranks. Alves himself cultivated such an image, which had widespread appeal among Angolans, despite the fact that a number of his close collaborators were white. A second explanation is that Alves was a wartime leader who saw himself, as he reportedly told Neto, as "the incarnation of the revolution" with a historical claim to lead the country.[83] Given the loose nature of the MPLA organization and the isolation of many *maquis* during the war, Alves had operated almost autonomously for years. The experience of Algeria earlier suggests that such a situation often spawns warlordism and later rebellions. Ideological differences between Neto and Alves have also been pointed to as a cause of the rebellion. Neto himself declared that Alves "wants to have the working class rule and rule alone and incessantly struggle against other classes,"[84] but it seems more probable that such a posture simply reflected the fact that Alves was appealing to the workers of the *musseques,* while Neto had many followers within the petty bourgeoisie. Whatever the causes of Alves' own actions, it is worth remembering that a similar phenomenon has appeared in some form in many other revolutions, from Trotsky in the Soviet Union, to the Ethiopian People's Revolutionary Party in Ethiopia. At a time when a revolutionary leadership begins to consolidate its power, transforming itself into an established government, an ultraleftist opposition easily arises, claiming that the revolution has been betrayed and presenting itself as its real voice.

The abortive coup's effects on the MPLA were manifold. First of all, the crisis was extremely demoralizing and confusing to party supporters. Secondly, it provoked a purge and a campaign of "rectification" in every national organization. Thirdly, the whole people's power movement was stopped dead in its tracks and all further elections setting up people's assemblies were postponed indefinitely. Fourthly, the need for a stronger, more homogeneous and centralized vanguard party was made manifest as never before. Finally, there were repercussions on the MPLA's ideology, some subtle, others flagrantly obvious, but all serving to strengthen the authoritarian and statist tendencies within the new Angolan political system. Some of these effects became apparent at the First Party Congress held in December 1977, when the MPLA formally converted itself into a vanguard Marxist-Leninist "labor party."

The MPLA was formally described as a "party of the working class" uniting in a "solid alliance the workers, peasants, revolutionary intellectuals, and other working people dedicated to the cause of the proletariat."[85] The creation of such a party would lead to the creation of a "revolutionary democratic dictatorship," in turn opening the way for the dictatorship of the proletariat "in the stage of building socialism."[86] Such a line of thinking was ideologically correct from a Marxist-Leninist point of view. It also made political sense as a refutation of Alves' claim that only the working class, i.e., his supporters in the *musseques,* had a right to lead the revolution. There was little mention of class struggle as central to the current stage of the Angolan revolution, apparently also in reaction to Alves' insistence on it. The MPLA was to undergo a "vast Rectification Movement" in order to remake it into a vanguard party with membership limited to militants thoroughly indoctrinated in Marxism-Leninism at "cadre training schools."[87] The Congress decided to draw a clear distinction among MPLA supporters, dividing them into categories of "militants," "aspirants," and "sympathizers."[88] The latter were to be relegated to membership in the mass national organizations. No one could become a militant before serving first as aspirant, receiving ideological training, and establishing his credentials as an exemplary worker.

The Congress also analyzed at great length what had gone wrong with the people's power movement. It even redefined the meaning of *poder popular* to demonstrate that, correctly interpreted, it was synonymous with "State Power." People's power did not mean direct democracy but indirect representation of the workers' interests by a "revolutionary state apparatus" and a vanguard party. The Law on people's power would thus have to be repealed because it "expresses a petty bourgeois and hardly correct concept of state power with illusory ideas about democracy and about the way the working masses should ensure and consolidate their political power."[89] The Angolan people had to understand that "the organs of the state apparatus are themselves organs of people's power" and that the party had to become "the leading nucleus of the organs of people's power acting on the basis of party resolutions."[90] Without mentioning Alves, the MPLA Congress blamed him for creating a parallel government "separate from and even opposed to the organs of the state apparatus and especially the central state organs."[91] There was nothing unorthodox about asserting this primacy of "state" over "people's" power in a Marxist-Leninist revolution. But in the context of the Angolan revolution, it meant the MPLA was beginning to downplay what had once been regarded as the very essence of mass participation during the anticolonial struggle.

Policies

Despite its preoccupation with politics even since independence, the MPLA has also devoted much time and energy to revising the economy and refashioning Angolan society along socialist lines. In so doing, it has been guided by its commitment to Marxism-Leninism but even more so by the concrete situation existing in the country and the limitations of manpower and know-how. Altogether, it has been relatively pragmatic in trying to adapt Marxism-Leninism to the circumstances in Angola.

1. Economic Policies

Like other African countries experiencing a sudden exodus of white settlers, Angola was bound to fall into some form of socialism very quickly. The Portuguese left behind thousands of abandoned farms and factories which the government had to deal with even before the October 1976 Central Committee resolutions opting for socialism. The policy toward nationalizations, initially spelled out in March 1976, stipulated that properties belonging to "saboteurs" and "traitors," to partisans of the FNLA and UNITA, and to those absent from the country for more than 45 days "without justification" would be seized without compensation.[92] It was also specified that the government could take over properties of those guilty of unauthorized repatriation of funds or reduction in production. Later, the government set as a goal the takeover of 80 percent of the country's 500 "heavy" industries by 1980.[93] Through a combination of nationalizations under this law and departures of Portuguese owners, the government ended by taking over a very large percentage of the country's industrial assets. By the time of the MPLA's First Congress in December 1977, the state already controlled 100 percent of enterprises in some fields (textiles, sugar, plywood production, and metal works) and over 50 percent in others (diamond production, ship building, leather footware, beer, match production, margarine production).[94] After putting several hundred abandoned properties under state control in mid-1979, Angola was probably close to its stated goal of nationalizing 80 percent of the country's major industries.

One of the most crucial areas in MPLA economic policy was relations with the multinational companies exploiting the country's mineral wealth, most particularly its oil fields and diamond deposits. The MPLA followed a very consistent pattern of trying to work out mutually acceptable deals with the multinationals, acquiring control but still relying on them for capital investment and expertise. It is interesting to note that in its dealings with Western oil companies Angola solicited the advice of the Algerian government, which had long sought to establish such a partnership. Like Algeria, Angola also made use of the American consulting firm Arthur D. Little, both to establish an oil code and to negotiate with the multinationals. Again, like Algeria, Angola first set up a state oil company, Sonangol, and then sought to transfer control of the oil industry to it through a series of agreements with the major Western firms already exploiting the country's deposits. A new oil law passed in September 1978 specified that Angola would either accept joint ownership or take over full control and then enter into production-sharing arrangements. Then in December 1978, Angola signed its first agreement with the American Gulf Oil Company, the major producer, resulting in the transfer to Sonangol of 51 percent of the shares, management, and production of the Gulf subsidiary in Cabinda. A second accord was signed in September 1979 with Texaco, establishing what was expected to be the future model for all dealings with foreign oil companies. Sonangol took over complete ownership of Texaco's concessions off northern Angola but signed a production-sharing deal with the company. Texaco remained as operator of the off-shore field and agreed to invest a total of $360 million in the expansion of its existing fields and exploration for new deposits. Initially Texaco was to get about 60 percent of the expected 50,000 barrels a day, but Sonangol's share would increase as production went higher.

These deals, and a dozen others in the making, established the crucial importance of the oil industry as the keystone of the new Angolan economy. Oil was to become by far the most important source of revenue for the government and the country's overall economic development. By 1980, the Sonangol-Gulf joint venture in Cabinda was generating most of the Angolan government's oil earnings of around one billion dollars, a sum estimated to be between 60 and 80 percent of its total revenues. With the addition of the Texaco fields and new ones discovered by Gulf in early 1980, Angolan earnings from oil alone will probably reach two billion dollars by 1983, a figure representing more than the country's entire GNP just after independence. Sonangol meanwhile also acquired a 30 percent interest in the country's main refinery, negotiated oil exploration deals with several French companies similar to the Texaco one, and was slowly extending its control over the internal marketing system.

Angola used the same businesslike approach in its dealings with Diamang, a consortium of Western and South African interests which exploited a 50,000 hectare concession in eastern Angola and was responsible for all of Angola's diamond production before independence. After output dropped to about 15 percent of its preindependence level, Diamang sought to get rid of its assets and above all its mounting debts by asking the Angolan government to nationalize the company outright. The government refused, however, and instead forced Diamang in August 1977 to enter a partnership in which Angola took 61 percent of the assets. Diamang would continue to market the diamonds. By and large, the Angolan government showed more interest in this type of agreement than outright nationalization when dealing with large Western firms, except Portuguese ones. In the latter case, emotional issues were often involved, resulting in a complete takeover.

Two major problems emerged in reorganizing the industrial sector, production, and the system of management. Nationalization did not automatically restore higher levels of production. The litany of problems was a familiar one: acute shortage of managers, technicians, and skilled labor; lack of spare parts; difficulty of obtaining raw materials; transportation problems. Carlos Rocha, serving as planning director in mid-1978, explained in some detail how all these stumbling blocks were affecting the economy and producing "incredible zig-zags" in the monthly production of individual enterprises.[95] The magnitude of the problem of managing hundreds of abandoned enterprises far surpassed the state's limited capabilities.

In addition to these problems, Angola faced the politically sensitive issue of whether the nationalized enterprises should be managed "collectively" by workers or "individually" by state-appointed managers. Such a conflict was not, of course, exclusive to Angola, but one emerging regularly in socialist countries. What was unique to Angola was that it became entangled in the struggle between Neto and Alves, with enormous repercussions for the character of socialism in the country. A form of workers' self-management started arising immediately after independence at the initiative of the workers simply trying to keep abandoned enterprises functioning in some fashion. But to the action committees and elements of the labor union, the *União Nacional dos Trabalhadores de Angola* (UNTA), worker management was an important principle to be defended against state interference. In 1976 and well into 1977, the "intervention committees" set up by the government to run the abandoned enterprises encountered stiff opposition from the people's power action committees and UNTA's own autonomous commissions. The result, as one minister put it, was "paralysis," encouraged by the "factionalists" (Alves and his supporters) intent on sowing discord between the workers and the MPLA.[96] Slowly, the MPLA quashed this incipient worker's management movement. In fact, since it was a political threat, the Netoists tried to destroy it completely. The March 1976 decree on nationalizations had provided for a limited amount of workers' participation in management. A resolution of the MPLA central committee in October of the same year, however, called for a revision of the decree "to substitute the present form of collective leadership with personal leadership" in the nationalized firms and "to give increasing importance to the role of the MPLA and UNTA within the enterprise to facilitate political work" as well as to "strive for increases in production, discipline, revolutionary vigilance and management ability."[97] The First Congress confirmed both the principle of "personal directorship," meaning dominant authority for the state-appointed manager, and that of direct MPLA control at the workplace.[98] In fact, after the party congress, the UNTA commissions were disbanded and party cells organized in the enterprises. These party representatives undertook alone, or with hand-picked UNTA members, to enforce discipline among the workers. The workers were left only with a very limited consultative role regarding management. These various measures, together with the defeat of the *poder popular* movement after the attempted coup by Alves, put an end to much of the labor unrest, but also effectively killed the self-management movement. Interestingly, a similar phenomenon had happened a decade earlier in Algeria when self-management was caught in the power struggle between Ben Bella and Boumédiène. On a much smaller scale in Ethiopia, all experimentations with workers' participation, even in the limited form of "workers' fora" floundered as the opposition tried to use the institution to denounce and undermine the military government.

MPLA policies in the agricultural sector were extremely cautious and limited in scope. In fact, outside the modern farm sector where the government had to cope with abandoned farms, very little happened. The Portuguese had abandoned 6,250 farms, but by mid-1978 the government was still only able to operate 1,500 because it lacked personnel.[99] Most Portuguese properties were made into state farms, with a small number converted into cooperatives. The state farms tended to be very large, because the government regrouped many Portuguese holdings into one *"Agrupamento de Unidades de Produção"* (Regrouped Production Unit) and ran them as a single entity in a centralized fashion. By mid-1978, there were 58 such AUPs, regrouping 450 farms and employing 175,000 workers.[100] The Ministry of Agriculture also controlled four huge agri-businesses formerly belonging to the Portuguese government or to Western consortia and employing another 150,000 workers.[101] The preference for state farms was strengthened by the failure of the cooperative movement, first launched in 1976. Only 300 "cooperatives" were formed, but apparently cultivation remained strictly individual, with the only "collective" aspect being government-provided services.[102] The cooperatives, moreover, were caught in the same struggle between Netoists and "factionalists" which destroyed the self-management movement in industry. According to the left-wing magazine *Afrique-Asie,* "the confusion existing within government and party organs, where factionalists would go in the opposite direction from all central directives, finally made it impossible even to make an accurate inventory of the number of existing cooperatives and their respective production."[103] As a result of all these problems encountered in forming cooperatives, the government lowered its short-term goals and decided to start again by forming "pre-cooperatives," sending out especially trained *dinamisadores,* or "dynamizing agents," into the rural areas to educate the peasants about the benefits of collective and modern methods of production. By mid-1978, there were reportedly 150 such precooperatives nationwide, with 15,000 to 20,000 members, and another 300 in the process of being organized.[104]

In the peasant sector, the government proceeded with extreme caution. It neither nationalized the land, as Ethiopia and Mozambique did, nor pushed for collectivation. "If now in the name of socialism," President Neto told an UNTA conference in October 1976, "we were to begin to expropriate the peasants, our people would at once feel they were being sacrificed to our socialist option."[105] While he did not deny that collectivization was the final goal, he argued that the process would be gradual, beginning with the formation of cooperatives. Socialism meant the abolition of private ownership of the means of production, but, he warned, "the road we have chosen... is long, complex and difficult." There was no sense, he said, in wasting paper and ink proclaiming "every week-end that the revolution is to arrive Monday morning."[106] In the short run, production rather than ideology was clearly the main preoccupation of the government. Nowhere was this more clearly illustrated than in the case of the abandoned Portuguese coffee plantations in northern Angola. An early attempt to run them as state farms with Cuban assistance failed. Subsequently, the government quietly encouraged the former Ovimbundu farm workers to return, settling them on the coffee estates as small owners. In effect, the Angolan government was creating what many Marxists would consider as a burgeoning kulak class.

None of the measures taken in the field of agriculture restored production rapidly. Food shortages in the cities remained very serious, and in 1978 Angola was still importing half of the staple foods sold in the market.[107] Export crops fared equally badly. The coffee crop in 1978 was 26,000 tons compared to 210,000 tons in 1973; pineapple, 4,400 tons against 55,000 tons; cotton, 1,000 tons compared to 79,281 tons; sisal, 15,000 tons against 60,330 tons, and sugar, 39,000 tons compared to 81,900 tons.[108].

These poor results were due to a variety of factors: shortage of personnel to run the farms, breakdown of the transportation system, and, most important, the fact that the country's breadbasket was the central highlands where UNITA guerrilla activity was greatest. In fact, the government was very alert to the fact that UNITA could easily exploit discontent with its farm policies, particularly among the Ovimbundus among whom it had its strongest support. This was one factor in the decision to resettle the Ovimbundu workers on the abandoned Portuguese plantations.

2. Political Organization

MPLA policy in setting up a new political organization and administrative infrastructure was influenced on the one hand by ideology and on the other by the negative political experience with the people's power movement. Both argued the need for a vanguard party of very carefully chosen militants. Far more effort went into establishing the new party than into reforming the old colonial administration, which ended up by becoming a major impediment to introducing radical socialist change in Angola.

The restructuring of the MPLA into a vanguard party of the working class was a slow, arduous process. As in all Leninist-model parties, the cell became the new base of the party in a hierarchical structure dominated by the 11-man Political Bureau and 45-member Central Committee. The MPLA decided, however, that the cells should be located primarily at the workplace rather than in the community at large, both to increase the party's effectiveness and control and to promote greater direct participation by the working class. The desire to change the "petty bourgeois" nature of the MPLA top leadership could also be seen in Neto's decision before his untimely death from cancer in September 1979 to broaden the Central Committee to 60 members, retaining the additional 15 places for peasants and workers. The "rectification campaign" decided upon at the First Congress aimed at sorting out "militants" from "sympathizers" and admitting only the most dedicated Marxist-Leninists, free from "fractionalism" as well as from "tribal, regional, and racist prejudices" and steeped in "the revolutionary theory of the proletariat."[109] This campaign proved a time-consuming task which the MPLA took very seriously. It set up a commission to screen candidates and established a national as well as regional party training schools to teach Marxism-Leninism. When the party finally released the new membership figures in early 1979, it became clear just how narrow the door to entry was. After 2,374 "rectification assemblies," 4,952 "sensitizing assemblies," and 1,572 "workplace meetings," attended by a total of over half a million Angolans, the new MPLA had 654 cells grouping just 8,750 militants and 6,338 aspirants. Sympathizers numbered only 3,386 while the MPLA youth organization had less than 4,000 members.[110] Numerous "rectification campaigns" also affected the other national organizations, particularly UNTA, as the party strove to weed out Alves' supporters and bring all institutions more firmly under its control.

The main mass organization in the country, as it turned out, was the People's Defense Organization (ODP). By 1979, the ODP had become a huge militia force of some 600,000 members existing in virtually every village throughout the country. Of this number, 50,000 were said to be fighting alongside the regular army against UNTA guerrillas and repeated South African incursions into southern Angola.[111] The size of the ODP seemed to reflect the conditions of insecurity still prevailing in many parts of the country, particularly the south. But it also served to embody the MPLA wartime tradition of the people in arms defending their revolution.

Despite the thoroughness of the party "rectification campaign, "fractionalism" continued to be viewed as a potential major problem. MPLA secretary-general Lara, for example, did not exclude the resurgence of this phenomenon in an interview in mid-1978, declaring it "part of the logic of revolutionary movements."[112] The fear of fractionalism had some noticeable effect even on MPLA ideological thinking, as the same interview made clear. Asked about the centrality of class conflict to the ongoing Angolan revolution, Lara called it "inevitable" and said the party was ready to make it "even more active, more biting and more conscious" as part of the process of creating a political consciousness in the country. But he cautioned against forcing the issue in an "ill-conceived manner," for as he explained, "we cannot at the same time want national unity and arouse false divisions and contradictions poorly understood by the people."[113] Therefore, he said, the class struggle would be carried on mainly within the confines of the party itself rather than the entire society. Once again the impact of the Alves affair was making itself felt, this time on the subtleties of the MPLA ideology.

Virtually all MPLA leaders complained repeatedly about the enormous difficulties they faced in converting the old Portuguese colonial administration into a new "revolutionary state apparatus" capable of carrying out the radical changes envisaged. A problem of both institutions and attitudes stood behind these difficulties, combining to create a phenomenon of "bureaucratism" which all decried but nobody could stem. In the first place, the acute shortage of MPLA cadres meant the party had to make use of what they called the "least compromised" Angolans who had served in the colonial administration but were still basically unmotivated by any revolutionary fervor and often indulged in passive resistance to the revolution. Apparently in the majority, these former colonial civil servants were hardly the stuff making for a "revolutionary state apparatus." The institutional aspect was much more serious, and here the effects of the Alves abortive coup were very evident. First of all, elections to establish people's assemblies nationwide were postponed until the fall of 1980, five years after independence. Secondly, there was a lingering fear that any new institution not tightly controlled by the party might be turned against it. As a result, the MPLA ended up by clinging to the old colonial administrative structure, which at least posed no threat. Even the old chieftancy system, under which the tribal chief wielded local power, was not scrapped. Thus, the countryside remained under the influence of traditional chiefs, complicating the introduction of any fundamental changes there.

In practice, then, the MPLA maintained much of the colonial state apparatus, a highly centralized and authoritarian system. Making "bureaucratism" even worse, the MPLA entrusted this centralized state apparatus with socialist tasks the colonial administration had never undertaken. In its drive to control the modern sector, the government tried to do everything. For example, the Ministry of Housing established a monopoly over all construction and even maintenance activity in the country, while the Ministry of

Trade tried to control entirely internal marketing. President Neto finally spoke out against this overcentralization, which risked paralyzing the country. He said the state had created its own "army of workers" in the construction industry to the point where Angolans could not find, or hire individually, even a carpenter or mason to do minor repairs on their homes, let alone build a house.[114] Similarly, the state had totally stifled private entrepreneurship in the transportation sector, vastly complicating the delivery of food crops from the countryside to the cities. He argued that allowing private enterprise in both these semiparalyzed sectors should not be viewed as a "political setback" in the revolution but simply a recognition that the state was not capable of doing everything immediately. He declared that it was particularly ill-suited to help the rural areas. "The state has made great efforts to resolve most problems, those of commerce, transportation, housing, and others," he said, "but at this time we must recognize it is not able to resolve, for example, most of the problems of the rural population."[115]

3. Social Services

Government policy in the social sector was strongly influenced by the political and social need to meet popular demands for previously nonexistent or scarce services and bore little relationship to its actual ability to deliver them. Even before the MPLA government was established, the principle of free education and medical services for the entire population was applied by the neighborhood action committees in a rudimentary form. The MPLA launched a nationwide literacy campaign in January 1976, while the civil war was still raging in the north and south. One of the guidelines of the campaign stated that factory workers, peasants in cooperatives and on state farms, and FAPLA soldiers should be given priority attention. By the end of 1976, 573,000 adults were enrolled in literacy classes.[116] A veritable explosion took place also in general education. Between 1973 and 1977, the number of children attending primary schools increased from about 340,000 to a little over one million, while at the secondary level it grew from 72,000 to over 100,000.[117] The quality of education inevitably suffered enormously, first because of the exodus of teachers and second because of the sheer numbers of students. According to a document on education produced for the first MPLA Congress, 52 percent of the 25,000 school teachers had only a fourth-grade education themselves and only 7 percent had "minimum teaching qualifications."[118] Nonetheless, the Congress set the highly unrealistic goal of putting the entire school-age population into schools by 1980, an objective the government was totally unable to meet. Making matters even more difficult, ideology dictated that the state take over completely the task of education, so that programs could be based on Marxism-Leninism. This meant the closure of all schools run by the Catholic church and Protestant missions, both of which had been mainstays of the colonial educational system. The exact proportion of total government expenditures devoted to education is difficult to determine, because of the way in which the figures are presented in the only budget published to date, that for the year 1978.[119]

The government also made a major effort to change the character of the health system and extend it to the entire population. The emphasis was on preventative rather than curative medicine, and the government carried out several mass inoculation campaigns affecting the vast majority of Angolans. Yet the means at its disposal were painfully limited in this field. There was only a handful of Angolan doctors and the government has had to rely heavily on foreign assistance to provide free medical service to the country. Cuba became a mainstay of the Angolan medical service. The MPLA First Congress stated there were 418 Cuban doctors and health technicians in Angola as of 1977 and indicated the figure would rise to about 900 in 1978. Cuban doctors were credited with having examined one million Angolans during the year 1977 as well as having performed 16,000 surgical operations and delivered nearly half of all babies born in health institutions (6,000 out of 14,850).[120] Providing health services obviously has been given special attention just as has education, but again the exact amount being devoted to health is not known.

Conclusions

Unlike that of Mozambique, the history of Angola has been one of discontinuity and crisis. War among the three nationalist movements and infighting among the top MPLA leaders have consumed the country for many years now. It seemed as of early 1980 that both these ongoing struggles had yet to run their full course. UNITA was still active in the south, and the death of President Neto had reopened once again the question of leadership within the MPLA.

UNITA and South Africa constituted still a major source of concern for the MPLA government, diverting its energies, resources, and attention time and again to the task of national defense. Despite repeated Cuban-backed FAPLA offensives against UNITA strongholds in southern Angola, Savimbi's Ovimbundu-based resistance to the MPLA government persisted with the help of arms and other supplies primarily from South Africa. The South Africans in addition were in a virtual state of war against Angola because of its support for the Namibian Southwest African People's Organization (SWAPO), which had guerrilla bases in southern Angola. Incursions by the South African army became commonplace, not only against SWAPO bases but occasionally even against Angolan economic targets. The delicate military and political situation in southern Angola made any attempt at introducing radical reforms that might stir the opposition of the Ovimbundu, the largest single ethnic group, a hazardous venture, and the MPLA was indeed extremely cautious in this regard. The threat from the FNLA in the north, on the other hand, was receding, thanks partly to an American-initiated reconciliation between the presidents of Angola and Zaire. Similarly, a separatist movement in Cabinda that had once caused fear that the oil-rich enclave might be detached from Angola had waned. What still remained was some distrust of the MPLA and a residue of sympathy for the FNLA among the Bakongo of the north. The government, as a result, was moving cautiously in implementing radical changes there.

Political discord and infighting within the top ranks of the MPLA continued even after the defeat of the Alves faction. In December 1978, President Neto shook up his government and the party by dismissing his prime minister and long-time ally, Lopo do Nascimento, as well as accepting the resignation of his vice prime minister, Carlos Rocha 'Dilolwa." Both were removed from the Political Bureau, and several other ministers were eliminated from the government at the same time. These changes reflected not only the difficulties the government was having in overcoming the economic depression still afflicting the country but also the unsettled nature of relations among the main MPLA factions and leaders. Less than a year later, the whole leadership issue was reopened by the death of President Neto himself while in Moscow undergoing treatment for cancer. To the general surprise of all outside observers, Neto was smoothly replaced by his young planning minister and former first vice prime minister, Jose Eduardo dos Santos. He controlled neither the party nor the army, the country's two most important institutions. His strongly visible asset was ethnicity: he was a black Mbundu like Neto while the party and army leaders were both *mestiços*. Whether dos Santos would succeed in consolidating his power remained unclear at the time of this writing, but three events suggested he was hard at work attempting to do this and might well succeed. The Second Party Congress scheduled for the spring of 1980 was put off until the end of the year, and one possible contender, "Iko" Carreira, the *mestiço* defense minister, resigned to go abroad for "professional studies" and was dropped from the Political Bureau. The second major rival, party secretary-general Lucio Lara, retained his post but was stripped of control over ideological education and propaganda. The continuing instability in the top ranks of the MPLA was reflected in the fact that as of early 1980 only five of the original 11 members of the Political Bureau elected in October 1976 still retained their position there.

Precisely what was behind all these political changes remained the subject of much speculation and relatively little certain understanding. The visible evidence pointed to a combination of ethnic, racial, and even intra-tribal Mbundu clan factors, with conflict over ideology or Angola's foreign policy serving a secondary supporting role. One pattern tentatively emerging was a shift away from the traditional Mbundu and *mestiço* dominance over the MPLA toward a broader alliance of ethnic groups and a preponderance of blacks, suggesting the party's underlying awareness of the need to expand its base of support within the country and to defuse the racial issue long haunting Angolan politics. In a sense, the MPLA in 1980 was still fighting to come to terms with its own history of ethnic and racial conflicts and within its urban and intellectual bias.

The political jockeying still underway in early 1980 made it difficult to reach firm conclusions about most future trends. One that was becoming quite pronounced, however, was a very strong statist tendency. Even more than ideology, "objective conditions" were pushing the country in this direction, undermining other forces that might have acted as a counterbalance. First was the presence of thousands of abandoned Portuguese properties coupled with an acute scarcity of trained Angolans to run them. The state was forced immediately to take a preponderant role in the management of these enterprises. Second was the political opposition to Neto's leadership, based precisely in those organs promoting direct popular participation in the economy and in the polity—the people's power commissions. This could hardly do other than turn the MPLA against the kind of highly decentralized and participatory system implicit in the people's power movement. The 1977 abortive Alves coup spelled the eclipse of this movement and at the same time strengthened enormously the MPLA's already existing penchant for tight centralized control over the economy and polity. Finally, the very nature of an oil-dominated economy greatly encouraged statism, as the Algerian example made so abundantly clear. For all these reasons, it seems probable that the statist tendency in Angola will not only continue to prevail but will become even more pronounced. Even were the Second Congress to rehabilitate the concept of people's power, the party seems destined to impose tight controls over any future elected assemblies.

Chapter VI
Ethiopia

Among the Marxist-Leninist countries in Africa we are discussing here, Ethiopia stands out as a unique case. Socialism there did not follow in the wake of a war of national liberation but was the outgrowth of an internal social upheaval. Class conflict was omnipresent and real, an everyday experience for most of the population rather than an abstract concept propounded by intellectuals as it tended to be elsewhere. While a military government suspicious of civilian involvement and reluctant to share power tried to control the process of revolution closely, there was in the end a great deal of unchecked and unauthorized popular participation, as various groups sought to settle their grievances, the peasants tackled broadside the problem of land reform and redistribution of wealth, and ethnic minorities struggled for recognition and power. More than any other African country, Ethiopia did not simply adopt Marxism-Leninism by a fiat of the leadership but also experienced a real revolution.

At the time events eventually leading to revolution erupted in early 1974, Ethiopia was a country ripe for change. It was ruled by an aging Emperor, whose concept of political modernization amounted to moving from feudalism to royal absolutism. It was wracked by old conflicts between peasants and landlords, the center and the periphery, and the Emperor and the aristocracy; it also faced a host of new problems spurred by incipient economic growth and modern education. In short, Ethiopia was marked by enough contradictions for all political observers to agree that the succession to Haile Selassie would be a painful one. But trouble set in even before the death of the Emperor and triggered the type of social revolution that occurs only rarely in history, a revolution that drastically altered social, economic, and political relations. Why it took on such dimensions is not an easily answered question. To be sure, it is possible to trace the course of events, to describe the underlying conditions and to point to the precipitating factors. But this does not mean, in our opinion, that the revolution was inevitable. While the underlying conditions existed, it also took a series of highly accidental events to trigger the process. A famine, the barracks revolt of a garrison over a broken water pump, a taxi drivers' strike over a stiff hike in gasoline prices, all these were accidents of history which might or might not have occurred at the same time. The fact that they did transformed Ethiopia's potential for revolution into an actual revolution. But even after the old order was openly challenged by army and civilians, and even after the Emperor's overthrow, there was still no certainty that the transformation would be so radical or so quick. It did not follow an overall plan and was not controlled by any one individual or group. It was aimed initially at broadening somewhat the base of political power and eliminating the monopoly over wealth by a small elite. It ended as an attempt at reshaping the entire society and reweaving the pattern of social relations. In the process, the revolution inevitably devoured a good many of its own children.

Steps Toward Revolution

The beginnings of the revolution have been narrated many times, and we will only resketch them very briefly here. A barracks revolt in early January at a small garrison in southern Ethiopia, sparked by lack of water and bad food, led to a similar venting of grievances by enlisted men and NCOs in other parts of the country. Their demands were highly specific and corporate: pay, food, conditions of service, schools for their children. But in all cases, the same pattern of soldiers and NCOs rising up against their higher ranking officers was repeated. By mid-February, unrest had spread to the civilian population. Students at Haile Selassie University went on strike against an educational reform. Then, teachers struck for higher pay and taxi drivers for higher fares. The country was suddenly in turmoil. The Emperor tried a bit of everything, giving in to some demands, ignoring others, replacing his prime minister, promising a new constitution that would make the prime minister responsible to Parliament. Unrest nevertheless persisted. The capital was paralyzed by a general strike, and the soldiers continued to agitate, progressively adding political demands to their specific corporate requests.

The next few months were marked by obscure behind-the-scenes maneuvering, as many groups tried to take advantage of the crumbling of the old regime. There never emerged in this period an organized, broadly based civilian movement bringing together all the participants in the strikes and demonstrations. Rather, the initiative passed on the one hand to the military and on the other to civilian elites trying to assert their power vis-a-vis the faltering Emperor. Within the armed forces, a series of committees emerged, by and large representing junior officers. Among the civilians, two groups vied with each other, one representing the old aristocracy trying to regain its lost power, and the other a new bourgeoisie seeking a political role for itself through liberal reforms. Civilians and military ran a close race until the end of June, when the military committees which had sprung up in the previous months managed to join forces, organizing a Coordinating Committee of the Armed Forces, Police, and Territorial Army and seizing power. In the following weeks, the Committee called upon the leading figures of the old regime to surrender themselves; most complied willingly, believing their imprisonment was only a temporary measure. The Committee then set aside the new constitution which had been readied by August and represented basically a bid for power by Ethiopia's new bourgeoisie. Finally, it deposed the Emperor on September 12 without a shot being fired in his defense.

Between September 1974 and the following March, the military's Co-ordinating Committee underwent enormous internal change. More moderate elements were forced out, and a radical and ruthless faction consolidated its hold. The Committee, renamed the *Derg,* or the Provisional Military Administrative Council (PMAC), took a series of policy decisions truly revolutionary in their impact, and much more far-reaching than even the most radical civilians had dreamed possible. But it also established a pattern of "revolution from the top" and a tradition of uneasy relations with all civilian groups.

For two months after the Emperor's deposition, the chairmanship of the *Derg* was in the hands of General Aman Michael Andom, Eritrean by origin, moderate in outlook, and autocratic in style of rule. Drawing on his Eritrean contacts, he devoted most of his attention to solving the conflict which for over ten years had pitted two Eritrean nationalist groups, the Eritrean Liberation Front (ELF) and the Eritrean People's Liberation Front (EPLF) against the central government. But neither his policy of seeking a political rather than military solution in Eritrea, nor his moderate outlook, and even less his authoritarianism, proved acceptable to his colleagues. At the end of November, a showdown took place. Aman first resigned and then was killed after he refused to surrender and the military attempted to capture him by force. This confrontation marked the triumph of the hard-liners, whose first decision on the same night as Aman's death was the sudden execution of the 57 most important political prisoners, all top officials of the old imperial regime who had surrendered peacefully during the summer months. The new *Derg* chairman, Brigadier General Teferi Bante, was a quiet, colorless man, chosen because it was assumed he would not try to amass power in his own hands but would defer to the *Derg* as a whole. Under him were two vice-chairmen, Major Mengistu Haile-Mariam and Major Atnafu Abate. The former was to emerge in February 1977, after many bloody conflicts, as the *Derg*'s strongman and the country's ruler. The hard-liners also chose military force as their solution to the Eritrean problem, and shortly after the elimination of Aman a new offensive was launched in the northern province to crush the ELF and the EPLF.

It was just a month after this showdown that the *Derg*'s first declaration concerning socialism was issued. It was a hazy statement, in which *hebrettesebawinet,* or Ethiopian socialism, was defined as "equality; self-reliance; the dignity of labor; the supremacy of the common good; and the indivisibility of Ethiopian unity."[1] Soon, however, socialism began to acquire a much more concrete content. In January, the *Derg* nationalized the major financial institutions, insurance companies, and 72 key industries. In March, it proclaimed a sweeping land reform declaring all land state property and organizing the entire rural population into "peasant associations." These were empowered to redistribute land among their members, set up co-operatives or collectives, organize their own defense and, in general, become the basic units of local self-government. The government called upon the 50,000 students already sent out to the countryside in early January to take responsibility for overseeing the implementation of the land reform. The final blow to the old economic order came in July when the *Derg* nationalized all urban land and rental properties and established elected neighborhood associations known as urban *kebeles* to take over the administration of local affairs. With these reforms, the revolution had entered its radical phase. There was no longer any possibility of going back to the *ancien régime,* and within one more year Marxism-Leninism was all but the official ideology of the military government.

The Conditions

The society giving birth to such dramatic change could, in many ways, have been used as a textbook illustration of Marx's explanation of revolution. Ethiopia was not only a feudal society marked by deep conflict between landlords and peasants, it was also a country in which the power of the landlords was beginning to be challenged by economic modernization, and above all by the growth of "capitalist" commercial farming, which altered the old pattern of land use and social relations. In addition, there were fissions not so neatly explained in Marxist terms, chief among them the existence of intense ethnic rivalries and a separatist movement stemming from Italian colonization in Eritrea. The Ethiopian empire was just that, a conglomerate of different ethnic and language groups, or "nationalities" as the Marxists would later call them, brought together by military conquest and the personal fealty of local potentates to the Emperor. Like all empires, Ethiopia had experienced changing boundaries over the centuries, finally reaching its present ones at the end of the nineteenth century through the conquest of large new territories to the south. These areas were inhabited mostly by a Galla, or Oromo, population different in its language, customs, and traditions from the Amhara and Tigreans of the empire's heartland. Western colonialism, too, had contributed to creating conflict. Eritrea, which the Ethiopian government considered its northern province, had been colonized by the Italians from the 1890s to World War II, and only reannexed to Ethiopia in 1952 as the result of a very controversial United Nations decision. The issue whether Eritrea was historically part of Ethiopia is an extremely intricate one. What matters most is that many Eritreans were convinced that their land should be a separate entity and that they started a guerrilla movement to achieve this in 1961. At the time of the revolution, Eritrea was in a state of war. To the southeast, too, in the corner of Ethiopia wedging into Somalia known as the Ogaden, Ethiopian sovereignty was openly contested. A movement known as the Western Somalia Liberation Front had been organized and armed by the Somali government, which lay claim to the region as part of a "Greater Somalia." Elsewhere in Ethiopia, ethnic conflict was not so open, but nonetheless existed as a potential threat, particularly in those areas of the south where the land was owned by absentee Amhara landlords and tilled by Oromo sharecroppers who had never derived any advantage from being Ethiopian subjects.

This large and conflict-ridden country, with its more than thirty million people, was only very loosely administered. The Emperor had sought to build a more bureaucratic and centralized administration, but Ethiopia was still far from having the apparatus of a modern nation-state. The provincial administration was understaffed, and local authorities—very often landlords—tended to have the last word. The road system of Ethiopia reflected the country's political reality: a star-shaped configuration of all-weather roads connected Addis Ababa to the provincial capitals. Further than that, roads were practically nonexistent, and so was modern administration.

The economy of Ethiopia, the world's fifth poorest country, revolved almost exclusively around the land. It was land that provided the livelihood of over 90 percent of the population and the wealth and power of the elite. Rents were high and a system of tenancy affecting millions of peasants was highly exploitative. Per capita income stagnated around $110 annually.[2] Little innovation had taken place in agriculture until the 1960s, when modern farms began to spring up around the capital. These provided food for the urban market and some exports but also increased social conflict by displacing sharecroppers through mechanization. Altogether, by the time of the revolution there were some 5,000 commercial farms in Ethiopia covering about three quarters of a million hectares.[3] But the dominant picture of Ethiopia was one of grinding poverty, ignorance, and disease.

The industrial sector was even less developed than in other African countries we have considered. It consisted chiefly of about 100 consumer goods manufacturers employing only 50,000 to 60,000 workers—in a country of thirty million.[4] Internal trade was mostly in the hands of small merchants, and transport outside the few roads relied on donkeys. The country exported coffee, small amounts of gold, hides, and skins, and, in recent years, pulses, worth altogether $200 million to $300 million annually.[5] Paradoxically, before the revolution, Ethiopia had enjoyed a very healthy balance of payments, despite the paltry amount of exports, because imports were limited largely to consumer goods for the small upper class and to agricultural machinery for the commercial farms.

Given the subsistence character of the Ethiopian economy, agriculture had to be the key to growth, but its development was impeded, as had been pointed out by many economic advisory missions, by the rigid land tenure system which actively discouraged peasants from introducing innovations to increase production. Land reform was advocated not only by Ethiopian radicals but by virtually all international organizations and foreign aid agencies in the country. Such a measure was a highly explosive issue, however: it would undermine the power of the ruling landed elite, call into question Amhara domination, and bring into the open a host of latent social and ethnic conflicts. For these reasons, the *Derg*'s decision to nationalize all land in March 1975 was a truly revolutionary move which in fact set loose a process nobody could control.

While the divisions in Ethiopian society were deep, and the potential for conflict enormous, there were no political organizations to represent the interests and aspirations of various groups and classes. The Emperor had actively discouraged such associations. While he finally allowed the formation of a labor union, this was closely controlled and under a very tame, conservative leadership. The only group which openly expressed dissent was the students, who for many years had demonstrated, struck, and agitated for reform. But the student movement never spawned an organized political force, as its members dispersed after graduation or were coopted into the system. The absence of any political organizations helps to explain why in the early months of the revolution the civilians were unable to coalesce into a coherent opposition movement. The most articulate and organized center of political activity and opposition to the Emperor was not inside the country, but outside. The Ethiopian students abroad, mostly in the United States and Western Europe, were free to organize, had more access to books, and therefore were better read and more articulate than their counterparts inside the country. They were also very far removed from Ethiopia and thus precluded from any concrete possibility of action, a situation which tended to encourage interminable and very abstract ideological debate. Virtually all of the politically active students abroad, and most of those inside, were Marxists, though this did not prevent them from being deeply divided into factions based on their respective admiration for the Soviet Union or China, their attitude toward the Eritrean question, and, more simply, personal rivalries. Many of these students came back to Ethiopia after the Emperor's overthrow to make their long-dreamt-of socialist revolution. Given the weakness of all organizations and the limitations of the political debate within Ethiopia, it is probably not surprising that most of the radical civilians who played an important role in the revolution, for or against the *Derg*, came from the ranks of these returnees. They participated in the formulation of policy, helped to organize a political party, wrote the clandestine antimilitary pamphlets, led the opposition groups and shared with the *Derg* responsibility for the violence and bloodshed which led in 1977 and 1978 to a period of revolutionary "red terror."

Ideology

When the *Derg* came to power in June 1974, it was not guided by a precise ideology and put forth no specific program. This was not surprising since the military committee was simply a conglomerate of representatives from the various branches of the armed forces selected for reasons internal to their respective corps and not because they shared a common political outlook. Even the proclamation of socialism in December 1974 did not amount to a very clear ideological choice, given the vagueness of the concept of *hebrettesebawinet*. But a Marxist outlook soon came to prevail, and by 1977 Ethiopia had officially accepted the Soviet interpretation of Marxism-Leninism verbatim, to the point that many ideological writings in the newspapers appeared under Soviet signatures and Soviet professors were in charge of teaching ideology at Addis Ababa University. The transition from Ethiopian to Marxist socialism was preceded by a period of intense ideological debate in late 1975 and 1976. Interestingly enough, this discussion followed the enactment of the major policy decisions shaping the character of Ethiopian socialism. The main purpose of the exercise thus was not that of paving the way for reforms, but rather of bringing about reconciliation between the *Derg* and various radical civilian factions in order to facilitate the formation of a political party.

During the fall of 1975, the *Derg* had established a close relation with a group of former Ethiopian students abroad, chief among them Haile Fida. These returnees were charged with forming a political party and were organized into a 15-man Political Bureau for that purpose. The best-known radicals in the country were also invited to join the Political Bureau, but some refused on the ground that the party was being organized from the top down—this was undoubtedly true—and thus that it could never become a genuine popular institution. Faced with a split in the ranks of the radicals and growing opposition from one faction, the *Derg* hoped that ideological debate would resolve the differences among the various groups and strengthen civilian support for itself. In the end, the debate had the opposite effect, confirming the division among civilians and sealing the hostility of one faction to the *Derg*. However, ideological discussion was quite important for the country. It did, in the opinion of the authors, contribute to the political education not only of the literate public but of the *Derg* itself. It also served to propagate Marxist ideas and influence the *Derg*'s concept of what should be done. While ideology did not make the *Derg* more radical, it did provide it with an overall, more coherent vision of the revolution.

The ideas expressed in the debate were never those of the *Derg* itself, but of two semiclandestine civilian groups. Even the Political Bureau did not enjoy official status at that time, although it was an open secret that it existed with the PMAC's blessing. One of the characteristics of this ideological debate was the lack of clarity of language and the abstractness of arguments. It simply represented the public continuation of a private debate among intellectuals that had started many years earlier among students in Ethiopia and particularly abroad. There was no attempt to make the issues more intelligible to a broader audience. The debate took place in the columns of the Amharic daily *Addis Zemen* and in a series of theoretically clandestine but in reality freely circulating pamphlets. Among these, *Democracia* was the voice of the anti-*Derg* faction, which eventually emerged as the Ethiopian People's Revolutionary Party (EPRP). *The Voice of the Masses* represented a pro-*Derg* faction, close to the unofficial Political Bureau, and dominated by Haile Fida's All Ethiopian Socialist Movement (MEISON).[6]

The discussion centered around three major issues, all representing burning political problems in the country at the time: the process of transition from feudalism to socialism, the basic concept of democracy, and the right of

Ethiopia's "nationalities" to self-determination. In practical terms, these related to the relationship between military and civilians, the channels and form of political participation, and the policy toward the separatist movement in Eritrea. Since the exponents of both sides claimed to be Marxist-Leninists, they all spoke the same language and started from the same assumptions but then went on to reach different conclusions when they applied the theory to the Ethiopian situation. Both the EPRP and MEISON started from the premise that a military regime was not a "people's government" by definition, and that only a party and government based on the working class in alliance with the peasants could usher in true socialism. Both parties, however, recognized that since an instantaneous transition from feudalism to socialism was unthinkable, Ethiopia would have to go through a phase in which party and government could not be based on the proletariat. This period of "national democratic revolution" would be marked by an alliance of all progressives. However, the two groups disagreed concerning whether the military could be considered a "progressive" force, with MEISON answering a guarded "yes" and the EPRP a definite "no." The latter faction's conclusion was based in part on its contention that the *Derg* was composed only of "elite officers," not of low-raking officers and NCOs as the other party claimed. In support of its position, the EPRP was circulating a partial list of *Derg* members which included names of captains and majors and left out those of sergeants and corporals.

While the EPRP's contention that the *Derg* was composed of a military elite was inaccurate, its perception that the revolution was being engineered from the top down was quite exact. Reluctantly, the EPRP admitted that some of the measures taken by the *Derg* were progressive. It would have been difficult in fact to argue against the land reform, which had destroyed the basis of the old regime's power, given concrete meaning to the revolution in rural areas, and brought about some improvement in the peasantry's standard of living. But in the implementation of the land reform, the EPRP claimed, the *Derg* had shown its true colors by refusing to allow the revolution to run its full course. The progressive students sent out to oversee the land reform had been hampered in their activities, imprisoned, or recalled to the capital. More specifically, they had not been allowed to encourage class conflict to the point of spurring the peasants en masse into armed struggle against the landlords. The EPRP also argued that the *Derg* had curbed popular participation, and thus a real revolution, because this would have threatened its monopoly over power.

To MEISON, the EPRP position was essentially anarchistic and its concept of unlimited democracy incompatible with socialism. "Anarchists are those who believe that the government is the source of existence of social classes, that when you destroy the government you destroy social classes. They (anarchists) do not believe in class struggle and oppose any government led by the workers."[7] In rejecting the "anarchist" position, MEISON implicitly accepted the notion that revolution should be engineered from the top, so long as the leadership was a progressive one. Here, then, was the crux of the difference between the two positions: they held diametrically opposite concepts of socialist democracy and of the overall revolutionary process. While both sides proclaimed themselves Marxist and rejected the Western notion of democracy and pluralism as a thinly disguised justification for bourgeois rule, the EPRP in the final analysis took what is often considered today by radicals as a "Trotskyite" stance, calling for unfettered direct participation by all the downtrodden. MEISON, on the other hand, interpreted democracy in a more orthodox Leninist light as carefully circumscribed and exercised indirectly through the intermediary of a vanguard party. Beneath all this theoretical jargon so often making the debate incomprehensible to all but a handful of well-read Marxists was the same basic issue that has divided socialist movements everywhere and is surfacing anew in the socialist African countries. A version of the Trotskyite position had emerged in Algeria in the form of the worker self-management system, in Mozambique among those advocating that socialism be based on the communal villages, and in Angola under the guise of the *poder popular* movement. In all these countries, what MEISON referred to as the "anarchist" position has lost out, or seems likely to do so, to the Leninist one.

MEISON and the EPRP also differed sharply concerning the problem of nationalities, although both appealed to Lenin's authority to justify their position. The problem of the nationalities was above all that of Eritrea, since the conflict among the various ethnic groups composing the population of Ethiopia had reached the most critical stage there. Both factions argued in favor of the "right of nationalities to self-determination," but while the EPRP said such a right must include the option of secession, MEISON held that it should be exercised only "within the limits of Ethiopian unity." In other words, right to self-determination meant at most regional autonomy. This was the position advocated by the *Derg*.[8] Moreover, the *Derg*, and possibly MEISON (although this is not clear to the authors) interpreted the concept of nationality to indicate a homogeneous ethnic and linguistic group. By that definition, the Eritrean population of some three million did not constitute a single nationality but was composed of several. Thus, if applied to Eritrea, the doctrine would have allowed the province to be carved up like the rest of the country into new regions. By accepting the doctrine of nationalities, the *Derg* was in practice seeking a way to define the Eritrean problem out of existence. The severity of the fighting in Eritrea never allowed the policy to be enacted. It is unlikely anyway that it would have provided the basis for a solution because both the ELF and EPLF consider Eritrea as a single "nation," regardless of the correct definition of a nationality.

The ideas of the EPRP and MEISON, while stemming from the same ideological source, represented in fact two irreconcilable concepts of revolution and political power. While the *Derg* claimed it was trying to find a synthesis of the two, it was in practice siding with MEISON, as was almost inevitable. Mengistu, then only a vice-chairman of the military council, used the debate in the end to strengthen his own position. With a major speech launching a "National Democratic Revolution" on April 20, 1976, he established himself as the radical ideologue within the *Derg*, the true Marxist guided by a program to which radical civilians, too, could adhere. He announced that the country was embarking on a revolution which would be led by the proletariat "in close collaboration with the farmers and support of the petty bourgeois, antifeudalist and antiimperialist forces, to guarantee to the Ethiopian people their right to freedom, equality, peace and prosperity as well as self-administration at various levels and unrestricted human and democratic rights."[9] At the same time, Mengistu declared that the formation of a party would be accelerated by setting up an organization, the Provisional Office for Mass Organizational Affairs (POMOA), to lay the groundwork.

The attempt at reconciliation failed, and the EPRP became an opposition group bent on overthrowing the government by force, while the *Derg* ruthlessly tried to hunt down its members and root out the organization. During the summer of 1976, the EPRP opened a *marquis* in central Ethiopia; in the fall it started a campaign of terrorism in the capital; and by early 1977 *Derg* and EPRP were pitted against each other in open warfare in the cities, leading to a period of "terror" in which thousands died. Despite the failure of reconciliation, however, the ideological debate was not inconsequential. It did, as we have argued, serve to politicize the public. Most important, it did provide the *Derg* with some guiding principles, which affected its policies in the following years. After the initial wave of reforms of 1975, the *Derg* in fact embarked upon a process of reorganizing the country politically, administratively, and economically in a quite systematic fashion, although its effects were blurred by the persistence of opposition and the wars in Eritrea and the Ogaden. What ideology provided in Ethiopia, in the final analysis, was a set of overall political and economic goals and a concept of the organization required to reach them.

Policies

The major policy decisions dealing the final blow to the *ancien régime* were announced and carried out before Marxism-Leninism was the country's official ideology and long before the Soviet Union played a significant role in Ethiopia. Nonetheless, these policies were unmistakably influenced by Marxist ideas, seeking radical structural change and assuming that the restructuring of the political system required first complete overhaul of the economy. The reforms created initially a very decentralized and participatory system, partly by intention and partly because of a snowballing effect the *Derg* found difficult to control. The thrust of later policy decisions was an attempt to establish an overall system of control, administration, and political participation, as well as to introduce the rudiments of economic planning. The acceptance of Marxism-Leninism, setting forth a centralized concept of authority and economic organization, certainly reinforced this thrust. But the centrifugal forces unleashed by land reform and various separatist or opposition movements made a strengthening of the central power imperative, irrespective of ideological considerations.

1. The Economy

The first decision affecting the economy was taken in January 1975 with the nationalization of financial institutions, the insurance business, and major industries. While important because it gave the government control over the country's tiny modern sector and also because it was the first concrete step toward socialism taken by the *Derg*, this measure did not really affect radically either the character of the economy or the distribution of power in the country. Only an agrarian reform could do that. Furthermore, these nationalizations were not accompanied by any attempt to introduce democracy in the workplace by instituting some kind of worker control. There had been no previous agitation for any kind of self-management in Ethiopia. While there had been labor unrest early on in the revolution, it had been aimed mostly at obtaining higher wages and better working conditions. The equivalent of the Algerian or Angolan spontaneous self-management movement never arose. The *Derg* itself was not interested in introducing worker participation. It simply replaced the old private managers with new state-appointed ones, and in some cases even asked the owners to stay on as managers. It also replaced the old labor union leadership, which had been closely controlled by the Emperor, with a new group, which it similarly sought to yoke. But after the nationalization of industry, demands for worker participation in management and an independent union arose, causing considerable strife between the military and labor leaders. Complicating matters, the EPRP and other antimilitary factions sought to use the labor union as a springboard for their activities. The nub of the conflict thus became civilian-military relations rather than the organization of the industrial sector to allow for worker management.

The keystone of the *Derg*'s revolution was the land reform, a measure which triggered a complex and open-ended process of change still unfolding. Legislatively, the land reform was shaped by three major proclamations. The first, in March 1975, nationalized all land and organized the rural population into "peasant associations."[10] The second, in December of the same year, spelled out in greater detail the powers of the associations.[11] The third, in June 1979, sought to accelerate collectivization by formalizing a process through which "producers' cooperatives," or peasant collectives, should be formed.[12] Each of these measures had unintended repercussions which provided stimulus for further change as well as acute conflict.

The initial proclamation was as simple a piece of legislation as it was momentous. Instead of placing a limit on the size of private properties or expropriating only those of the old aristocracy, it simply nationalized all land and gave use rights to those who were presently cultivating it. This approach avoided the necessity of measuring and registering holdings. Since land registers were very incomplete, most fields unmeasured, land litigation a way of life in Ethiopia, and personnel trained to do surveys practically nonexistent, the decision to nationalize everything cut through all knots at once and enabled immediate action. Moreover, the *Derg* made the reform self-enforcing by calling upon the peasants to carry it out themselves rather than waiting for the slow processing of titles and claims by bureaucrats. The proclamation created an institutional framework for the reform by stipulating that the peasants should come together into associations, with one being created for every 800 hectares of land. Each association would then redistribute land among its members (the upper limit was set at 10 hectares per family) and form cooperatives. But the importance of the associations went beyond land redistribution. They became virtually local units of government, filling a vacuum left by the demise of the landlords and the absence of formal bureaucratic administration below the district level. The second proclamation, published a few months later, recognized openly this governmental role of the associations by giving them formal jurisdiction over some local administrative and even judicial tasks. In practice, then, the creation of the associations responded to the very practical and immediate need to improve administration in rural areas. But it also satisfied the ideological objective of giving "power to the people" by making them directly responsible for their own affairs.

The reaction of the peasants to the land reform proclamation was by and large extremely positive. In the southern regions where tenancy and landlord absenteeism had prevailed, the reform was heartily welcome. Small holders, particularly in the northern part of the country, were far more suspicious of the government's real intentions. Generally, there was far more enthusiasm for land redistribution than for collectivization. The success of the reform could be measured by the swift progress made in forming associations. By the end of 1975, they already numbered over 18,000 and by 1978 there were 28,583 grouping 7.3 million peasant families, virtually the entire rural population. Compared to the experience of other African socialist countries in reorganizing the peasantry, the Ethiopian accomplishment was extremely impressive. The main reason was the high degree of social conflict marking the countryside of Ethiopia and the very real exploitation by the landlords, making the peasants eager for change. Also important were the efforts of the 50,000 university and high school students put in charge of supervising the formation of the associations. The students were enrolled in a "Development Through Cooperation Campaign," better known as the *zemacha,* whose twin objectives were to arouse the peasantry from their centuries of servitude and to spread the benefits of literacy and modern knowledge to the countryside.[13] Despite the enormous responsibility they were given as agents of revolution, the students were antagonistic to the *Derg*, which they tended to regard as a military dictatorship irremediably opposed to a "people's government." Thus in implementing the land reform they pursued their own goals, trying above all to promote immediate collectivization in disregard of the *Derg*'s more cautious approach that such a radical step might well be counterproductive and turn the peasants against the government. The military's fears were not without some reason, for in some cases the peasants did react violently to the students' efforts to create instantly Chinese-style communes. In the end, the students' confrontation with the *Derg* on the one hand and the peasants on the other led to their progressive withdrawal, or flight, from their posts and eventually to the collapse of the campaign. But by the time this happened, the land reform was well launched, the peasant associations were in place, and the landlords were in flight.

The land reform did, as intended, radically redistribute power and wealth in Ethiopia. It also had other, less desirable consequences. Many parts of Ethiopia went through a period of virtual civil war because of the land reform, with former landlords manipulating the peasants to come to their support. Particularly in the strongly Christian Amhara areas, landlords had some success in convincing their tenants that the land reform was all a plot to take the land from the Christians and give it to the Moslems. In other areas, particularly where the landlords had been Amharas and the tenants Oromos, the reform contributed to the strengthening of ethnic resentment. Most importantly, it led to considerable problems of food supplies and strife among the peasants themselves.[14]

It was initially predicted by many observers that land reform would lead to general famine in Ethiopia. While there was no such catastrophic occurrence, the problems mounted over the years. Production of food grain stagnated, oscillating between 4.7 million tons and 5.5 million tons between 1974 and 1978.[15] Furthermore, as the government noted, "the contraction in food grain production was accompanied by increased stock holding by farmers, increased on-farm consumption, disruption of the marketing network, and transport difficulties."[16] A state marketing organization created after the land reform did not operate efficiently. Efforts to make available more consumer goods in rural markets so that the peasants would have an incentive to sell their grain were frustrated by the shortage of such goods and the difficulty of distribution. As a result, in 1978 Ethiopia imported about twenty-five million dollars worth of grain in addition to 80,000 tons of relief food made available by international aid donors for drought-stricken areas of the country.[17] Marketing problems and the tendency of the peasants to withhold grain from the market in order to drive prices up were of great concern to the government. But there were no easy answers to resolving them, particularly in the midst of war and considerable counterrevolutionary activity led in part by the dispossessed landlords.

Another problem arising from the land reform was conflict within the peasant associations themselves. The root cause was the scarcity of land. During the first year of the reform, the peasants continued to cultivate the same plots as before by government order. Thus, some held much more land than others. In the following years, the associations came under pressure to redistribute plots among their members in a more equalitarian fashion. But, as one study concluded, there were no overall criteria for such redistribution and no institution to facilitate it.[18] The somewhat sketchy information available suggests that most associations never tried to distribute all the land in equal shares but simply to reduce inequality somewhat by setting an upper limit on the size of individual holdings. Dissatisfaction thus remained. The first consequence of this land hunger was the whittling down of the size of the communal fields initially set up at the instigation of the *zemacha* students.[19] Even this limited process of land redistribution, moreover, was confined above all to those areas where tenancy had dominated. There was virtually no effort at equalizing plots in those northern areas of the country where the peasants were small-holders. Even from the existing information, it is clear that the land reform performed no miracles. Inequalities remained both within associations and among them. The leadership of the associations, particularly in the north, was somewhat skewed toward the better-off peasants, although it had become more representative with time. And communal farming was at best a very marginal activity. However, changes were still taking place within the associations, and already in three years Ethiopia had taken giant strides in its agrarian reform.

To the *Derg* and civilian radicals, the pace of collectivization was particularly disappointing. The study mentioned earlier concluded that the land reform had led to the proliferation of small private holdings, rather than to the formation of the Chinese-style communes its authors seemed to have in mind. In fact, as we have already mentioned, the size and number of the communal fields had dwindled. More important, very little progress was being made in the formation of cooperatives. Producers' cooperatives, in which members held at least 75 percent of their land collectively, numbered only 21 in 1978, with another 22 being set up. Service cooperatives, where land remained privately held and only the purchase of inputs and marketing were done on a group basis, numbered 343, with another 1,846 in the process of being organized.[20] Service cooperatives were concentrated in the coffee-growing areas, where peasants produced for the market rather than for self-consumption. The government's mounting frustration with all these problems was reflected in a speech by Chairman Mengistu in September 1978 denouncing "rampant individualism" among the peasants and the perpetuation of the "old anarchic relationship between the buyer and the seller." Because of the "petty bourgeois tendencies of the peasantry," he warned, Ethiopia risked moving "not towards socialism but towards capitalism."[21]

In order to speed up collectivization, counteracting this excessive individualism, the *Derg* issued a new proclamation in June 1979. The decree spelled out the steps by which the peasant associations would be transformed progressively into collectives. It directed first that a single "producers' cooperative" should be established in each peasant association. Adherence to the cooperative was to be strictly on a voluntary basis, though, with a minimum of three peasants needed to form one. The others were expected to join as the advantages of the new system of farming became evident to them. The producers' cooperatives were supposed to go through three stages, beginning with the common exploitation of only part of the peasant association's land and ending in the collectivization of all of it as well as with common ownership of all farming tools and animals. The peasants would be allowed to retain a small kitchen garden, but its size would be reduced from a fifth of a hectare initially to only one tenth. Members of the new cooperatives were to be paid according to the work they did, but part of the income was to be set aside for reinvestment and "communal life." In order to encourage the peasants to join producers' cooperatives, the decree stipulated that their members had a *de jure* right to hold all executive positions in the peasant associations. Finally, in a bid to gain a measure of central control over the new cooperatives, it decreed that they were to "produce and submit annually on a standardized form, a work plan to the government for approval before implementation."[22]

There could be little doubt about the intent of the proclamation: it aimed not only at ending individual cultivation of land but also in bringing the collectives under government control and eventually within the framework of an overall planning system. The proclamation, however, was written in such a way as to allow the government to back out of a direct confrontation with reluctant peasants, since it underlined that they did not have to join the cooperative unless they wanted to do so. By putting leadership of the peasant associations in the hands of cooperatives' members, however, the proclamation placed those peasants who elected to cultivate individually at a clear disadvantage. In the weeks following the proclamation, rumors mounted that the *Derg* was determined to collectivize the entire country in a three-year "great leap forward," a claim the government repeatedly denied as malicious.[23] It was too early at the time of this writing to know what the outcome of the measure would be. While the government might back away from a confrontation for a time, it seemed likely to push for collectivization again later, in the same way as China did in its attempt to form peasant communes. It does not seem on the basis of available information that the *Derg* initially pushed very hard. By March 1980, there were reported to be only 89 collective producers' cooperatives with a membership of 11,300.[24] Furthermore, government officials were repeatedly stressing the "voluntary principle" underlying the collectivization campaign, apparently reacting to a number of incidents of peasant armed opposition to it, particularly in the south. There can be no doubt that the land reform has now entered its most difficult stage, and that relations between the military government and the peasants have reached a real time of testing.

The key issue for the agricultural sector of Ethiopia is undoubtedly the future of the peasant associations, which encompass about 99 percent of all cultivated land. But there also exists a state-farm sector. The state farms first came into existence in the immediate aftermath of the land reform when it was decided not to break up the largest nationalized private commercial estates and the foreign-owned plantations, altogether numbering probably around fifty. In the following years, some more land was opened up as state farms in southwestern Ethiopia, but even with that, this sector accounted in 1978 for only 73,000 hectares and about 2 percent of all food production.[25] The state farms were very important for sugar and industrial crops such as cotton, however, Furthermore, even the small amount of grain they produced was crucial, since all of it was controlled by the state and could be used to feed the urban areas where food shortages were a problem.

On the whole, the land reform did more to meet the *Derg's* goals of destroying the power of the landed class and redistributing income in favor of the peasantry than to increase production. During the first few years, the military council's policies were determined primarily by political rather than economic criteria. But this approach could not continue indefinitely. The economy was running down, food shortages were becoming chronic, and the country's once large foreign exchange holdings ($300 million plus) were rapidly being depleted. These problems did not all stem from the *Derg*'s economic policies. The wars in Eritrea and the Ogaden, political unrest, and persistent drought in some areas of the country all contributed to the economic deterioration. The 1978/79 budget illustrated just how costly the prosecution of these wars had become: about 55 percent of all recurring government expenditures ($750 million) was earmarked for defense and internal security. The *Derg* nonetheless recognized the pressing need to focus on the economic situation, most specifically on the agricultural sector. The same budget programmed $300 million for development, with $120 million going for capital investment in agriculture, plus an additional $86 million just for rural roads, compared to only $35 million for industry, mining, and tourism combined.[26]

The government's primary focus was on aiding the peasant associations. This it tried to do through two programs. First, it planned a major expansion of the existing agricultural extension service (EPID) to reach out to all the 28,000 peasant associations. This was scheduled to be launched in 1980 and to be financed by the World Bank, the Swedish International Development Agency, and the International Fund for Agricultural Development. The project called for a total investment of $73 million over two years.[27] The second program, financed by the Ethiopian government, involved the training of "village agents" to serve as links between EPID and the peasant associations. The project called for the training of three agents for each association, a total of almost 75,000 for the entire country.[28] These agents were to be selected by the associations from among their members, attend a one-month course, and then return to work in their respective villages. They would be trained in the rudiments of agronomy, animal husbandry, soil and water conservation, and the organization and management of cooperatives. These measures made clear the government's commitment to a strategy of rural development based primarily on the associations rather than on state farms.

To emphasize its concern for development, the *Derg* announced a new *zemacha* in October 1978, issuing a "Proclamation to Provide for the Establishment of the National Revolutionary Development Campaign and Central Planning."[29] This second *zemacha* was seen as the beginning of a long-term, planned, economic development effort with peasant agriculture serving as the base and industrialization viewed as ultimately essential to establish a socialist economy but relegated to secondary importance for the immediate future. The decree established a Central Planning Supreme Council, under the chairmanship of Colonel Mengistu, which was in reality a nationwide organization composed of a Congress, an Executive Committee, a Secretariat, a Provincial Development Campaign and Planning Office, plus similar offices at the regional and district levels. These various bodies brought together representatives of the central and regional administrations, military corps, and mass organizations at all levels. They were all very top-heavy, with representatives of the labor union and other mass organizations heavily outnumbered by military officers and administrative officials. Considering the growing number of officers being appointed to top administrative positions, the military emerged as the dominant force in the entire organization. The function of the new Council was to design and supervise the implementation of development plans in all fields. The new campaign was thus very different from the first. It was not a crash program depending on the goodwill and enthusiasm of largely unsupervised students. Rather, it was the creation of a state planning apparatus linking the various institutions developed during the revolution, bureaucratic in nature and dominated by the military. It was nonetheless realistic in its underlying assumption that development could only emerge from a long-term, sustained, and carefully coordinated effort.

The initial economic targets of the campaign were to increase peasant production by 350,000 to 400,000 tons, amounting to seven or eight percent of the total, and to open up another 82,000 hectares of state farmland, practically doubling the size of this sector and boosting its production by 170,000 tons. Another 100,000 hectares of state farmlands were to be readied for 1980.[30] In industry, the main goal was simply to increase utilization of the existing capacity of the 132 state-owned factories, accounting for 90 percent of total production, by about 40 percent.[31] In the export sector, the chief objective was to increase to 100,000 tons the main cash crop, coffee, which provided the country with most of its foreign exchange earnings.[32] The targets were extremely ambitious, probably beyond the country's capabilities given the war situation. Nonetheless, government officials were claiming at the end of 1979 that the two-year *zemacha* had met 93 percent of its planned target in industry and 99 percent in agriculture during the first year; industrial production was said to have increased by 30 percent and that of agriculture by 17 percent. Coffee exports were reported to have reached 85,000 tons, while the overall real growth rate of the economy was estimated at 5.2 percent in the period 1978 through 1979 compared to a negative one of .9 percent the preceding year.[33] But the cost of enlarging the state farm sector was, in the view of outside Western economists, not commensurate with the production benefits; many of the 13 new farms were proving to be costly operations, and the entire sector had run up $47 million in debts to the state by the end of 1978. These failings of the state farms led to a government decision the following year to bring back some of the old foreign companies to provide management for several of the nationalized industrial plantations. While the future of this sector remained uncertain at the time of this writing, it appeared likely that the difficulties being encountered would serve to reinforce the already clear commitment to a policy of development based on the peasant associations and small-holder peasant agriculture.

Another aspect of the *Derg's* economic reforms worth mentioning here was its effort to redistribute wealth through a new income and taxation policy. The land reform and other nationalizations drastically reduced or eliminated altogether income coming from rent and profits, but they did not affect salaries, which were in themselves a source of enormous inequality in Haile Selassie's Ethiopia. The minimum daily wage of an unskilled worker had been just one birr ($.50) and the average monthly pay for a government guard or usher 40 birr ($20.00). By contrast the monthly salary of a minister was 1500 birr ($750), plus a 750 birr allowance ($375), or a total of 2250 birr ($1125), giving a formal ratio of better than 50 to 1 within the civil service. But top salaries in the banks, insurance companies, and even the government airlines under the imperial government ran as high as 6,000 to 8,000 birr ($3,000 to $4,000), creating a ratio of 200 to 1 in the worst extreme of salaries under the old system. The revolution modified these extremes considerably but did not dramatically increase the income of the lowest paid workers. While the *Derg* did establish a new minimum wage of 1.50 birr ($.75) for unskilled labor, it rejected the labor union's demand for a 3 birr ($1.50) minimum. On the other hand, it gave a very substantial salary increase to middle-level civil servants, bringing the minimum monthly wage for a high school graduate up from 280 birr to 420 birr ($140 to $210). It left unchanged the top civil service and parastatal salaries. However, in late 1978, the *Derg* decreed a new tax policy imposing a highly progressive income tax on all salaries and increasing dramatically the maximum rate from the old 16 percent under the imperial government to 85 percent on all incomes over 3,750 birr ($1,875). In addition, another form of unofficial taxation was imposed by the *kebeles,* which solicited regular contributions from all residents for local projects and virtually forced those with the highest incomes to contribute the largest proportion of the total cost. There can be no doubt that the net effect of all these changes was a considerable leveling of the highest incomes and thus a substantial narrowing of the gap in the extremes of wealth. Because of the *kebele* unofficial taxes, however, it is impossible to determine precisely the ratio in the extremes of incomes under the new system. It was obviously still sizable and the minimum wage of the lowest-paid workers was only slightly improved. The major beneficiary of all these changes seemed to have been the middle income civil servants.

2. Political and Administrative Organization

The most striking aspect of the political institutions set up under the *Derg* lay not in what was created, but in what was missing. In early 1980, Ethiopia stood as a unique example of a Marxist-Leninist country without a political party. It had many of the trappings of a party—an ideological school, trained cadres, a skeleton cell structure, at one point even a political bureau. But the party itself, as a full-fledged organization with the power of decision making, simply did not exist. While its imminent formation was repeatedly announced, it always failed to materialize. The absence of the party has been pointed to by detractors of the regime as the most conclusive demonstration that the *Derg* is just another dictatorial military junta, not a group of revolutionary officers trying to usher in socialism. Given the scope of other reforms, we think that such an interpretation constitutes a vast oversimplification. There were some very concrete obstacles to the formation of a party in Ethiopia, and two of these deserve some detailed discussion: the first was a structural problem common to many African countries, namely the difficulty of forming a party holding a monopoly of power after power has already been seized and is being exercised by other institutions, particularly the army; the second is an issue specific to Ethiopia, namely the complexity of the relationship between the military and civilians.

Any group taking over control of a country must immediately set up some system to make decisions and see to their implementation. More often than not in the history of postindependent Africa, such a system has consisted of a military council or committee relying on the existing administrative apparatus. Subsequently, there usually develops pressure to create a party, both because this is fashionable and because of the felt need to mobilize public support. In practice, a party formed after the takeover of power usually turns out either to be redundant or, more seriously, a threat to the already ruling council or committee. As a result, it rarely thrives. There are a number of examples of this phenomenon in Africa. In Algeria, the FLN, which had practically collapsed in the civil war at independence, was still in the process of being reorganized 18 years later and appeared unlikely to ever displace the military as the ruling institution. In Mali, the military officers who overthrew Modibo Keita in 1968 took a decade to move to some form of party rule. But even then, the military overshadowed the party leaders and an officer became the president. The same happened in Upper Volta. This does not mean that the transition from a nonparty to a party regime is impossible, but simply that it is very difficult and that the military tends to remain the ultimate arbiter. The difficulties encountered by the Ethiopian military council should be looked at partly in the context of this broader African experience.

The deep distrust and rivalry between military and civilian radicals severely compounded these inherent structural difficulties. Just after the proclamation of the National Democratic Revolution in April 1976, the *Derg* created the Provisional Office for Mass Organizational Affairs (POMOA). It also organized a party school to train cadres and provide Marxist political education for civil servants and other government personnel. POMOA was heavily infiltrated by MEISON, which tried to use the Provisional Office as a power base to challenge the *Derg*. This resulted in the abrupt demise of MEISON as an ally of the *Derg* in the summer of 1977 and a purge of POMOA which left it greatly weakened. The party school, which had also been controlled by MEISON, underwent a change of personnel but continued functioning. By early 1979, it had trained some 7,500 people in three-month courses on Marxism-Leninism, with another 500 undergoing training at that time.[34] While not all people who had received training were destined to become party cadres, many being simply civil servants, there began to exist in Ethiopia a reservoir of personnel with formal Marxist political education.

After the demise of MEISON, the *Derg* did not abandon efforts to form a party, but changed its tactics somewhat. Rather than rely on one group, it decided to bring together under one umbrella the various Marxist-Leninist factions that had come into existence in semiclandestinity. The first initiative at unifying the various radical parties was taken by the civilians themselves, with the *Derg* looking upon it favorably. Five factions issued a communique in February 1977 announcing the formation of a Union of Ethiopian Marxist-Leninist Organizations and proclaiming their intention to work toward a complete merger. The plan failed in the end because of bickering among the factions apparently based on differences in their social base and in their attitude toward the *Derg*; personal ambitions and rivalries among leaders of the various movements also helped to keep them apart. The social base of each was probably the major reason, however. One of the groups, Revolutionary Flame *(Seded)*, recruited its members mostly from the army and was led by a *Derg* member. The Labor League (*Wez Ader*) was also considered to be close to the Military Council and, in fact, a tool used by it against MEISON. Eventually, however, it too turned against the military, and tried to use the labor union as a springboard to power. MEISON itself was supposedly strongest among the Oromo people and had a predominantly Oromo leadership, including Haile Fida himself. A fourth faction, the Ethiopian Oppressed Revolutionary Struggle (I.Ch.A.T.), was also Oromo-led, demonstrating that ethnic divisions were not the sole determinant and simple personality clashes between leaders were also a factor. Finally, there was the Marxist-Leninist Revolutionary Organization (Ma. Le. Ri. De.), a tiny group appealing above all to the students and youth.[35]

The best efforts of the *Derg* to overcome these schisms among the civilian radicals failed. By mid-1978, the Union of the Ethiopian Marxist-Leninist Organizations was comprised of only three of the original five factions, and even they appeared as far away from a merger as ever.[36] The result was that the *Derg* gave up on this approach and decided to try another. In Mengistu's own words:

> Although Marxist-Leninist organizations and individual communists who stand genuinely for the revolution have struggled for ideological and organizational unity, many were those who focused their attention on the form rather than on the lasting union of the progressives. Struggle made it evident, therefore, that the working class party cannot come into being through the merger of organizations.[37]

In December 1979, the *Derg* announced the formation of a new Commission for Organizing the Party of the Working People of Ethiopia (COPWE). This time Mengistu did not rely upon civilians but named himself chairman and appointed trusted officers to other top positions. The task of the new Commission was again to prepare the way for the formation of a "party of the working people." This was described in somewhat broader terms than just the working class, however. The party was to embrace those earning their livelihood "not from the sweat of others but by their own labor and toil" and also those "shedding their blood for Ethiopian unity and for the well-being, process and victory of the revolution."[38] In other words, the party was to include soldiers. All militants would be recruited into the party only as individuals and not as members of other organizations, an obvious bid to bypass the various bickering Marxist factions. It also appears that the party will be a vanguard rather than a mass one, although this was not explicitly stated in the chairman's speech.

Mengistu was very defensive about the fact that the party was still not officially in place. "Today," he admitted, "when the formation of the Commission ... is being disclosed, many revolutionaries and supporters of the revolution are bound to wonder why the party itself should not be set up once and for all." His answer was that "objective conditions" and the low level of political consciousness among Ethiopians did not allow this yet. Interestingly, the speech also contained a rather stinging attack on those who criticized Ethiopia and the *Derg* for not having a party: "Our nascent revolution which erupted spontaneously has achieved so many victories, which were not attained by radical socialist revolutions under the leadership of famous communist parties," he declared.[39] Since among the critics were not only radical civilians but also the Cubans and the Soviets, the statement was in effect a warning to Ethiopia's socialist allies that the *Derg* intended to move in its own manner and at its own pace toward establishing a party. Some 18 months earlier, Cuba had tried to force Mengistu into speeding up the formation of the party by clandestinely bringing back into the country Negedde Gobeze, one of the discredited MEISON leaders, in order to open negotiations about the formation of the party. The Cuban ambassador was asked to leave the country following the incident.

Given the difficulty the *Derg* has previously encountered in working with civilians, there is no reason to expect that the formation of the latest

Commission heralds the imminent establishment of a party. There is even less reason to believe that the party will soon, if ever, become more powerful than the army. Ethiopia is likely to remain for some time yet in the anomalous situation of being a socialist country without a ruling political party. This does not mean, however, that the country has been left without channels for political participation. Partly by design, partly by necessity, and partly because of the centrifugal forces set loose by the revolution, Ethiopia has a far more decentralized and participatory system than the other Marxist countries we have discussed earlier. The basic new institutions of the Ethiopian revolution have been the peasant associations in the countryside and the neighborhood associations in urban areas. Both the rural and urban associations have proved at times very difficult for the *Derg* to control, particularly the peasant ones.

There is a parallel between the decentralization of Ethiopia under the *Derg* and the decentralization of Ethiopia under the Emperor. Neither central authority tolerated formal checks on its authority. The Emperor was an "absolute" and not a constitutional monarch. But this did not mean that his writ ran unlimited; on the contrary, in the provinces, imperial authority was only nominally represented through the intermediary of semiautonomous local authorities. Similarly, the *Derg* did not accept any formal limitations on its authority; it gave no open role to the civilians and procrastinated in forming a party. But the *Derg*'s authority, like the Emperor's, was stymied in the provinces by the weakness of the administrative apparatus, which did not reach far beyond the district capitals. The centralization and authoritarianism which prevailed at the top could not be easily replicated at the bottom. There, the problem was rather an excess of decentralization bordering on total autonomy.

After the revolution, the weakness of the formal administration at the local level allowed for a considerable amount of democracy in the Western sense of an expression of the local will and of self-government. The peasant associations were for a time after the student *zemacha* almost completely autonomous and, if anything, abandoned too much to their own ways and decisions. The peasants elected their own representatives to run the associations and decided pretty much on their own whether, and how, to go ahead with land distribution. This was not so much because the *Derg* was committed to local self-government as because it had no way to exercise authority over the 28,000 peasant associations. The result of this local democracy was not always what the *Derg* and its radical civilian advisors had hoped for. As we have seen, the peasants, left to themselves, were not overly enthusiastic about collectivization of their land. They also tended to elect to the leadership of their associations the wealthier peasants. For example, one study found that in Sidamo Province the associations initially were dominated by the kulaks and that only after repeated intervention by local authorities did the leadership become more representative of the peasants as a whole.[40] Another probably less reliable study carried out by students concluded that around Addis Ababa the leadership of the peasants' associations was often in the hands not only of richer peasants but of those connected by blood ties to the former landlords.[41] The conservative bias was more pronounced, according to all available information, in the northern part of the country, where most peasants had owned some land. There, traditional authorities, including Coptic priests, continued to play a dominant role in the peasants' associations.

The *Derg* first sought to extend central administrative control over the peasant associations by forming "Revolutionary Administrative and Development Committees" composed of local administrators, personnel of various ministries working in the provinces, and representatives of the peasant associations.[42] There is unfortunately no study of how successful these committees were in integrating the central administration and the self-governing associations. There is considerable circumstantial evidence, however, that they have not overcome the historic gap, and that the associations continue to be unable to influence formal central government decisions, while the *Derg* finds it very difficult to impose its will on the peasantry. Continuing resistance to collectivization, repeated government accusations of rampant peasant "individualism," and the chronic difficulty in extracting grain from the associations to supply the urban areas all point to the persistence of local autonomy. On the other hand, the *Derg* continues to announce decisions, such as the third phase of the land reform, which were certainly not taken in consultation with peasant representatives. The all too real autonomy of the peasant associations is one of the most striking features of the Ethiopian revolution. Yet, it is also one of the chief obstacles, in the minds of radicals in the *Derg* and among civilians, to the consolidation of the country into an authentic Marxist-Leninist system. Unless the associations are brought under closer central government control, there cannot be much collectivization, effective central planning, or "democratic centralism" in the country.

While the autonomy of the peasant associations posed the most serious problem because the peasantry constituted more than 90 percent of the population, a similar conflict between central authority and local semi-autonomous groups emerged in other areas as well. The urban neighborhood *kebeles* became for a time a veritable battleground between the military government and its principal civilian opposition, the EPRP. In the 1977 to 1978 period, control of the *kebeles,* particularly in the capital, was regarded by all sides as crucial to their fate. Some of the *kebeles* were infiltrated by the EPRP, others by MEISON or by some of the various minor Marxist factions. MEISON apparently hoped to use the *kebeles* and their militias against the military government, and the *Derg* had to mount a "red terror" and purge the neighborhood associations of all opposition elements before it could even consider itself safe in the capital. In the process, thousands died. Throughout the first six years of the revolution, curbing participation and integrating local institutions into an overall political system have remained crucial, still-unresolved issues. The revolution has oscillated between complete authoritarianism on the part of the *Derg* and near anarchy whenever mass participation blossomed.

3. Social Services

Derg policies regarding social services are probably more important for what they indicated about the depth of change in government than for what they accomplished in practice. The government of Haile Selassie had never regarded it as a duty to provide the population with at least basic services concerning health and education. The PMAC did, but it did not command the means to fulfill its acknowledged obligations. Before the revolution, Ethiopia had an illiteracy rate of 95 percent, one of the world's highest levels of infant mortality, and the lowest life expectancy (39 years) of any country. Famine was a recurrent problem, and the most recent one in 1973 through 1974 had been allowed to claim at least 100,000 victims before the imperial government even acknowledged a crisis and allowed an international relief effort to be mounted. The callousness demonstrated by the old regime in the face of that disaster had served greatly to discredit it morally, particularly abroad.

Because the famine was so recent and burning an issue, one of the first concerns of the *Derg* in the area of services was assistance to famine victims. A Relief and Rehabilitation Commission was set up as early as 1974 to coordinate Ethiopian and foreign efforts in this sector. Over the years, it distributed grain, organized food-for-work programs, and even carried out some resettlement projects to move famine victims to the more fertile parts of the country or to irrigated land. While most of the money and food were provided by foreign donors, the Commission made a major effort to monitor the food supply situation throughout the country and to coordinate relief. In addition to distributing grain, between 1974 and 1978 the Commission spent some sixty-five million dollars for rural road construction, agricultural development, digging of wells, and resettlement projects.[43]

Education posed a major challenge. In 1974, only one-fifth of primary school age children were in school, and only 5 percent of the total population could read. Literacy teaching had been originally envisaged as one of the primary tasks of the students involved in the first *zemacha*, but it had been overshadowed by the land reform. At any rate, the problem was of such magnitude that no crash program could have made much difference. But conventional education could only bring about very slow and costly progress. In 1978, the government budgeted $108 million for primary and secondary education, a respectable amount in a total budget for capital and recurrent expenditures of about $1 billion.[44] Such an effort meant that the number of children in primary school increased to 1.3 million, or 50 percent more than in 1974.[45] But there were still only 5,000 elementary schools in the entire country[46]—there were, by contrast, 28,000 peasant associations, not to mention towns and cities. It was from this dismal situation that the idea arose that primary education should become the responsibility of the peasant associations; proposals were circulated to the effect that they should build the schools and pay the teachers, while the Ministry of Education concentrated on the preparation of teaching materials and the training of teachers. While the idea had not been implemented by the time of this writing, the cost and difficulty of the central government trying to provide for all education suggested it might move eventually to pass some of the burden on to the associations.

The problem of health was equally immense. As Mengistu stated succinctly: "Ours is a country where still the rate of mortality of those below one year of age is 200 out of a thousand, where there is only one doctor for every 80,000 people and where there is one bed for every 3,000 patients."[47] The $42 million budgeted by the PMAC for 1978 was a significant effort, but just a drop in the bucket in relation to the magnitude of the problem.[48] Generally speaking, while the *Derg* talked openly of the dreadful social conditions existing in the country and the need to do something about them, the slim resources available to it were consumed mostly by the military to carry on the wars in Eritrea and the Ogaden and for internal security. Raising agricultural production was recognized as the second priority and improving social services only the third.

The "Red Terror"

Just as no other African socialist or Marxist country has undergone such prolonged internal turmoil as Ethiopia, so no other has ever experienced anything like the "Red Terror" unleashed by the military government in a bloody bid to crush the armed civilian opposition to its rule. For many outsiders, the Ethiopian revolution has come to mean little more than the red terror which gained enormous notoriety abroad for the *Derg* in late 1977 and left the impression that bloodshed was its hallmark. It is a distorted perception, in the sense that the revolution brought much more than bloodshed to Ethiopia, as we have tried to show. But there is no doubt that Ethiopia experienced a period of terror during which thousands were killed, as the *Derg* openly espoused the use of "revolutionary red terror" to combat what it called the "white terror" of the "counterrevolutionaries." It is not our intention to condone or justify such indiscriminate use of violence. However, it is necessary to understand the causes of this phenomenon in order to come to grips with the full drama of the Ethiopian revolution.

Red terror was not used to force a reluctant peasantry into collectives or to exterminate a social class considered inimical to the revolution. It grew out of the struggle for leadership of the revolution and was used by the *Derg* primarily against the various civilian Marxist factions, such as the EPRP and MEISON, and the royalist and conservative Ethiopian Democratic Union as they turned to force of arms to oppose and seek the overthrow of the military government. Indiscriminate killing of civilians by the *Derg*'s various security forces has also been periodically resorted to in Eritrea either in retaliation for EPLF and ELF assassinations of progovernment individuals or in an effort to intimidate the population there into ceasing its support for the Eritrean nationalist cause. The *Derg* has at times used a similar tactic against Somali civilians in the Ogaden. But there was never an official recognition or endorsement of such killings.

There were really two separate waves of red terror, the first in the months following the assassinations of General Teferi in February 1977 and the second subsequent to the killing of Major Atnafu in November of the same year. Both power struggles were used by Mengistu to consolidate his position by eradicating not only his closest rivals within the *Derg* but centers of general opposition throughout the country as well. In the first instance, he declared the revolution was passing from the defensive to the offensive, announced a policy of "arms and democracy to the broad masses," and organized the urban *kebele* militia squads to root out EPRP cells in every neighborhood.[49] MEISON, which at the time was nominally supporting the *Derg*, immediately set about to infiltrate the 6,000-strong militia which sprang up in Addis Ababa and to use this armed force for its own ends. The result was general warfare in the capital and other cities among armed bands sent out by the military and the various civilian factions, each acting to assassinate the other's supporters and unleashing an indiscriminate wave of killings. No Ethiopian felt safe from possible assassination, deliberate or mistaken, as first dozens, and then hundreds died at the hands of often unknown assassins. The EPRP rose to the occasion by mobilizing students and youth to hold antigovernment demonstrations which triggered the first really brutal measures of mass repression by the military at the end of April, when somewhere between 500 and 1,500 young people were shot down on the streets of Addis Ababa or rounded up to be executed later. The intrafactional strife continued throughout the summer months and finally saw MEISON turn from being the hunter to becoming the hunted as its leadership broke with Mengistu and sought to challenge his authority by force of arms and assassinations.

The height of the red terror was yet to come, however. The catalytic event was Atnafu's execution November 11, after which the doctrine of "spreading red revolutionary terror" to eliminate the opposition was elevated to the level of official *Derg* policy. When two American congressmen, Don Bonker and Paul Tsongas, visited the Ethiopian capital in mid-December they were appalled by the wave of killings under way and the *Derg* tactic of leaving bodies of their assassinated victims in the streets with signs marking them as "counterrevolutionaries" attached to their clothes. The two were moved to comment that "bloodshed permeates the present system" and a "reign of terror" grips the city.[50] Just how many died in the four-month period following Atnafu's elimination, or indeed in the 15-month span of red terror from April 1977 to June 1978 is pure guesswork. Amnesty International gave a "reasonable estimate" of the death toll during the worst two months of December 1977 and January 1978 somewhere between 2,500 and 3,000 with another 1,200 to 1,500 killed in the following two months.[51] In addition, they claimed somewhere between 30,000 and 100,000 suspects were held in *kebele* jails for one to two months of "political indoctrination" during which many were tortured and beaten.[52] A Swedish medical group issued a report saying that it was "very probable" that at least 10,000 Ethiopians were killed for political reasons in the course of 1977 and cited an Ethiopian oppostion claim of 30,000 deaths in political violence since the revolution's beginning.[53] Strangely, the lowest estimate came from the US State Department, which in its 1978 annual report to Congress on human rights violations in countries receiving American aid estimated that only 3,000 were killed in the red terror.[54] The truth probably lay closer to 10,000 for the two waves of red terror. Whatever the grisly toll, the fact remains that a phenomenon of red terror on such a scale is totally unprecedented in the history of African socialist and Marxist experiences and can only be understood in the light of the bitter infighting that took place not only between the *Derg* and its civilian opposition but even among the various Marxist factions claiming to be supporting the revolution.

External Influences

The adoption of Marxism-Leninism as Ethiopia's official ideology took place progressively over a period of about three years. Marxist notions were first propagated by civilians without an official role; they were then appropriated by members of the *Derg*, as reflected for the first time in Mengistu's National Democratic Revolution speech; and they were finally elevated to the level of an official ideology after the Soviet Union became Ethiopia's main ally and provider of arms in mid-1977. The question thus arises whether the adherence to Marxism-Leninism can be considered genuine or is simply a facade adopted for convenience' sake, a lure used to attract the Soviet Union or indeed a requirement imposed by the Soviets as the *quid pro quo* for their support. The answer inevitably is somewhat mixed. As we perceive it, there is a genuine commitment on the *Derg*'s part to certain policies which are in accordance with, and inspired by, the ideology. On the other hand, one may well question whether the present high pitch of Marxist-Leninist rhetoric would ever have been attained without the Soviet and Cuban presence. While there is no evidence that the Ethiopian government's policies were in any way modified after the Soviet Union became its major foreign ally, there can be little doubt of a much greater open commitment to the ideology.

Until mid-1976, the Ethiopian revolution owed nothing to external intervention. The major policy decisions shaping socialism had been taken by the *Derg* on its own. The reforms were influenced by Ethiopian Marxist civilians acting as advisers, but these individuals could only propose and try to convince, while the *Derg* had the final say. In other words, there was absolutely no indication that the military government's policies were imposed or even significantly influenced by outsiders. In fact, Soviet and Chinese officials the authors came to know while living in Addis Ababa more often than not were openly alarmed at what they regarded as the all too radical nature of the *Derg*'s reforms, fearing that they would trigger more problems and opposition than the military government could cope with. This was particularly true of the land reform, which jumped many of the steps the Chinese and Soviets had gone through in their own revolutions. Ironically, the major foreign presence in Ethiopia throughout the formative months of the revolution was the American one. The Soviets were still watching with interest and some puzzlement from the sidelines at the unfolding course of events, while the Cubans had only a minimal diplomatic presence in the country. Not until February 1977, when Colonel Mengistu purged his opponents within the *Derg*, eliminated its chairman, General Teferi, and personally took over as leader did the Soviets and Cubans send a clear signal indicating their readiness to support the Ethiopian revolution.

By this time, the internal situation was shifting rapidly against the *Derg*, and another source of support other than the United States was becoming a matter of life or death. The war in Eritrea had escalated greatly, since the nationalists there knew that they would never have a better chance for victory than at a time when Ethiopia was in turmoil and at odds with its major foreign ally. For the same reasons, Somalia was preparing an offensive in the Ogaden, the south-eastern corner of Ethiopia it claimed as part of the "Greater Somalia." Faced with wars on two widely separated fronts and a great deal of unrest at home, the *Derg* desperately needed arms. The American government, which had until then provided Ethiopia with the bulk of its weapons and military training, liked neither the *Derg*'s radical reforms at home, nor its tilt to the East abroad, nor its human rights record and was unwilling to rush arms to its defense on the scale it wanted and increasingly needed to survive. The Soviet Union was, on the other hand, willing to provide massive amounts of weapons and advisers and Cuba even combat troops, on condition Ethiopia cut its military ties with the United States. This is precisely what happened in April 1977 when the U.S. military aid mission was expelled and the American communications center in Asmara was closed down. Subsequent Soviet and Cuban military assistance allowed the *Derg* to repel the full-scale Somali invasion of the Ogaden launched in the summer of 1977 and to stop the steady progress of the Eritrean nationalist movements toward a clear victory in the northern province. While Ethiopia did not fully succeed in crushing either the Eritrean or Somali insurgents, it at least was able to contain both struggles. But since neither war was totally won, Ethiopia remained heavily dependent upon Soviet arms and the 13,000 to 15,000 Cuban combat troops still stationed in the country three years later. Such a heavy dependency obviously exposed the *Derg* to Soviet and Cuban interference. Yet, it seems that the influence of these countries was never commensurate to the size of their presence and that it was felt most on foreign issues of least import to the *Derg*, as we shall see in a later chapter in greater detail.

Conclusions

The Ethiopian revolution is still very much an unfolding process, and it would be hazardous to attempt to make predictions as to its final outcome other than to exclude a return to the *ancien régime* or a total rejection of socialism. With wars still under way in Eritrea and the Ogaden, foreign troops stationed in the country, tensions persisting over collectivization, and the issue of the "nationalities" still unsettled, the revolution obviously has not reached a point of equilibrium. Furthermore, some of the factors affecting its future are particularly unpredictable, being linked as they are to much wider issues. The fate of the armed conflicts in Eritrea and the Ogaden, for example, is very much dependent on Soviet willingness to continue providing arms indefinitely and possibly, too, on the extent of American military aid to Somalia in return for US access to Somali ports and airfields. Barring Ethiopia's territorial disintegration as a result of dramatic changes in the international context, it seems that the main issue of the revolution in the next few years is not whether Ethiopia remains as a socialist country officially adhering to the principles of Marxism-Leninism, but what such an adherence will come to mean. There are today contradictory indications. The *Derg* has demonstrated over the years an unmistakable tendency toward authoritarianism and a drive for centralized control. Marxism-Leninism, particularly the Soviet interpretation prevailing in Ethiopia, has provided it with a theoretical justification for this posture. If there is only one correct solution to each problem, if economic development demands central planning, if the peasants are too "petty bourgeois" to be trusted to make their own decisions, then there are good reasons for the *Derg* to continue directing the revolution from the top down. On the other hand, the "objective conditions" existing in Ethiopia are such as to make it extremely unlikely for a tightly centralized system of control to become a reality. These conditions fit the Marxist concept of historical change as a dialectical process of conflict among classes much better than the Leninist concept of social transformation engineered through central control and planning. The society is far too divided politically, and national institutions are far too weak, for central control to be easily consolidated. Thus, it seems probable that in the foreseeable future, Ethiopia will remain fairly decentralized in the sense that semiautonomous centers of power will continue to exist. In this regard, Ethiopia is noticeably different from the other Marxist and socialist countries we have discussed so far. There, the "objective conditions" have favored centralization, even when ideology promoted a more democratic and participatory system. In Ethiopia, Marxism-Leninism may be increasingly interpreted in an authoritarian fashion and the *Derg* ever more dictatorial, but conditions still favor uncontrolled, and even excessive, participation. The conflict between authoritarianism and participation in Ethiopia is not only one between two interpretations of Marxism, as is the case, for example, in Mozambique, but also one between ideology and existing conditions. As a result, socialism is less likely to mean a completely centralized, state-controlled system in Ethiopia than in any of the other countries we have discussed.

Chapter VII
Nationalism and World Revolution

Nowhere have the Communist leanings of the African Marxist-Leninist states been more pronounced and worrisome to the United States than in their foreign policy. Americans might not know what was going on inside Angola, Mozambique, or Ethiopia, but they might well be cognizant of these countries' close ties to the Eastern bloc and the large contingent of Cuban troops stationed in two of them. The prevailing American view of Communist involvement in Africa in 1980 was that the Soviet Union and its allies had taken advantage of the continent's troubled political waters to impose communism on struggling regimes seeking outside support to survive. The American reaction, as typified by Undersecretary of State for Political Affairs David Newsom in testimony before Congress in October 1969, was that the Communist presence in Africa represented a "threat" not only to US interests but to "the long-term interests of the African states as well."[1] In his view, the linkage between certain African states and the Communist world was an unnatural and fundamentally unwanted one that constituted a "clear and unwarranted extension of the global competition to Africa."[2] Such an American interpretation was not only dangerously ethnocentric and self-serving, it also obscured, probably deliberately, the ideological basis of these ties. Furthermore, it ignored that the African Marxist states saw themselves pitted in an ongoing struggle against Western imperialism and capitalism and were thus naturally drawn to the Soviet Union. The fact of the matter, however disagreeable it might have been to American policymakers, was that a growing number of African states viewed the evolution of international relations through a similar, if not identical, ideological prism.

This said, it nonetheless remained true that as of 1980 the relationship between the Soviet Union and its new African allies was complex, unsettled, and still fumbling for a point of equilibrium. For all the rhetoric of solidarity, there was a residual distrust of the Soviet Union as a superpower among these African countries, all too aware of their own weaknesses. The alliance between the Soviet block and its ideological allies in black Africa did not fall into any existing pattern. Certainly, it was nothing like that between the Soviet Union and the Eastern European nations deemed under the Brezhnev doctrine to have "limited sovereignty." Nor was it similar to the Soviet-Cuban relationship, because the African Marxist-Leninist states were nowhere nearly as dependent on Moscow, while the Soviet commitment to them was not as clear yet, either. Nor did Afghanistan provide a parallel, since none of these regimes had been installed through a Soviet military invasion. The three countries we have studied here—Mozambique, Angola, and Ethiopia—had all signed 20-year treaties of friendship and cooperation with Moscow, but it was still far from clear what they meant; similar agreements with other African countries such as Somalia and Egypt had, after all, been cast aside in the past with great alacrity. Spelling out the nature of this complex relationship is the task of this chapter. We shall begin first by examining the Soviet, and to a lesser extent Cuban, attitude toward their new Marxist-Leninist allies and then look at the African viewpoint on the same relationship.

The Soviet Outlook

The Soviet attitude toward the evolution of events in Africa generally and the rise to power of a growing number of Marxist leaders more specifically has been one of simultaneous great hope and persisting doubts. On the one hand, the Soviets would obviously have liked to interpret the new wave of Marxist-Leninist regimes as a fulfillment of their own prophecy about the whole world eventually turning to communism. On the other hand, their own often bitter experience with a first generation of now fallen African radical regimes in the 1960s instilled a large degree of caution and lowered their expectations. These doubts were reinforced by their ideological conviction that feudal and precapitalist African societies could not really be transformed directly into socialist ones.

Probably the best recent expression of Soviet optimism about contemporary events in the Third World came in an article by B. Ponomarev, secretary of the Communist party Central Committee and one of its chief writers on international affairs, published in *Kommunist* just after the Soviet invasion of Afghanistan in late December 1979.[3] Entitled the "Invincibility of the Liberation Movement," the article heatedly refuted the American contention that the meddling "hand of Moscow" was responsible for the recent communist successes in the Third World, arguing instead that these were a manifestation of "the development, in breadth and depth, of the worldwide revolutionary process." In Ponomarev's view, the turn of events in Vietnam, Cambodia, Cuba, Nicaragua, Afghanistan, Iran, Ethiopia, and the former Portuguese African colonies had to be explained by "objective historic factors" and understood as part of "an implacable process... of replacing the obsolete, reactionary, oppressive regimes by progressive ones, most frequently those with a socialist orientation."[4] The African liberation movements were singled out for special praise and seen as a confirmation of the Soviet thesis that the capitalist international order had plunged into a "deep crisis" and was declining while the world socialist order was prospering and expanding. This changeover, according to Ponomarev, constituted "the basic content of the modern era," and was not a result of Soviet meddling. "A revolution requires a revolutionary situation which cannot be created artificially from without... the roots of revolution and its motivating force are always in national soil." Moreover, "one cannot force a revolution on anyone," and the Soviet theoreticians from Lenin onwards had always rejected the idea of "the exporting of revolution."[5] All the new progressive regimes had come to power because their countries were ripe for revolution, not because of Soviet interference. But, he added, "obviously it is no matter of indifference to Soviet citizens what sociopolitical orientation the various currents in the developing world adhere to."[6]

> Sympathies for the persons who are fighting for true freedom are natural for Marxist-Leninists and internationalists. And wherever such forces exist and fight, they can rightfully count on our solidarity and support.[7]

The Ponomarev esssay articulated well both the Soviet viewpoint on the current course of international affairs and the rationale and timing for interference under certain circumstances to push events along further in the desired direction.

Cuban leader Fidel Castro has been even more explicit in justifying the need for a certain degree of Communist activism in the Third World, and especially Africa, to help the revolutionary process along. In an interview with a prominent radical African magazine following a 40-day tour of the continent in 1977, Castro described Africa as "imperialism's weakest link today" and added:

> Perfect opportunities exist there for the transformation from quasitribalism to socialism without having to go through the various stages that were necessary in other parts of the world. . . . If we are militant revolutionaries, we must support the antiimperialist, antiracist and anticolonialist struggle. Imperialist domination is not as strong here as it is in Latin America.[8]

A few months later, Castro sent 16,000 combat troops to Ethiopia on the second major Cuban expedition of military forces to Africa in support of the "antiimperialist struggle." Castro's remarks expressed the positive Third World assessment of the potential for socialism even in highly underdeveloped societies. In his view, African countries were capable of leaping from "quasitribalism to socialism" directly.

The Soviet Union, by contrast, took a position on this issue which was looked upon as patronizing by radicals in the Third World. While arguing on the basis of Lenin's writings that capitalism was not a precondition for socialism, the Soviets contended nonetheless that most developing countries were not ripe for socialism and had to go first through a period of transition. In Moscow's eyes, even the most radical African regimes were simply "revolutionary democracies" or countries on the "noncapitalist" road.[9] The Soviets did not accept the contention of African leaders that they had embarked upon "socialist revolutions" and argued instead that they were simply leading "national democratic revolutions," whose purpose could at best be the creation of the necessary preconditions to make a socialist revolution possible at the later stage. Nothing has shaken this basic Soviet thesis about the limitations of the African socialist regimes, not even the new wave of self-proclaimed Marxist-Leninist ones in the 1970s. About the only ideological concession they have made is one of terminology. Instead of the negative expression "noncapitalist" regimes and the "noncapitalist" road of development, terms which African Marxists found belittling, they began talking about "socialist-oriented" states and putting forth what they called a "theory of socialist orientation."

A good, recent restatement of the old Soviet thesis in its new guise was contained in a 1979 article written by Anatoli Gromyko, son of the Soviet foreign minister and head of the African Institute in Moscow.[10] Basically, there was little new in the analysis, but it captured nicely the ambiguous Soviet reaction to the wave of Marxist regimes, both their exhilaration with this phenomenon and their persisting doubts about its authenticity. Gromyko began by noting that a wide belt of "socialist-oriented states" existed across Africa and Asia with a combined population of 150 million. Most of them, he noted, were located in Africa, where "over a dozen" countries, accounting for 30 percent of the continent's territory and nearly 25 percent of its population, now fell within this category. He declared that some of the African socialist-oriented countries were ahead of the Asian ones in chosing a "socialist option" and even "making faster progress in this direction" because of the "particular historic features" of the African continent, notably the weaker economic and social position of the local bourgeoisie.[11] Gromyko nonetheless expressed the same Soviet concerns about what the trend meant and whether it might not be ephemeral. He noted, for example, the very different circumstances allowing for the successful development of socialism in the equally backward Soviet Central Asian republics "under the guidance of the Communist Party of the Soviet Union" and outside the "world capitalist economy."[12] The African socialist-oriented states, on the other hand, "have not completely extricated themselves from the capitalist world's economic fold and are still tied to it by many economic tethers."[13] Furthermore, the reforms in such countries as Algeria, the Congo, Guinea, Tanzania, Angola, Mozambique, Benin and Madagascar were not being carried out under a "working-class dictatorship" and "the leadership of Marxist-Leninist parties," but rather by "revolutionary democrats whose advanced sections often go over to scientific socialism."[14] Tribalism, the absence of class formation and presence of "precapitalist," often even "prefeudal," socio-economic formations and the high degree of illiteracy were all viewed as additional major obstacles. About the best one could hope for, according to Gromyko, was success in undertaking "presocialist reforms." In fact, he added:

> It would be more correct to speak of a particular socialist trend or a combination of such trends, prevailing, developing or asserting itself in a complex battle involving many difficulties.[15]

These official Soviet doubts were shared widely by their allies, with the notable exception of Cuba. Even officially recognized African communists echoed them, showing the greatest concern for the steadfastness of the "revolutionary democratic leaderships" of the socialist-oriented regimes. A document published after a meeting of official African Communist and workers' parties in late 1978, entitled "A Communist Call to Africa," was most explicit in expressing concern that the revolutionary democrats were "subject to vacillation between socialism and capitalism." As a consequence, the document said, "the possibility that some revolutionary democrats may seriously reverse their progressive social policies is very real."[16] An even more cogent summary of Communist doubts about their new African allies could be found in the writings of East German theoreticians. A 1979 article in *Deutche Aussenpolitik* noted that

> because of the still weak social base, the inconsistencies ... in thinking and behavior of predominantly petty bourgeois-peasant forces of leadership, the lack of experience and cadres, and not least of all on account of the strong economic positions and the ideological influences which imperialism continues to dispose of in these countries, the development of the countries with a socialist orientation is by no means irreversible. Changes—conceivably of a precipitous nature—are possible.[17]

By comparison with the Soviet, East German, and official African Communist cautious embrace of the African "revolutionary democrats," the Cuban reaction was warm and free of conditional ideological reflections. Castro was far more willing to accept these revolutions as authentic and to understand their peculiarities. For him, Angola, Mozambique, and Ethiopia stood together alongside Vietnam, Laos, and Afghanistan as "new revolutionary bastions" in the worldwide struggle against Western imperialism.[18] He expressed particular admiration for the Ethiopian experience which he regarded as embodying aspects of both the French and Bolshevik revolutions and of being a "true revolution." While African and European Marxists had the gravest doubts about the character of Colonel Mengistu and his belief in Marxism-Leninism, Castro described him as a "calm, intelligent, bold, and brave" person with "exceptional qualities as a revolutionary leader."[19] The success and consolidation of the Ethiopian revolution was regarded by Castro as "extremely important" for all of Africa. Clearly the presence of a military person at the head of a revolution, so bothersome to European and African Marxists, constituted no problem for the Cuban leader, himself a military revolutionary. Similarly, the difficulties the African Marxist regimes were experiencing in building vanguard parties was something Castro could appreciate, having taken a decade himself to implant one at home. Castro clearly found it far easier to identify with the African socialist revolution than either the soviets, East Germans, or African Communists encumbered with all their heavy, uncompromising ideological baggage.

Soviet Bloc Policy

Soviet bloc policy, strangely, did not reflect very accurately the doubts the Soviets and their East European allies seemed to have about the permanency and authenticity of the African Marxist-Leninist states. Given these doubts, the downfall or wavering course of a number of socialist-oriented leaders in the 1960s (Ben Bella, Nkrumah, Keita, and Touré), and the turnabouts of other countries in the 1970s (Egypt, the Sudan, and Somalia), one might have expected an even greater caution on the Soviets' part and a mounting reluctance to make a substantial economic, political, or military investment. This has not been the case, however. Indeed, the Soviets have, if anything, accelerated their efforts to cement alliances through treaties, secure the Marxist-Leninist regimes in power, and work out a coordinated strategy of assistance with their bloc allies, most notably the East Germans and Cubans. The Soviet Union signed a 20-year Treaty of Friendship and Cooperation with Angola in October 1976, with Mozambique in April 1977, and with Ethiopia in November 1978, despite the failure of similar earlier agreements with Egypt and Somalia. East Germany, for the first time in its fast developing relation with Africa, concluded very similar treaties with the same countries. Two of them were signed during the visit of the East German Chairman, Erich Honecker, to Angola and Mozambique in February 1979 and the third during his trip to Ethiopia in November of the same year. The Soviet Union, East Germany, and Cuba have also reached numerous agreements on cultural, trade, scientific, military, and economic cooperation with their three closest African allies, establishing a broad framework for assistance.

The coordination of policy among these Eastern Bloc countries was one of the most striking new developments of the late 1970s in their dealings with Africa. It indicated that both East Germany and Cuba had come of age in their international relations and that the Communist world was more committed to pressing its cause on the continent. Precisely how this three-way cooperation between the Soviet Union, East Germany, and Cuba came about, and who influenced whom, is beyond the scope of this study. It does appear that Cuba's motives and the history of its relationship with the African Marxist-Leninist states were of a different nature than those of the Soviet Union and East Germany. Nonetheless, there seemed to have emerged a general understanding about which country would provide what, not only to the Marxist-Leninist states but to the continent in general. The division was based essentially upon the resources and special capacities of each donor country. The Soviets provided almost all the arms and took overall responsibility for military assistance, the Cubans sent the bulk of both military and technical personnel, and the East Germans concentrated on improving these regimes' security and police. The Cuban contibution was way out of proportion to that country's size or wealth and truly astounding. According to US government estimates, Cuba in 1978 accounted for 37,275 of the 41,680 Communist military personnel in Sub-Sahara Africa and provided 10,970 civilian technicians compared to the 7,640 from the Soviet Union and Eastern Europe. The Soviet Union, for its part, sold or gave $1.3 billion worth of arms to black Africa between 1973 and 1977 and then a record $1.2 billion in 1978 alone, almost all of it for Ethiopia.[20] East Germany, finally, was training the security and police forces of Ethiopia, Mozambique, and Angola as well as sending some arms to Mozambique.[21]

The concentration of Soviet bloc assistance on the military and security forces clearly reflected a special concern for the political stability of their allies and a determination to keep them in power. The Soviet Union has also sought, however, to institutionalize these socialist-oriented regimes by helping to establish a strong vanguard party. A third objective has been to work for the creation of a larger stratum of convinced Marxists to provide a stronger social and political basis for them. This has meant emphasizing education and indoctrination in Marxism-Leninism. The Soviet experience in Africa during the 1960s has undoubtedly been the determining factor in the choice of emphasis. Nkrumah, Keita, and Ben Bella might well have eventually created acceptable facsimiles of Marxist-Leninist systems had they survived long enough, but they didn't because of very weak parties and of armies they could neither control nor convert their way of thinking. There was every indication that the Marxist leaders of the late 1970s fully agreed with the Soviets and Cubans in giving close attention to the military, the security forces, and the training of political cadres. This was as much in their own as in the Soviet or Cuban interest and should not be looked upon as an imposition of "foreign" communist influence on their revolutions. There was, however, one area of potential conflict with the Soviet Union stemming from the presence of military leaders in a number of the Marxist-Leninist states.

African military regimes have constituted both a political and ideological quandary for the Soviet Union. The Soviet experiences with ruling officers in the Sudan, Egypt, Algeria, and Somalia have all shown that in the end nationalism prevailed over Marxism-Leninism. On the other hand, the national liberation struggles in Mozambique and Angola have given birth to avowedly Marxist military-civilian regimes. These, however, have yet to prove the steadfastness of their commitment. To date, from the Soviet point of view, no African government, be it military, civilian, or mixed, has proven to be reliable as an ally or in its commitment to Marxism-Leninism. The Soviet thesis thus treats the military as it does all other "progressive" elements in African countries, namely as part of a petty bourgeoisie which by definition has an equal chance of turning radical or reactionary. Military officers who take power, according to the Soviet thesis, eventually have to decide which social groups they intend to side with. Some of the officers "sooner or later become mainly the instrument of the international and local exploiting classes" and end up using their force "to strike a blow at the developing revolutionary forces."[22] On the other hand, "democratic officers" interested in carrying out a "national democratic revolution" will join forces with other progressive forces and seek the support of the working class. Which type of officer prevails seems to be almost a matter of chance and of the internal power struggle within the military.

The Soviets have shown uncertainty not only about the progressive orientation of ruling officers but also about the suitability of the military as one institution for carrying out a revolution. Even when cooperating closely with military regimes, they have insisted that these governments create a vanguard party and make it, rather than the army, their base of power. This issue has been most delicate in countries where progressive officers came to power without the help of a political party and saw the Soviet insistence on building one as an attempt to push them to the sidelines. There has been really only an example in Africa of something resembling the kind of transition the Soviets have in mind, and that is Somalia. In 1976, Mohammed Siad Barre dissolved the Supreme Revolutionary Council and transferred power to the new Somali Revolutionary Socialist Party after seven years of pure military rule. The transition was imperfect, however, because army officers continued to play a dominant role in the party's political bureau and central committee. More paradoxically from the Soviet viewpoint, this party proved as unreliable an

TABLE I

Trade with the USSR and the East European Council for Mutual Economic Assistance (CMEA) (in millions of $)

African socialist	Total exports to USSR	%	Total imports	%	Total exports[1]	%	Total imports[1]	%
Algeria	52.9[2]	0.8	99.4[2]	1.27	34.9	0.56	209.7	2.67
Guinea	NA	NA	NA	NA	NA	NA	NA	NA
Tanzania	1.01[2]	1.86	1.15[2]	0.96	2.89	0.53	5.99	0.49
Zambia	.6[2]	0.07	.6[2]	0.15	3.6	0.46	1.3	0.2
African Marxist								
Angola	NA	NA	NA	NA	NA	NA	NA	NA
Benin	NA	NA	.32[2]	0.09	NA	NA	NA	NA
Congo	2.35[2]	0.73	1.11[2]	0.42	1.32	0.41	1.03	0.38
Ethiopia	.57[2]	0.18	5.51[2]	1.06	6.19	2.0	4.96	0.95
Guinea-Biss	.06[2]	0.63	.01[3]	0.04	NA	NA	.13	0.24
Madagascar	9.32[2]	2.64	3.02[2]	0.88	4.93	1.40	2.45	0.71
Mozambique	NA	NA	NA	NA	.70	0.24	3.10	.52
Somalia	8.69[2]	9.64	4.46[2]	1.30	NA	NA	NA	NA

SOURCE: *Direction of Trade Yearbook* (1978).
[1] These figures do not include the USSR.
[2] Extrapolated annual data.
[3] 6 months or less of reported data, 6 months or more extrapolated.

ally as any military regime. Within 18 months of the transition, Somalia broke its ties with the Soviet Union, canceled the Treaty of Friendship and Cooperation, and turned to the United States for assistance. Thus the example of Somalia would seem to suggest that the mere existence of a party provides no guarantee that a country will be a reliable partner of the Soviet bloc. The general Soviet experience with the institutionalization of power in the party rather than the army, and the specific case of Somalia, must have been disheartening and disillusioning. But the Soviets have not changed their approach and still consider the formation of a vanguard party to be the best proof of a regime's dedication to socialism.

The Soviets have shown much less concern for building up the economies of the African Marxist-Leninist countries than for strengthening their military or political institutions. Neither economic assistance nor trade have served as important tools of Soviet policy. Moscow has devised no preferential trade policy to lure African countries into its orbit, although its friendship treaties all incorporate the principle of "most-favored-nation treatment." Nor has it offered any African Marxist-Leninist state a long-term fixed price for its main

TABLE II
Trade with the USA and the EEC
(in millions of $)

African socialist	Total exports to USA	%	Total imports from USA	%	Total exports to EEC	%	Total imports from EEC	%
Algeria	3361.00	54.00	411.50[1]	5.20	2328.50	37.00	5103.50	65.00
Guinea	60.64[1]	20.70	30.91[1]	13.20	120.45	41.00	160.44	68.50
Tanzania	77.75	14.30	53.02	4.40	236.10	43.40	595.17	49.40
Zambia	109.50[1]	14.00	44.30[1]	6.90	348.10	44.70	266.40	41.70
African Marxist								
Angola	218.50[1]	20.60	34.70[1]	4.40	134.00	12.60	297.70	38.10
Benin	.36[1]	0.80	12.40[1]	3.30	17.40	38.30	190.80	51.00
Congo	77.73	24.30	9.7	3.60	122.90	38.40	195.00	73.10
Ethiopia	96.70[2]	31.70	26.950[1]	5.20	71.80	23.50	214.40	41.40
Guinea-Biss[3]	NA	NA	.043[3]	0.080	2.42	22.70	33.97	64.40
Madagascar	101.70[1]	28.80	10.12[1]	2.90	136.39	38.60	218.82	63.70
Mozambique	38.00[1]	13.40	22.22[1]	3.70	78.89	27.70	149.27	25.00
Somalia	.27[1]	0.30	22.44[1]	6.50	17.76	19.70	187.98	54.30

SOURCE: *Direction of Trade Yearbook* (1978).
[1] Annual data derived from partner country.
[2] Extrapolated annual data.
[3] 6 months or less of reported data, 6 months or more derived from partner.

export commodity the way it did to Cuba for its sugar. The weakness of Soviet economic and trade policy may indeed turn out to be the Achilles' heel of their relationship with Africa. As Tables I and II illustrate, the African Marxist-Leninist and the African socialist states have all remained thoroughly integrated into the international capitalist order, although in some cases the main trading partner may have changed from the former colonial power to another Western country. The best illustration of this is Algeria where the United States has displaced France as the main importer of Algerian oil and gas. Just as radical African regimes have continued to trade with the West while reviling it in international fora, so the Soviets have shown no compunction in trading with African governments at opposite ends of the political spectrum. As Table III shows, through 1978 the Soviet Union had more trade with Egypt than any other African country despite its public denunciations of President Anwar Sadat's regime ever since he broke his political and military ties to Moscow in 1972. Libya and Algeria were also important partners, and this made somewhat more sense in terms of Soviet political relations with the continent. But Ghana, Morocco, and Nigeria, consistently major Soviet trading partners in Africa in the late 1970s, were certainly not socialist. Furthermore, the Soviet Union signed a $2 billion phosphate deal with Morocco in 1978, an agreement destined to catapult that conservative, pro-Western country into first place in terms of Soviet imports from Africa. According to the agreement, the Soviets would develop and equip an entire mine producing 10 million tons of phosphate a year and be paid for their investment in phosphates.

TABLE III
Largest Trade Volume with USSR
(in millions of rubles)

	1973	1974	1975	1976	1977	1978
	1) Egypt	1) Egypt	1) Egypt	1) Egypt	1) Egypt	1) Egypt
T	541.1	728.1	710.3	530.6	492.4	345.5
I	277.2	301.3	262.0	199.8	203.3	147.5
E	263.9	426.8	448.3	330.8	289.1	198.0
	2) Algeria	2) Algeria	2) Algeria	2) Algeria	2) Algeria	2) Algeria
T	116.8	171.7	247.0	190.3	162.8	158.6
I	64.7	110.3	112.3	131.4	123.4	51.8
E	52.1	61.4	134.7	58.9	39.4	106.8
	3) Morocco	3) Nigeria	3) Nigeria	3) Morocco	3) Ghana	3) Algeria
T	54.4	91.9	108.3	105.6	116.9	139.6
I	28.3	21.5	24.3	55.3	11.8	88.3
E	26.1	70.4	84.0	50.3	105.1	51.3

TABLE III (continued)

	4) Libya	4) Morocco	4) Morocco	4) Ghana	4) Morocco	4) Ghana
T	44.5	87.1	86.9	81.2	105.2	114.2
I	14.1	54.1	45.7	16.9	55.9	4.8
E	30.4	33.0	41.2	64.3	49.3	109.4
	5) Guinea	5) Ghana	5) Ghana	5) Nigeria	5) Libya	5) Morocco
T	43.7	49.9	57.0	50.5	97.7	104.0
I	41.8	25.3	10.7	23.9	20.8	56.6
E	1.9	24.6	46.3	26.6	76.9	47.4
	6) Nigeria	6) Libya	6) Cameroun	6) Guinea	6) Angola	6) Nigeria
T	39.9	28.5	36.6	50.1	79.6	92.2
I	11.0	28.5	1.9	23.3	69.2	75.4
E	28.9	NA	34.7	26.8	10.4	16.8
	7) Ghana	7) Ivory C.	7) Guinea	7) Cameroun	7) Guinea	7) Ethiopia
T	37.7	28.2	34.1	36.7	53.1	68.5
I	9.7	8.6	19.7	3.3	24.8	64.2
E	28.0	19.6	14.4	33.4	28.3	4.3
	8) Somalia	8) Guinea	8) Ivory C.	8) Ivory C.	8) Nigeria	8) Ivory C.
T	12.6	27.3	32.7	24.3	34.8	65.6
I	11.5	22.4	13.2	9.6	34.5	6.1
E	1.1	4.9	19.5	14.7	0.3	59.5
	9) Tunisia	9) Somalia	9) Somalia	9) Somalia	9) Cameroun	9) Angola
T	11.2	18.8	26.5	23.4	33.4	57.4
I	5.8	16.8	22.2	18.7	4.9	47.8
E	5.4	2.0	4.3	4.7	28.5	9.6
	10) Ivory C.	10) Tunisia	10) Libya	10) Angola	10) Ivory C.	10) Guinea
T	10.1	17.1	18.8	19.7	31.0	47.5
I	3.9	8.1	18.8	5.3	5.7	20.6
E	6.2	9.0	NA	14.4	25.3	26.9

SOURCE: Ministry of Foreign Trade, USSR.

T Total
I Imports
E Exports

The pattern of Soviet bloc economic assistance correlates somewhat better with its political and military commitments on the continent. But its aid still remains a distant second to that coming from the West even in the Marxist-Leninist countries. As David Albright has pointed out, Moscow has traditionally given less assistance to sub-Sahara Africa than to any other Third World region and the amount actually dropped from 13 to 4 percent of the total between 1954 and 1974.[23] The share of North Africa, where the Soviets have had much more important political relationships with Algeria, Egypt and Libya, plummeted from 34 percent to 9 percent.[24] China, the Soviet Union's main Communist rival in Africa, has given nearly as much as the entire Eastern bloc of nations combined to sub-Sahara Africa, or $2.3

billion of the $4.8 billion flowing from all Communist countries between the years 1954 and 1978.[25] (Western nations, by contrast, provided directly and through various multilateral lending institutions like the World Bank a total of $5.1 billion in 1977 alone.)[26] In the 1954 through 1978 period, the most favored nations of the Soviet bloc in black Africa have been Guinea ($322 million), the Sudan ($305 million), Ethiopia ($200 million), Ghana ($199 million), Somalia ($170 million), Mali ($113 million), and Angola ($105 million). But none of these countries has received anywhere near as much assistance as those in North Africa. Morocco, for example, has been given a grand total of $2.2 billion, most of this accounted for by the 1978 phosphate deal, and Algeria $1.2 billion.[27] The most interesting question at the present time is whether the Soviets and their allies perceive any special reason to increase their assistance to the new group of Marxist-Leninist states which have come into being since the mid-1970s. This question leads us to a more detailed examination of the evolving economic relationship of Angola, Mozambique, and Ethiopia with both the Soviet bloc and the West.

1. Angola

The Soviet-Angolan alliance was sealed by the October 1976 Treaty of Friendship and Cooperation providing for cooperation in all fields and requiring the two countries to coordinate their positions in case of "danger to peace." It also provided for military cooperation "in the interests of strengthening the defense capability of the High Contracting Parties," terminology that seemed to imply unspecified Angolan assistance to the Soviet Union as well as Soviet aid to Angola.[28] The bulk of all direct Soviet assistance has gone for arms and military training. The Soviets, according to US calculations, provided $340 million in arms by 1977 compared to only $17 million in economic assistance through 1978.[29]

The main communist country helping the MPLA since long before independence has been Cuba. In addition to the 19,000 Cuban combat troops still stationed there as of 1979, there were also 8,500 Cuban technicians of all kinds and the latter number was expected to climb to 10,000.[30] This represented by far the largest contingent of Cuban technical aid personnel anywhere in Africa. Cuban doctors and nurses constituted the backbone of the entire Angolan medical system. Their technicians were helping to repair war-devastated bridges and roads throughout the country. Cubans were also engaged in the construction of urban housing, the running of abandoned Portuguese farms and factories, and they were sprinkled throughout the government ministries as advisers. Cuban military personnel were helping to train the new Angolan army and the massive militia force as well. On the isle of Pines in Cuba, 2,000 to 3,000 young Angolans were being instructed in the three Rs, technical skills, and revolutionary fervor. Western analysts have set forth no estimate of the value of Cuban technical assistance, but it most certainly leads that of the communist countries helping Angola to get back on its feet. The only aid agreement the dollar amount of which has been published was one announced in 1979 for $25 million worth of road construction and urban housing projects for the following year. It was not known what proportion of Cuban assistance was being financed by loans, provided free under grants, or paid for by Angola itself. By the summer of 1980, however, many Angolans were openly complaining about what they perceived as the high cost of Cuban aid. Nor was it known whether the Soviet Union was subsidizing, directly or indirectly, a portion of the Cuban military assistance, or whether Angola was meeting all of the cost.

The second most important source of Communist foreign aid to Angola has been Rumania. Of the total $105 million in Soviet bloc credits obtained through 1978, $75 million came from Rumania, $17 million from the Soviet Union and the remaining $13 million from other bloc nations.[31] Rumanian aid came in the form of a line of credit extended to Angola under an overall cooperation agreement signed in 1978. It is intriguing to speculate whether there was any special political significance to this loan from a country which has developed a reputation as the maverick of the Soviet bloc by fighting to maintain a degree of independence from Moscow in its foreign policy just as President Neto was increasingly doing at that time.

The effectiveness of this Eastern bloc aid was mixed or still unclear. The Soviet Union devoted most of its direct assistance to helping Angola revive its fishing industry and probably benefited from its investment far more than the intended recipient, having the right initially to 85 percent of the total catch in Angolan waters. The agreement was later renegotiated on terms more favorable to Angola and a joint fishing company established to share the catch more equitably. The value and nature of the Rumanian aid program remained to be seen, no major undertaking having been announced as of early 1980. Other East European countries had signed agreements for various projects but none had been completed. Hungary was committed to setting up a bus assembly plant and providing $6.5 million in component parts. Poland was building a plant in Luanda to produce tractor-trailers. The Cuban record was mixed. Their medical assistance was impressive by any standards, but Cuban advisers attempting to reorganize the abandoned Portuguese coffee and sugar plantations into state farms in the north met with very limited success. On the other hand, Cuban assistance in the urban housing sector and the building of prefabricated units outside Luanda were apparently quite effective. The Angolans, for their part, have welcomed economic cooperation with the Eastern bloc and tried to extract more without, however, agreeing to or seeking an exclusive relationship. So far, they have not gone beyond assisting as observers at meetings of the East European Council for Mutual Economic Assistance (CEMEA).

Interestingly, the Angolan government followed the same cautious policy in its economic relations with the West; it sought aid, trade, and investment but joined none of its institutions. As of 1980, Angola did not belong either to the International Monetary Fund or the World Bank, the two principal multilateral Western financial and aid organizations. After initial talks with the European Economic Community about membership in the group of 57

African, Caribbean, and Pacific countries benefiting from preferential tariffs and substantial aid under the Lome Convention, the MPLA government finally refused to sign the new Lome II agreement in October 1979. Thus, it belonged to no trade community, economic group, or aid and financial institution identified as a "tool" of either the East or the West. The main sources of multilateral assistance were the various United Nations agencies, the African Development Bank, and the Arab Bank for Economic Development in Africa, though none of these was providing a significant amount. Angola was nonetheless establishing ties with western economies by striking a large number of bilateral deals with individual Italian, French, Belgian, Austrian, Brazilian, Swedish, and American companies willing to set up joint companies and make investments in the country's economic development. The largest of these joint ventures involved American and French oil companies, notably Texaco, Gulf and ELF-Aquitaine, which together were committed to invest over $430 million. These government-to-company deals accounted for by far the largest proportion of the foreign contribution to the Angolan economy.

In its trade relations, Angola remained totally oriented toward the West, but it did radically shift the direction of its exports away from Portugal and to the United States. The latter country imported directly $218.5 million worth of goods, mostly oil, from Angola in 1978. Indirectly, it imported much more. IMF trade figures for 1978 showed $398.5 million of Angolan exports to the Bahamas and $180 million to the Virgin Islands.[32] These figures could only represent Angolan oil being imported by American-owned Caribbean refineries before being shipped onward to American markets. Altogether, then, nearly four-fifths of all Angolan exports were directed to the United States. Angola thus was one of this country's most important trading partners in Africa and a significant source of non-Arab oil, despite the American government's steadfast refusal to recognize the MPLA.

Angola's other new trading partner was neither a communist nor a Western country but a Latin American one, Brazil, which had been among the first to recognize the MPLA in the midst of the civil war. Brazil was reported to have provided Angola with $350 million worth of food and services between 1976 and 1979.[33] Bilateral trade between the two countries soared from $4 million in 1975 to over $400 million in 1979.[34] Under an accord signed in mid-1979, Brazil was to take 15,000 barrels of oil a day the following year and its state oil company, Petrobras, was to drill for new deposits in Angolan waters and provide technical training for the Angolan oil company, Sonangol.[35]

2. Mozambique

Mozambique's ties with the Communist world were unique in several respects. It was the only country of the three we are considering here where China was *persona grata* and played nearly as important an economic role as the Soviet bloc. Also, Mozambique had received far less military assistance, although it had signed treaties of friendship with both the Soviet Union and East Germany as well as military accords with three other bloc nations—Cuba, Hungary, and Bulgaria.[36] Through 1977, the Soviet bloc only provided $40 million worth of arms, although this figure probably increased subsequently in response to Mozambican requests for help in facing escalating Rhodesian air and ground attacks.[37] The Soviet bloc military presence remained nonetheless relatively small, with only 1100 personnel in the country in 1978, of which two-thirds were said to be Cubans.[38] The number was already reduced to 700 by January 1980 as the Rhodesian war wound down with the negotiation of a political settlement there.[39] Communist economic aid to Mozambique was estimated at $82 million through 1978, of which China accounted for $60 million, the Soviet Union $5 million, and other Eastern bloc nations $17 million.[40] While higher estimates have appeared in US intelligence reports, they have been later retracted as erroneous.[41] The question which needs to be posed, then, is why Mozambique had received so little given its strategic location in southern Africa, its need for outside protection, its commitment to Marxism-Leninism and the strength and unity of its vanguard party.

The answer lay partly in Frelimo's preindependence relations with the Soviet bloc and partly in its general attitude toward all foreign presence in the country after independence. Frelimo was never very close to the Soviet Union during its long national liberation struggle, because it had close ties with China and this rankled Soviet sensitivities. Similarly, Cuba played virtually no role in aiding Frelimo and had scant contact with its leaders. The main Eastern bloc state to have helped Frelimo in its guerrilla war against the Portuguese was East Germany, which in 1969 inaugurated its whole military assistance program to Africa by providing arms and other aid to the Mozambican and Angolan nationalists. After independence, necessity forced both Mozambique and the Soviet Union to reevaluate their relations. Like Angola, Mozambique began to look to the Soviet Union and its allies as its major defense against the threat posed by the far superior South African and Rhodesian military forces. Moscow, for its part, was very aware of the country's geopolitical value in southern Africa and on the Indian Ocean and also had an interest in countering Chinese influence. Their new-found alliance was cemented by a Treaty of Friendship and Cooperation, virtually identical to the Soviet-Angolan one, signed in April 1977 during a visit by President Nikolai Podgorny.[42] Again like Angola, Mozambique also signed a friendship treaty with East Germany in February 1979 almost identical to the Soviet one. It provided for military cooperation "in the interest of strengthening the defense capabilities" of both countries and committed both parties to "immediate contacts" in the event of a situation that threatens or violates peace."[43] In addition, Mozambique also signed military cooperation accords with Hungary and Bulgaria, constructing in appearance a broad Soviet bloc shield to protect it from South African military might. But despite this heavy dependency upon the bloc for its defense, Frelimo deliberately avoided the stationing of troops from any communist nation in its country. While Frelimo officials have never said so publicly, they remain in private sharply critical of the large Cuban military presence in Angola. Despite the casualties and damage inflicted by the Rhodesian army and air force, they never regarded a Cuban combat role inside Mozambique as an acceptable counterweight. Instead, they made use of two Tanzanian battalions to help defend Mozambican territory and sent some 250 of their own troops inside Rhodesia to aid ZANU guerrillas and respond in kind to the Rhodesian attacks.

Soviet bloc assistance in the economic sector slowly but steadily expanded, with Cuba and Eastern European countries taking the lead, most notably East Germany. The Soviets once again seemed to be primarily seeking fishing deals and, after much friction over the size of the catch Soviet vessels were taking out of Mozambican waters, the two countries signed an accord in April 1979 setting up a joint company in which Mozambique held a 51 percent interest. The Soviets also committed themselves under a protocol signed in late 1978 to help, together with the Bulgarians, to expand the Limpopo Agro-Industrial Scheme to cover eventually 314,000 hectares of irrigated land. As of 1979, however, the Bulgarians were providing most of the assistance in the form of advisers. Bulgaria in addition had pledged to help in the construction of a hydroelectric dam at Massingir on the Limpopo and to provide assistance in the construction industry. East Germany was involved in a wide range of trade and aid activities, including the provision of agricultural equipment, the construction of a truck assembly plant at Beira, technical assistance in the expansion of the metallurgical and metal-mechanical industries, and the exploitation of gold and copper deposits in the north. Cuban assistance, if American estimates of their personnel serving in Mozambique are correct, was greatest in the military field where there may have been as many as 800 advisers at the peak in 1978.[44] Cubans were also helping in the agricultural sector and above all in the area of education. By mid-1979, Mozambique had sent 2,800 secondary school students to Cuba to complete their studies.

Whatever the precise value of Soviet bloc aid, it was far from meeting alone Mozambican needs in any but the military field. President Machel's stated hopes of establishing an "exemplary relationship" with the Soviet Union were not likely to be fulfilled in the economic area.[45] There was no indication the Soviets were ready to make a sufficient commitment. On the other hand, the Mozambicans discovered during the first five years of independence that Western assistance was important and probably even indispensable to their economic survival. For example, UN figures showed that actual aid dispensed during the one year of 1978 and identified as coming from Western nations amounted to over $90 million.[46] The Scandinavian countries, led by Sweden, have become the major source of outside assistance to the agricultural sector, while the United States, forbidden by Congress from giving aid, led in the provision of grain and other food supplies in the form of disaster relief. Even in the absence of World Bank, IMF, or

European Economic Community assistance under the Lome Convention, the West had dispensed far more aid by 1980 than all Communist countries, including China. Furthermore, it will be recalled, the biggest single loan offered to Mozambique from any country was a line of credit of over $100 million from South Africa.

The failure of the Soviet bloc to provide more aid and the overriding necessity to obtain foreign assistance on a far more massive scale, drove the Mozambicans to reappraisal of their relations not only with the West but with private international capital, particularly American. As before independence, the United States continued to be a leading trade partner of Mozambique together with Japan, the United Kingdom, West Germany, and Portugal, although the latter country was becoming less important. Western nations and Japan took anywhere from 70 to 80 percent of all Mozambican exports in the 1975 to 1980 period. By early 1980, the Mozambican government was actively courting American business firms, first allowing Business International to organize a seminar in Maputo for potential investors and then sending a delegation to New York to attend a similar conference organized by the African-American Institute. Just how successful this opening to the West and to the United States would be remained unclear at the time of this writing. Mozambique still had not joined any of the main Western financial or aid institutions, like the World Bank or the IMF. But economic necessity was nudging it in the direction of establishing ties at least with the European Economic Community. None of this seemed to harbinger in any way the abandoning of its commitment to Marxism-Leninism or its military ties with the East. Rather, like so many of the other African socialist or Marxist countries, Mozambique was developing a strong economic relationship with the West, even while continuing to tilt toward its "natural allies" in its political and military orientation.

3. Ethiopia

Ethiopia's relationship to the Soviet bloc is one of enormous complexity. The Ethiopian military regime made its revolution without any outside help, but then only managed to preserve the territorial integrity of the old empire with massive Soviet and Cuban military assistance. The Soviets saw in Ethiopia with its class conflicts a much greater revolutionary potential than in any other African country, even shades of their own revolution. They were mindful, too, of its geopolitical importance, but they remained deeply distrustful of the military regime. The sum total of these conflicting trends was an enormous Soviet bloc military program, its largest ever in Sub-Sahara Africa, a growing economic aid program, and very uneasy political relations. Soviet military assistance, which began in 1977, had well surpassed one billion dollars by 1980, according to American calculations.[47] Although in theory the arms were sold to Ethiopia, a good portion of the cost seemed destined to become a grant, since the Ethiopian economy could not possibly generate such a large amount of money for repayment.

The geographic location of Ethiopia directly on the Red Sea and close to the Straits of Bab el-Mandeb, its proximity to the Arabian Peninsula, its potential control of the Blue Nile waters flowing through the Sudan and Egypt, and its suitability as a staging area for other activities in both the Arab and African worlds doubtlessly enter into Soviet strategic thinking. As one American scholar observed as far back as 1963, there was nothing new about Moscow's view of Ethiopia as a "postern gate" into the African continent: the czars felt very much the same way.[48] It is an interesting and generally forgotten historical footnote to the Soviet-Ethiopian relationship that the Russians provided advisers and "large consignments of arms, rifles, rounds of ammunition, and cannons" to Emperor Menelik during the European scramble for Africa and his struggle to hold off invading Italian forces at the end of the 19th century. The last emperor of Ethiopia, Haile Selassie, remarked during his visit to the Soviet Union in 1959 that "our country remembers with eternal gratitude the speedy help in the form of arms which the people of this country gave to us at the time of our decisive struggle with imperialism."[49] Twenty years later, the first leader of postimperial Ethiopia, Colonel Mengistu, would similarly comment during a visit of Soviet Party Chairman Alexei Kosygin to Addis Ababa that "the broad masses of Ethiopians . . . have found in the Soviet Union and a true friend and ally in a period of terrible ordeals and of clashes between revolutionary and counterrevolutionary forces."[50] The Russians, to be sure, were not the only ones to provide Ethiopian emperors with advisers and arms to help them hold the empire together, or even expand it. In times past, Ethiopia's rulers sought to use in turn the Portuguese, French, British, and most recently the Americans for exactly the same purpose. It may be worth noting as well that the discarding of a no-longer-needed ally was very much part of the Ethiopian tradition.

The Soviet-Ethiopian relationship began with a secret arms deal signed in December 1976 and valued at between one hundred million and two hundred million dollars. The following May, after Colonel Mengistu had severed his military and political ties to the United States, he traveled to Moscow and signed a "declaration" of friendship with the Soviets as well as various economic, scientific, cultural, and probably also military agreements. The amount of additional military aid made available to the Ethiopians in 1977 has been estimated at close to four hundred million dollars.[51] The next step was an agreement on economic and technological cooperation concluded in September 1978. Not until November of that year during a visit by Mengistu to Moscow did the Soviets actually seek, and the Ethiopians agree, to sign the standard 20-year Treaty of Friendship and Cooperation providing the overarching framework for their alliance. As in Angola and Mozambique, East Germany followed, signing a similar treaty with Ethiopia during Honecker's trip to Addis Ababa in November 1979 and taking over the training of the police and the security forces. By 1980, the Soviets had helped to build the Ethiopian army into sub-Sahara Africa's largest, with around

250,000 regular troops and militiamen, and also the best equipped with modern weapons, including the first Mig-23s provided to any black African state. Soviet arms, their 1200 advisers and the commitment of 16,000 Cuban combat troops in late 1977 enabled the Mengistu government to defeat the regular Somali forces engaged in the war over the Ogaden region and to push back the Eritrean guerrillas who had at one point taken control of every town except the provincial capital of Asmara and the port of Massawa. Without this massive Soviet and Cuban assistance, Ethiopia almost certainly would have lost both Eritrea and the Ogaden, and the Mengistu regime would have fallen. Thus the Ethiopian national, and Mengistu's personal, debt to these two communist countries was enormous, and he repeatedly acknowledged his thanks to "proletarian internationalism."

While the keystone of the Ethiopian-Soviet bloc relationship was military, there was also an expanding economic aspect to it. By the end of the 1970s, the bloc's economic assistance programs began to reflect the far greater interest of Moscow in Ethiopia than in either Angola or Mozambique. According to Mengistu himself, a plan had been drawn up providing for $300 million in investments by Soviet bloc countries in Ethiopia's economic development, primarily in the industrial sector.[52] The Soviet Union was apparently meeting one portion of this commitment under an old, largely unused $100 million loan extended to Ethiopia in 1959. Only a fraction of it, around fifteen to twenty million dollars, had been utilized by the time of the revolution to build an oil refinery in Assab and establish a technical training school. In April 1979, the Soviets made an additional commitment of roughly eighty-five million dollars (60 million rubles), bringing the total outstanding amount of credits to around one hundred seventy million dollars. The credits were earmarked for a wide variety of projects, including a major expansion of the Assab oil refinery, a large irrigation project in the Awash valley, the setting up of 15 tractor and agricultural machinery repair shops and 31 storage warehouses, the construction of a 600,000-ton cement factory (in Dire Dawa) and a tractor assembly plant, exploration for oil and gas, and the provision of 2,000 new scholarships to supplement the 1,500 already offered. Probably the most significant economic assistance extended by the Soviets was an unpublished agreement in early 1980 to provide Ethiopia with an unknown amount of oil at reduced prices. Already in 1979, after a second major hike in world prices, Ethiopia was spending around one hundred ninety million dollars on oil imports. This was more than 40 percent of the value of its export earnings that year.

The other three major Soviet bloc sources of economic assistance to Ethiopia were East Germany, Czechoslovakia and Cuba. The first country signed a $20 million loan for plant equipment and other aid to industry, mining, transportation, and agriculture in 1977 and another in 1979 for $2 million to help expand the Assab port. East Germany also provided 1000 tractors and set up a maintenance plant to service them. One study of East German activities in Africa showed Ethiopia to be its most important trading partner on the continent, with coffee becoming the main barter item for tractors and other assistance.[53] Czechoslovakia, for its part, signed a $46 million loan in early 1978 to provide for the construction of several industrial plants. Part of the loan would be invested in a $90 million textile factory, of which Czechoslovakia would finance 10 percent, East Germany 31 percent, and Ethiopia the remainder. Finally Cuba, as in Angola and Mozambique, provided 500 medical personnel and scholarships for 2,000 to 3,000 Ethiopian students in schools on the Island of Pines. On paper, East bloc pledges to Ethiopian probably came close to the three hundred million dollar total that Mengistu had mentioned, if the new oil subsidy was included. But there was no indication how rapidly the Soviets and their Eastern European allies intended to fulfill their commitments. In the past, they demonstrated a penchant for announcing important agreements and then taking an extraordinarily long time to implement them. This was the case for the 1959 Soviet loan to Ethiopia, of which only about one-fifth was spent in 20 years. It was also true of the Soviet $170 million aid program for Somalia, part of which never materialized.

Mengistu has been mindful that the West remains an important source of assistance, too; in the same speech in which he announced Ethiopia would obtain $300 million from socialist countries he noted that various Western countries and international organizations had already made available virtually the same amount between 1974 and 1978. There was no indication that Ethiopia had any intention of breaking its ties to Western financial institutions like the World Bank and the IMF, to which it had belonged for years and from which it had substantially benefited. Its relations with the Bank were nonetheless tense between 1977 and 1980 because of Ethiopia's failure to compensate various Western companies for their nationalized interests. Three new loans worth a total of $148 million were thus affected, including one for the main Ethiopian agricultural extension program to assist the peasant associations. The Ethiopians were carefully nurturing their relations with the European Economic Community, on the other hand, and showing no great interest in joining the East European CMEA grouping. The EEC had made available to Ethiopia $120 million over a five-year period under the Lome I Convention, more money than it could actually absorb. As of September 1979, it had utilized only 35 percent of the total.[54] Even more than Mozambique or Angola, which had not signed the Lome Convention or joined the World Bank and the IMF, Ethiopia was fully integrated into the international capitalist world order and its institutions. The pattern of its trade was only one further confirmation of this; the United States remained the principal market for Ethiopian coffee and together with Western Europe accounted for around two-thirds of all its exports and imports through 1978. Thus, Ethiopia's economic orientation was even more at odds with its political orientation than was the case for the other two countries.

The African Outlook

A first-time visitor to Ethiopia, Mozambique, or Angola in 1980 might easily have concluded that these three countries had already become an integral part of the communist world. Red flags fluttered everywhere alongside the national colors, and red tended to dominate in the bunting and decorations at official ceremonies. In Addis Ababa, enormous portraits of Marx, Lenin, and Engels completed the decor on Revolution Square. In Maputo, the Frelimo Party emblem included a five-pointed red star, the symbol of proletarian internationalism, and superimposed on the flag was a crossed hammer and a hoe standing for the worker-peasant alliance. The party flags of the other two countries carried similar socialist symbols. Bookstores and bookstalls in all three countries offered a wide selection of the writings of the three communist forefathers—Marx, Engels, and Lenin—while the Internationale was often sung at public rallies and party meetings. Everywhere, the words "Western" and "imperialist" were used interchangeably, while for the first time in black Africa leaders like Mengistu and Neto were publicly declaring that the goal of their revolutions was the establishment of socialism and communism. The inevitable impression left on the visitor would have been one of Communist fraternity and irreconcilable hostility to the West. Beyond the rhetoric and the choreography, however, the relationship between the Marxist-Leninist countries and the Soviet bloc was filled with nuances and unstated reservations. These were the result of intense nationalism on the one hand and of African and Third World solidarity on the other. Essentially, there were three threads running through the foreign policy of the Marxist-Leninist African countries: solidarity with all socialist countries and movements, referred to as "proletarian internationalism;" nationalism, which had fueled their anticolonial struggles but also made them leery of the Soviet Union as a superpower; and "Third World solidarity," which looked beyond the Pan-Africanism of the 1960s to seek the unity of all developing countries in a quest for a new international economic order.

1. Proletarian Internationalism

In this three-tiered relationship combining elements of Communist internationalism, nationalism, and Third World solidarity, the former seemed most pronounced and was of greatest concern to the United States. The Soviet thesis of a "world revolutionary process" and of "proletarian internationalism" was subscribed to wholly by Angola, Mozambique, Ethiopia, and most of the other Marxist-Leninist governments as well. The MPLA Central Committee report to the First Congress asserted, for example, that "a revolutionary process of historic dimensions is taking place: it is the stage of the universal transition from capitalism to socialism, started by the Great October Socialist Revolution."[55] The Angolan revolution was seen as "an integral part of the confrontation between the socialist and capitalist systems," and "the ever closer cooperation between the world socialist system and other present revolutionary forces" was viewed as determining the "future path of the development of mankind."[56] To these African countries, the Soviet Union stood as "the main bastion of mankind in the struggle for peace, democracy, and social progress,"[57] and the Eastern bloc nations as "our natural allies," the term used by both the Angolans and Mozambicans. As Frelimo stated:

> They are our natural allies ideologically, politically, diplomatically, economically, and socially. We defend the same cause, we struggle for the same goals. The experience of the liberation war as well as our present fight to strengthen our defense capacity shows that the socialist camp is still our strategic military rearguard, our base of support.[58]

In Ethiopia, the bloody struggle to carry out a revolution was held as proof of the country's "antifeudal, antiimperialist, antineocolonialist stand and its readiness to stand alongside the socialist community of the world, working class movements and progressive forces."[59] In fact, Mengistu went so far as to define Ethiopia as an "integral part" of the "socialist commonwealth," a statement the Soviets refused to echo.[60]

Not surprisingly, the African Marxist-Leninist countries held a view of "nonalignment" that in fact brought them closer to the Soviet bloc. Like the Soviets, they rejected the Western idea that nonalignment meant equidistance from the two opposing blocs in the world and they asserted the communality of interests among all socialist countries in the struggle against Western imperialism, colonialism, and neocolonialism. Mozambican President Samora Machel perhaps expressed this view of nonalignment in the most dramatic terms at the Havana meeting of nonaligned states in September 1979.

> Some often forget that we are no longer in the era of the cold war.... Peace reigns today in Europe as it does between the superpowers. But it is in our region... that wars, aggressions, plots organized by imperialism, coups d'etat, assassinations are being unleashed.... How, then, can we accept a nonalignment conceived for a situation which no longer exists today? The cold war of yesterday, which motivated many actions of the nonalignment movement, is today a burning war raging here in Africa, in the Arab world, Asia, and Latin America, destroying and pillaging.... How can one ask us to be at an equal distance in our relations with our principal adversary, which burns, bombs, kills, and massacres, and those who aid us to better defend ourselves, resist and triumph.[61]

The alignment of the Marxist-Leninist states with the Soviet bloc was thus rooted not only in a shared ideological outlook on the world but in an acutely perceived need for protection against what were viewed as direct, or indirect, Western machinations to undermine them. It seemed no mere coincidence that the African countries that signed treaties of friendship and cooperation with the Soviet Union and East Germany had all come under repeated military attack and attempts at subversion by their neighbors. As Frelimo saw it, "our political alliance with the socialist countries constitutes an important strategic factor for dissuasion of the aggressive plans of imperialism" and was particularly important at a time when "the enemy is providing atomic weapons to South Africa and strengthening its military presence in the Indian Ocean."[62]

Influencing greatly this perception of nonalignment and of the importance of the socialist camp were the very concrete and positive benefits of "proletarian internationalism" to their own revolutions. The late President Neto regarded Soviet, Cuban, and Yugoslav military assistance as "the principal force" accounting for the MPLA victory in face of invading South African troops during the Angolan Civil war, but also pointed out the importance of inter-African solidarity: Guinea-Bissau, Guinea, Mozambique, Nigeria, and Algeria had all provided either arms or combat troops to the MPLA struggle against its pro-Western and South African opponents.[63] But the country emerging as the great hero of the African Marxist-Leninist countries was Cuba. The MPLA hailed Cuban military aid as a shining example of "the practice of internationalist solidarity."[64] Mengistu praised in the warmest terms repeatedly the "unflinching internationalism" of Fidel Castro helping the Ethiopian revolution to prevail over its internal and external enemies and regarded the solidarity of the Ethiopian and Cuban peoples as "sealed in blood."[65] The African countries that benefited from proletarian internationalism saw themselves in turn becoming the providers of aid to other progressive movements. Mengistu clearly stated that he intended to repay his debt to the Soviets and Cubans in this manner:

> We promise to carry forward consistently the torch of proletarian internationalism as a way of repaying for the support that has been given to us by the People's Democratic Republic of Yemen, Democratic Germany, Czechoslovakia, Hungary, Bulgaria, Poland, Rumania, Yugoslavia, Libya, and other socialist and progressive forces.[66]

Even in the midst of the Eritrean and Ogaden wars and considerable internal opposition, Mengistu began carrying out his promise by training guerrillas for the Patriotic Front in Rhodesia, the Southwest Africa People's Organization (SWAPO) in Namibia, and the African National Congress of South Africa. Out of a similar conviction and sense of revolutionary internationalism, the MPLA extended considerable assistance to the Patriotic Front and particularly to SWAPO, and also allowed the Zairian opposition group, the National Front for the Liberation of the Congo, to organize and launch attacks twice into Zaire's southern province. Frelimo, for its part, sent about 250 of its regular troops to fight inside Rhodesia alongside guerrillas of Robert Mugabe's Zimbabwe African National Union. The price both Angola and Mozambique paid for their assistance to the Front and SWAPO has been considerable. At the end of the Rhodesian war, for example, President Machel announced that Rhodesian forces had attacked the country 350 times between 1977 and 1980, killing 1,335 Mozambicans and injuring another 1,500. Damage to property, equipment and infrastructure was estimated at fifty million dollars, while the cost of Mozambique's adherence to the international boycott of Rhodesia was estimated at five hundred fifty million dollars in lost revenue from the transit trade, services, and tourism.[67] The latter figure represented the value of almost two years of exports. Angola suffered just about as much from South African attacks; by mid-1979, the government there was reporting 1,383 persons killed, 813 of them Namibian and Zimbabwean refugees, another 1915 wounded and $300 million in damages.[68] Yet both countries, like Ethiopia, derived an enormous sense of pride and self-esteem from their sacrifices that served both to reaffirm their commitment to internationalism and to repay their debt to it.

It appeared extremely likely that more instances of "proletarian internationalism" involving the African Marxist-Leninist states, the Soviet Union, and Cuba would be forthcoming in the future. Castro himself warmly endorsed the idea of an "anti-imperialist front" of "African revolutionary comrades." The Soviets were less enthusiastic, warning against the formation of "miniblocs" of any kind on the African continent. This was apparently in reaction to the creation of the Western-supported Inter-African Force composed of troops from moderate African states, which helped Zairian President Mobutu Sese Seko during the Shaba crisis of 1977 and 1978. Yet, it was difficult to believe that the Soviets would not eventually welcome the establishment of a radical inter-African force should the need arise to rescue a threatened ally. In a similar manner Mengistu in particular appeared to have ambitions of playing one day the role of an African Castro in the spreading of revolution on the African continent. He had an army with the experience, the technical skills, the manpower and material to do so, if the Soviets provided the logistical support and Ethiopia's internal wars were resolved.

The proletarian internationalism of Ethiopia, Angola, and Mozambique was also manifested in the votes they cast at the United Nations on key East-West issues and in their support of Castro's drive to pull the nonaligned movement closer to the Soviet Union. On the most confrontational East-West matters, the three countries consistently voted with Moscow. They were the only three African states to reject a resolution in January 1980 calling for the "immediate, unconditional, and total withdrawal" of Soviet troops from Afghanistan.[69] Subsequently, three more radical African countries, Libya, the Congo, and Madagascar, showed their acceptance of the Soviet-installed Karmal Babrak regime by receiving its delegations or making statements in support of it. On another vote of great importance to them, recognition of the Vietnamese-backed Kampuchea government of Heng Samrin in September 1979, the Soviets were able to marshal the support of 13 African states. In fact, all of the self-proclaimed Marxist-Leninist or socialist countries sided with the Soviet Union, except Angola and Somalia. (Angola was simply absent for the vote, as it often was in this period, and Somalia was at that time actively courting the United States to obtain military assistance.)

Within the nonaligned movement, Angola, Mozambique, and Ethiopia joined Cuba in trying to push this amorphous grouping of 95 nations and liberation fronts closer to the Soviet bloc by emphasizing its anti-Western and particularly anti-American bias rooted in the Third World's struggle against imperialism, colonialism, and neocolonialism. At the Sixth Nonaligned Summit held in Havana in September 1979, President Machel was particularly eloquent as has already been seen in arguing the case against "equidistance" and for a closer alliance with the socialist countries. Castro entrusted Mozambique with the chairmanship of the conference's economic committee responsible for drawing up the final resolutions. Mozambique and Benin took the lead with Cuba in the effort to keep the fallen Pol Pot government from Kampuchea out and get the Heng Samrin regime seated. Benin called for expunction from the record of the Egyptian foreign minister's speech defending the Camp David accords with Israel, and Angola, Mozambique, Benin, Ethiopia, and Guinea-Bissau joined the Arab radical states in seeking to have Egypt expelled altogether from the nonaligned movement.

There is no doubt, in conclusion, that the idea of "proletarian internationalism" had a strong impact on the foreign policies of the African Marxist-Leninist countries. It was not an empty formula, but a real commitment to helping other countries and movements fighting battles similar to their own. Very disturbingly from the Western point of view, this commitment led them automatically to side with the Soviet Union on many issues. But, as we shall see next, there were also countervailing forces to this internationalism which introduced at times considerable strain in Soviet-African relations.

2. Nationalism

Willing as Ethiopia, Mozambique or Angola were to make considerable sacrifices to help other countries or liberation movements, they drew the line firmly at sacrificing any of their national independence or autonomy. Voluntarily aligning themselves with the Soviet Union to further the cause of world revolution was one thing. Accepting any limitations on their sovereignty or interference from the Soviet Union was quite a different thing. Both the MPLA and Frelimo wrote into their party programs not only their commitment to Marxism-Leninism but also principles clearly articulating a spirit of national independence. The MPLA Party document, for example, stated that among the guiding principles of its foreign policy were "the safeguarding of political independence," a policy of nonalignment "in respect to the military blocs set up in the world," and the forbidding of foreign military bases on the national soil."[70] In Mozambique, Frelimo stressed proletarian internationalism as one of its "immutable principles," but it also made it clear that in its commitment to building a "world antiimperialist front" it intended to maintain an "independent foreign policy" and that it demanded respect for the principle of "sovereign equality" and the "reciprocity of benefits" in state-to-state dealings with all countries.[71] Nor did Frelimo accept to side automatically with the Soviet Union in its quarrel with China. While acknowledging that China had made "mistakes" in its foreign policy, party leaders also argued that they did not intend to act as the "supreme conscience of the revolutionary movement" and emphasized that "each party is sovereign and free and has the right to make its mistakes."[72] Moreover, in a pointed reference to the predominance of Chinese over Soviet military assistance to Frelimo during its national liberation war, they declared that they would "never forget those who supported us when times were hard."[73] Perhaps the most open assertion of nationalism was made by President Neto shortly before his death, when he began saying publicly it was "necessary at all times to defend the independence of the country" from outside influence.[74]

In Ethiopia, the spirit of nationalism ran deep, rooted in the country's long history and its pride in having repelled Turks, Egyptians, and Italians, thus avoiding, alone in Africa, real colonization. It seems no mere happenstance that the original and never abandoned slogan of the Ethiopian revolution was "Ethiopia Tikdem," "Ethiopia First." The original meaning of Ethiopian socialism included "the indivisibility of Ethiopian unity," and whatever socialism came to signify later in Ethiopia, it still incorporated that principle. The Soviets discovered very soon how burning was the spirit of nationalism affecting all the principal actors in the Horn of Africa—the Somalis and the Eritreans as well as the Ethiopians—having attempted and failed to settle the conflicts among them by creating a Red Sea federation of Marxist-Leninist republics. Even Fidel Castro's personal intervention and his "shuttle diplomacy" between Addis Ababa and Mogadishu were to no avail. Proletarian internationalism was defeated by its historically most tenacious adversary, nationalism.

The real test of the strength of nationalism in Ethiopia, Angola, and Mozambique was what they actually did, or refused to do, in response to Soviet and Cuban pressure. Despite their enormous indebtedness to military assistance from the Soviet Union for their very survival, neither the Ethiopian nor the Angolan government gave it bases or even extensive facilities such as they had enjoyed in Somalia. Soviet reconnaissance planes flying over the southern Atlantic made use of Angolan airports and their warships regularly put in at Angolan ports. But there was no confirmation of any formal agreement permitting the Soviet military to use Angola as a home port for its ships and aircraft. The same held generally true in the case of Ethiopia, although the government there apparently agreed to allow the Soviets to anchor a floating drydock used for repairs in the Dahlak Islands off Massawa. Mozambique for its part flatly refused just after independence a Soviet request to establish facilities in the country, and when the South African press alleged such a base existed on a small island off Maputo, the Mozambican government flew the entire Western diplomatic corps out there to prove the report was false. It was, of course, difficult to know whether secret understandings had been reached between these countries and Moscow regarding access to air or naval facilities in their countries in a time of East-West crisis. American officials hinted in official testimony that such understandings existed, without however flatly saying so. Under Secretary Newsom, for example, told Congress that the Soviet naval forces had "facilities and rights" in Ethiopia and Angola and that a small Soviet West African patrol made use of ports in Angola, Guinea and Benin.[75] The extent of the Soviet access seemed in any case to be no greater than that which the US government was seeking to obtain from Kenya and Somalia in early 1980; the Americans were intent upon gaining not only access but also permission to stockpile vast military supplies and to station personnel to look after them. There was no indication by 1980 that the Soviets had acquired such a permanent logistical base anywhere in sub-Sahara Africa since their ouster from Somalia.

Aside from this obvious reluctance to abet the expansion of the Soviet military might into the African continent, the Marxist-Leninist states on several occasions went directly against Soviet policy objectives. Throughout the long national liberation struggle in Zimbabwe, Mozambique and the Soviet Union backed different factions of the Patriotic Front. Frelimo wholeheartedly supported Robert Mugabe's Zimbabwe African National Union (ZANU), allowing it to locate its headquarters and rear bases in Mozambique. Both the Soviet Union and Cuba, on the other hand, distrusted ZANU because of its links to China and assisted primarily Joshua Nkomo's Zimbabwe African People's Union (ZAPU). Mozambique remained steadfast in its support and toward the end of the Rhodesian war it was the Cubans who changed their position and began training and arming ZANU guerrillas. Later, both Mozambique and Angola cooperated extensively with the West in seeking negotiated political settlements in Zimbabwe and Nambia, a tact the Soviet Union could scarcely welcome. Ironically, British-led Western efforts to end the Rhodesian war led eventually to the rise to power of Robert Mugabe. While this result was hailed by African Marxists, it represented a stunning political defeat for the Soviet Union, which not only had had to watch the West make peace in Zimbabwe but was then faced with a Marxist African leader it had consistently opposed. As a result, the Soviets initially had great difficulty opening an embassy in Zimbabwe after its independence.

A second blatant example of resistance to Soviet pressure came in the

Horn of Africa, where the *Derg* rejected Soviet and Cuban entreaties to join a Marxist Red Sea Federation as we have already mentioned above. Moreover, Colonel Mengistu pursued a deliberate policy of seeking to impose a military solution in Eritrea, despite Cuba's opposition to this approach expressed in the refusal to allow its combat troops to be deployed there. Even the Soviets became unhappy with the *Derg's* policy once it was clear that the Ethiopian army could not swiftly crush the Eritrean nationalist movement. By 1980, the Soviets were pressuring Mengistu once again to seek a political solution and even initiated their own contacts with the Eritreans in an attempt to arrange peace talks. A third example of discordant policies was the 1978 reconciliation between Angola and Zaire following the second Shaba crisis, engineered partly by the United States. President Neto and Mobutu agreed to halt their support to each other's opposition. It was doubtful that either the Soviet Union or Cuba favored a policy which served to strengthen the Mobutu regime which they regarded as the archtype Western puppet.

3. Third World Solidarity

The third thread running through the foreign policy of the African Marxist-Leninist states was Third World solidarity. On some political issues, even the most radical African countries demonstrated that they saw themselves at odds with all the superpowers, or even occasionally closer to the United States than to their "natural allies.' On almost all economic issues, on the other hand, they identified with all underdeveloped nations in their struggle with the industrialized North, of which the Soviet Union was a part, for the creation of a new international economic order. The voting record of the Marxist-Leninist states at the United Nations was particularly revealing in this respect; on a wide range of questions, they voted just like capitalist-oriented African countries such as Kenya and the Ivory Coast, indicating a commonality of interests among developing countries transcending their ideological orientation. Sometimes the Soviet Union and the United States found themselves closer together in their thinking as superpowers than either did vis-a-vis its "natural" allies in Africa. While generalizations are always hazardous, it did seem that on resolutions concerning the role of the United Nations in world affairs, the African Marxist-Leninist countries actually tended to be closer to the United States than the Soviet Union; on resolutions involving the principles of self-determination and human rights in African they opposed the United States. On the matter of disarmament, they identified with the Third World against both superpowers. But the question that most clearly showed the Third World orientation of the African Marxist-Leninist regimes was that of the new international economic order. A few examples will illustrate these patterns:

- On the question of additional money for the upkeep and expansion of the United Nations' premises in New York, the African Marxist-Leninist states voted in 1977 together with all other African states in favor of spending more.

The United States agreed, while the Soviet Union and Cuba voted against the appropriation (see Table IV).[76]

- On the issue of the United Nations' responsibility for the decolonization of the Western Sahara, the right of the people there to self-determination,

TABLE IV
Political Issues

	1980 Afghanistan	1979 Cambodia	1978 Southern Africa: Human Rights	1977 UN premises	1978 Western Sahara A & B
African					
Algeria	Yes		I-Yes	Yes	A-Yes
					B-No
Tanzania	Yes		I-Yes	Yes	A-Yes
			II-Yes		B-No
			II-Yes		
African Marxist*					A-Yes
					B-No
Benin	Not Par		I-Yes	Yes	A-Yes
			II-Yes		B-No
Congo	Not Par		I-Not Par	Yes	A-Yes
			II-Abst.		B-No
Ethiopia	Yes		I-Yes	Yes	A-Yes
Mozambique	Not Par		I-Yes	Yes	B-No
			II-Yes		A-Yes
Somalia	Not Par		Not Par I & II	Yes	B-No
					Not Par
Other African					A-Abst.
Ivory Coast	Yes		I-Yes	Yes	A-Abst.
			II-Yes		B-Abst.
Kenya	Yes		I-Yes	Yes	A-Yes
			II-Yes		B-No
Other non-African					
Cuba	Yes		I-Abst.	Abst.	A-Yes
			II-Abst.		B-No
USSR	No		I-Abst.	Abst.	A-Yes
			II-Abst.		B-Abst.
USA	No		I-Yes	Abst.	A-Abst.
			II-Yes		B-Yes

*Later advised the Secretariat it had intended to vote in favor.

TABLE V
FINANCING OF THE UNITED NATIONS EMERGENCY FORCE AND OF THE UNITED NATIONS DISENGAGEMENT OBSERVER FORCE—1976-1978

Resolution number	31-5 B	31-5 C	31-5 D	32-4 B & C	33-13 B	33-13 C	33-13 D	33-13 E	33-13 F
African Socialist Algeria	Not Par	Yes	Yes	Yes	Not Par	Not Par	Not Par	Yes	Yes
Tanzania	Yes	Yes	Yes	Yes	Yes	Not Par	Not Par	Not Par	Yes
African Marxist* Benin	Not Par	Yes	Not Par	Yes	Not Par	Not Par	Not Par	Not Par	Not Par
Congo	Yes	Yes	Yes	Not Par	Not Par	Not Par	Not Par	Not Par	Not Par
Ethiopia	Yes	Yes	Yes	Yes	Yes	Yes	Yes	Yes	Yes
Mozambique	Yes	Not Par	Not Par	Yes	Not Par	Not Par	Not Par	Not Par	Not Par

Somalia	Yes	Yes	Yes	Yes	Not Par	Not Par	Not Par	Yes
Other African								
Ivory Coast	Yes	Yes	Yes	Yes	Not Par	Not Par	Not Par	Yes
Kenya	Not Par	Yes	Yes	Yes	Yes	Yes	Yes	Yes
Other non-African								
Cuba	Yes	Abst.	Abst.	Abst.	Abst.	Abst.	Abst.	No
USSR	Yes	Abst.	Abst.	Abst.	Abst.	Abst.	Abst.	No
USA	Yes	Yes	Yes	Yes	Yes	Yes	Yes	Yes

*Angola does not appear because its representative was absent for most votes.

and an appeal to all nations to refrain from actions impeding a peace mission by the Organization of African Unity, African countries regardless of their political persuasion voted alike unanimous and in agreement with Cuba and partially so with the Soviet Union, while the United States sounded a discordant note (see Table IV).[77] The same pattern was found concerning human rights in South Africa.

TABLE VI
Disarmament Issues

	1977 1) Nucl. Weapons Systems: Limitation and Reduction.	1977–1978 2) Prohibition of Nucl. Weapons in Latin America: I and II.	1978 3) Military Budgets: Reduction.
African Socialist			
	Yes	I-Yes	Yes
Tanzania	Yes	I-Yes II-Yes II-Yes	Yes
*African Marxist**			
Benin	Not Par	I-Yes II-Yes	Yes
Congo	Not Par	I-Not Par II-Abst.	Yes
Ethiopia	Yes Par	I-Yes II-Abst.	Yes
Mozambique	Not Par	I-Yes II-Yes	Yes
Somalia	Not Par	Not Par I & II	Yes
Other African			
Ivory Coast	Yes	I-Yes II-Yes	Yes
Kenya	Yes	I-Yes II-Yes	Yes
Other non-African			
Cuba	Yes	I-Abst. II-Abst.	Abst.
USSR	No	I-Abst. II-Abst.	Abst.
USA	No	I-Yes II-Yes	Abst.

*Angola does not appear because its representative was absent for most votes.

- On the issue of funding for the United Nations Emergency Force and the United Nations Disengagement Observer Force stationed in the Middle East, the African Marxist states consistently supported additional appropriations, as did the United States and conservative African countries, while the Soviet Union and Cuba, with one exception, either abstained or voted against resolutions coming before the world body in 1976, 1977, and 1978 (see Table V).[78]
- On the issue of the prohibition of nuclear weapons in Latin America, they voted in December 1977 in favor of it, together with the United States, while both Cuba and the entire Soviet bloc abstained. Only the Congo sided with the Soviets (see Table VI).[79]
- On a resolution before the same UN session in favor of the limitation and reduction of nuclear weapons systems, they voted with all other African countries, and this time even Cuba, against the two superpowers.[80] On the more general question of reducing overall military budgets, they were again in agreement with other African countries in favoring it, while the two superpowers voted against the resolution. This time Cuba stood alongside the Soviet Union (see Table VI.)[81]

Turning to economic issues, the African Marxist-Leninist states felt as strongly as all the other African ones that industrialized nations should accelerate the transfer of real resources to the developing world on a "predictable, continuous and increasingly assured basis" and that they should increase their aid to .7 percent of GNP. Resolutions on this problem before the General Assembly in 1976, 1977, and 1978 saw the United States the only nation voting outright against them while the Soviet Union abstained and Cuba voted in favor with other developing Third World nations (see Table VII).[82]

Similarly, on a 1976 resolution urging developed nations to accelerate the redeployment of some of their industries to developing countries, the Marxist-Leninist states stood on the side of virtually all other Third World countries in supporting it, while the United States was again alone in voting no. The Soviet Union abstained and Cuba again joined the Third World bloc (see Table VII).[83]

This same pattern existed on another 1976 resolution calling for a reexamination of Third World countries' debt burden and a revision of the industrialized nations' approach to find a "general and effective solution" to relieve poor countries of it (see Table VII).[84]

These voting patterns demonstrated beyond any doubt the existence of a distinct African and Third World position among the Marxist-Leninist states concerning many crucial issues. This solidarity should not be confused with the Pan-Africanism of the 1960s, however, which was built around the concept of a separate African identity and of a communality of political, economic, and cultural interests which all countries on the continent shared by virtue of being African. The solidarity of the Marxist-Leninist states extended to all developing countries on the assumption that all shared the same economic interest in the conflict with the industrialized ones and the need for a new economic order. At the same time, they recognized and

TABLE VII
Economic Issues

	1976 Industrial Redeployment in favor of developing countries	1976 Debt Problems of developing countries	1976 & 1978 Transfer of real resources	1978 Finance for development
African Socialist				
Algeria	Yes	Yes	1976-Yes	Yes
			1978-Yes	
Tanzania	Yes	Yes	1976-Yes	Yes
			1978-Yes	
African Marxist*				
Benin	Yes	Yes	1976-Yes	Yes
			1978-Yes	
Congo	Yes	Yes	1976-Yes	Yes
			1978-Yes	
Ethiopia	Yes	Yes	1976-Yes	Yes
			1978-Yes	
Mozambique	Not Par	Not Par	1976-Not par	Yes
			1978-Yes	
Somalia	Yes	Yes	1976-Yes	Yes
			1978-Yes	
Other African				
Ivory Coast	Yes	Yes	1976-Yes	Yes
			1978-Yes	
Kenya	Yes	Yes	1976-Yes	Yes
			1978-Yes	
Other non-African				
Cuba	Yes	Yes	1976-Not Par	Yes
			1978-Yes	
USSR	Abst.	Abst.	1976-Abst.	Abst.
			1978-Abst.	
USA	No	No	1976-No	Abst.
			1978-No	

*Angola does not appear because its representative was absent for most votes.

accepted the existence of widely different political interests between socialist and capitalist states in Africa as elsewhere. Third World solidarity was, as we have already argued, only one of several elements of their foreign policy, nationalism and proletarian internationalism being equally important driving forces.

Conclusions

The foregoing analysis of Ethiopia, Angola, and Mozambique reveals a far closer relationship between them and the socialist, namely Soviet, bloc of nations than has heretofore existed anywhere in black Africa except perhaps temporarily in Somalia. These African states were drawn to the East by a sense of shared ideology, the perception of a common external enemy, and a vital need for military protection. On the other hand, they soon found cause for keeping a certain distance from their principal "natural ally." The Soviet Union rankled sensitivities with its refusal to accept these countries as Marxist-Leninist states. Occasional Soviet interference in the internal affairs of their African allies, the unfavorable economic deals they offered, and their requests for military facilities all raised questions about the possible costs of too close an alliance with the Eastern bloc. Like the United States, the Soviet Union also tended to view in East-West terms issues the African Marxist-Leninist states perceived primarily as North-South ones. Finally, the Soviet Union proved unwilling, or unable, to provide the economic aid, the technology, and the terms and volume of trade the African countries regarded as vital to overcoming their underdevelopment and dependency.

The African Marxist-Leninist countries had already concluded by 1980 that the Soviet bloc did not offer a viable economic alternative to the international capitalist order and they thus developed a bifurcated foreign policy. Economic necessity dictated continuing ties with the Western countries while political convictions and military imperatives pulled them toward the Soviet bloc. This bifurcation of political and economic interests was the most salient characteristic of the foreign policy of Angola, Mozambique, and Ethiopia. Nationalism and Third World solidarity provided a counterweight to proletarian internationalism and assured a degree of independence from the Soviet Union that their geographical distance served only to reinforce. Trade with, and aid from, the West similarly suggested that the kind of exclusive and totally dependent relationship such as Cuba has evolved with the Soviet Union was not likely to repeat itself in the case of the African Marxist-Leninist states. Despite their ideological affinities to the communist world and their military dependence on the Soviet Union, there was scant evidence that these states wanted to take the same road into the Eastern bloc as had Cuba, or that "objective" international conditions were forcing them to do so. What was emerging, in fact, was a search for a new, more independent relationship between committed African Marxist-Leninist countries and the Soviet Union. By analogy to the quest of some European communist parties for a new, more autonomous Eurocommunism, we will call the emerging stance of the African Marxist-Leninist states "Afrocommunism," a concept we shall discuss more thoroughly after analyzing its domestic components in the next chapter.

Chapter VIII
The Case for Afrocommunism

In early 1980, the three principal Marxist-Leninist states of black Africa demonstrated clearly that they were still unsettled political and economic systems. In Angola, the issues raised by the death of President Neto remained unresolved: black nationalism was still a potentially explosive issue, a covert struggle for leadership continued, and the tension between two diametrically opposed tendencies, people's power and state power, had not been assuaged. In Mozambique, the future status of the communal villages had not yet been defined, leaving many open questions about the nature of Mozambican Marxism-Leninism, and Frelimo was returning some small businesses to their private owners in its search for a realistic balance between its commitment to a centrally planned and controlled economy and its very limited managerial capacity. In Ethiopia, the struggle to form a party and find a *modus vivendi* between military and civilians continued unabated, while the government was still testing how far and fast it could push collectivization of the peasantry. In such circumstances, it might well be argued that conclusions about the Marxist-Leninist African states were at best premature. There was no doubt that fundamental issues were still being fought out and that as Marxist-Leninist systems they were in their infancy. Instability remained a potential problem, although not more so than in other African countries. The choice of Marxism-Leninism by itself did not obviate the problems wracking the entire continent for the previous 20 years—economic stagnation, rising expectations, ethnic conflicts, separatist movements, border conflicts and internal struggles for power among competing elites. While justifications for caution were legion, there were nonetheless good reasons to attempt drawing some conclusions about Marxism-Leninism in Africa. Autopsies may be more easily performed than vivisections, but they come too late to be of any help in dealing with the problem at hand. Scholarly caution may be a safe posture, but in a situation where judgements are being made and acted upon daily by policymakers such caution also relegates the scholar to irrelevance.

The judgments already rendered about the African Marxist-Leninist states are numerous and diverse. Curiously, they share one point in common, namely that they dismiss the importance of ideology. This, we would contend, is a serious mistake. We discussed in the preceding chapter how the Soviet Union has been reluctant to accept these countries as full-fledged members of the socialist commonwealth, labeling them instead as "revolutionary

193

democracies" or at best "socialist-oriented" regimes. Not surprisingly, American views are more varied, and it is possible to distinguish three basic ones which can be defined, without any attempt at originality, as the conservative, liberal, and radical outlook.

The conservative view, ironically, is the only one that takes the African Marxist-Leninist states seriously, to the point of viewing them as positively a threat to the United States. But it holds erroneously that they are little more than extensions of Soviet and Cuban influence into the continent, "puppet" regimes having no life or vitality of their own and heavily dependent on outside communist support for their survival. What is fundamentally missing in the conservative approach is any understanding of the internal roots of the phenomenon or of the economic and social problems of African countries generally which make Marxism-Leninism such an appealing ideology at present. Former Secretary of State Henry Kissinger, for example, considered Angola and Ethiopia simply as Soviet beachheads for further intervention on the continent and saw American failure to stop the rise of the MPLA to power as a surrender to Soviet expansionism, a prelude to the Soviet invasion of Afghanistan. Addressing a meeting of newspaper editors in Washington in April 1980, he argued that because the communist push had not been resisted in Angola, there existed a large "Soviet finger" stretching from Luanda through Addis Ababa and pointing threateningly at the Middle East.[1] As for the internal dynamics of these countries that led to the emergence of Marxist-Leninist regimes, Kissinger was simply not interested.

The liberal view, on the other hand, depicts the African Marxist-Leninist countries as much less dangerous to the United States. But it, too, is somewhat oblivious, by mistake or intention, to the impact of ideology on their internal characteristics. The most outspoken exponent of this approach was former UN Ambassador Andrew Young, who argued that all radical African countries, no matter their rhetoric, were basically African nationalist rather than Communist. We have already noted the existence of a strong nationalist strain in the Marxist-Leninist countries, serving to drive a wedge between them and the Soviet Union even while they preached and practiced proletarian internationalism. But nationalism does not preclude socialism on the domestic front, as history shows, nor commitment to the spreading of revolution abroad. While it is accurate to speak of the persistence of nationalism in the Marxist-Leninist states, this is only one side of them. The other is the ideological conformity and the policies stemming therefrom—the building of vanguard parties, the attempts at collectivizing agriculture, the nationalization of most of the economy, and the close alignment with the Soviet Union on geopolitical issues—all phenomena which simply cannot be explained in terms of nationalism.

The radical view, not surprisingly, is not found among politicians but only among committed intellectuals. The problem with this outlook is the strong element of utopianism underlying it. The radicals' conclusions about the Marxist-Leninist states are usually negative, much more so than the Soviet ones. The Soviets were simply cautious, but accepted the self-defined Marxist African leaders as at least "revolutionary democrats." Western radicals are inclined to see them simply as petty bourgeois dictators. This view is expressed most often concerning Ethiopia, where the military leadership offers a ready target, but many of the same accusations could also be levelled against Angola and Mozambique. The thrust of the radical argument against Ethiopia is that "state power" is not based in the right social classes; it is not rooted in the proletariat, the peasants and the revolutionary intellectuals, but rather in the petty bourgeoisie or the military. This is usually taken to mean that the former classes have been excluded from exercising power directly. In the same perspective, the Angolan leadership is not revolutionary either, because far from relying on the working classes and allowing them to participate directly in government, it has crushed the whole *poder popular* movement. Even in Mozambique, by such standards, power is being accumulated in the hands of the state bureaucracy to the detriment of the revolutionary forces themselves. The argument may well be factually correct. But the question then arises whether power is ever exercised directly by the proletariat and the peasantry. Even Lenin saw the "dictatorship of the proletariat" being filtered through the intermediary of the professional cadres of a vanguard party. Because it disregards fundamental questions and accepts facile assumptions, the radical view in the end is merely a utopian one and thus of little help in understanding these countries.

All these views of the Marxist-Leninist African states have a degree of truth to them. Ethiopia, Angola, and Mozambique are not socialist paradises where power is literally in the hands of workers and peasants; they are fiercely nationalistic in spirit, but they are also far closer to the Soviet Union than to the United States. None of the views we have summarized offers, however, an overall picture of the African Marxist-Leninist systems. It is this picture which we shall try to sketch here.

The Impact of Ideology

It is not possible to understand the essential character of the African Marxist-Leninist countries without an appreciation for the fundamental impact of ideology. Ideology has determined the choice of institutions, the thrust of foreign relations, the direction of major policy decisions, and has even created the major dilemmas these countries are facing today. Marxism-Leninism is having a far greater impact than African socialism. The latter was never more than a vague ideal, a set of values its proponents believed should motivate the behavior of Africans in the modern-day world. Even Nyerere's *ujamaa,* probably the most elaborated version of African socialism, was not a blueprint for economic and political action outlining institutions, policies, and concrete goals. Marxism-Leninism, on the other hand, is much more specific. It prescribes institutions and policies and, perhaps more importantly, a method for analyzing reality as well as for changing it. It is a very logical theoretical system, and it is the rigor of its logic that accounts for both its appeal and the strong impact it has on policies. We are not arguing that Marxism-Leninism accurately describes the African reality or that it provides all the answers to the continent's economic and political problems. But it claims to do so and through a logic many African intellectuals have found very convincing. In fact, Marxism-Leninism has come close at times to being transformed into a system of pure deductive logic without any empirical underpinnings.

There are multiple examples of the very deep influence Marxism-Leninism is having in Mozambique, Angola, and Ethiopia. It explains, for example, why Ethiopia has tried to collectivize agriculture in the midst of two wars and in the face of the resurgence of ethnic movements throughout the country. The ideology argued that it was imperative to head off the formation of a kulak class which would in turn give rise to a "petty bourgeois" individualism undermining socialism. It explains, too, why Mozambique and Angola viewed their state farms as a superior form of economic organization rather than as a gigantic managerial nightmare. State farms, in the logic of Marxism-Leninism, advanced the cause of socialism by creating a proletariat, lent themselves to centralized economic planning, and contributed to the spread of a "mentality of efficiency." It explains additionally the painstaking labors in all three countries to try to build serious vanguard parties. At times, the acceptance of the ideology has verged on the absurd. Frelimo, for example, proclaimed the leading role of the working class and the unreliability of the peasantry in the socialist revolution. Historically, however, its greatest support came from the peasants while urban workers played virtually no role in the national liberation struggle and even indulged in "petty bourgeois" unionism. In Angola and Mozambique, the ideological prescription that the party must be small and pure has helped to alienate segments of the population which initially supported the liberation struggle but subsequently found themselves cast aside as unreliable "petty bourgeois."

Our emphasis on the ideological orthodoxy and even rigidity of the Marxist-Leninist African states contradicts statements often made about the growing "pragmatism" of their leaders. For example, President Machel has been described as a "pragmatic Marxist" because he was willing to enter into trade agreements with South Africa, courted American investment, and allowed the reopening of small private stores. President Neto was viewed in the same light when he argued that the government should not attempt to run everything immediately and that there was a role for private truckers in the paralyzed transportation system and for private carpenters and masons in the construction industry. Prime Minister Robert Mugabe, upon coming to power in Zimbabwe, was invariably referred to as a pragmatic Marxist because he moved cautiously in implementing economic or social reforms in an attempt to avoid a white coup d'etat. All these leaders have been pragmatic at times. Their pragmatism, however, has been more akin to that of the Soviet New Economic Policy (NEP) of the early 1920s than to the American meaning of the term. In that period, the struggling Soviet government liberalized somewhat the economy and encouraged American and other Western businesses to come invest in the country. Similarly, the pragmatism of the African Marxist-Leninist states has so far been applied to the choice of means and the pace of reforms but not to the final goals of socialism and communism. There is no evidence yet that the "pragmatic Marxists" are in any sense becoming social democrats. Pragmatism has undoubtedly affected the timing and pace of reform and even dictated the undoing of some socialist measures. Machel in early 1980 announced the denationalization of some small businesses, particularly grocery stores and restaurants, when he found the state paralyzed by inefficiency in trying to run them. "The state should not sell matches," he remarked in defense of his decision.[2] But he upheld the principle of state control over the main means of production and continued the policy of nationalizing troublesome Portuguese-run industries. Colonel Mengistu decided not to press hard for rural collectivization in 1975 and again in 1979 after issuing the proclamation outlining the various steps that would lead to it. But there was no indication of a backing off from the pursuit of the ultimate goal of collective agriculture. It should be recalled in this regard that both China and the Soviet Union, too, manifested moments of great pragmatism, and even retreat, in implementing their socialist policies in the face of economic difficulties and stubborn resistance.

The common ideological commitment explains the similarities of the major institutional and policy choices made by these three countries. In the political realm, Angola, Mozambique, and Ethiopia have all opted for a single-party system with the party being a vanguard rather than a mass one. This is true even in Ethiopia, where for the complex political reasons we have discussed above the party is still a skeleton only. There is no doubt that eventually even Ethiopia will have its vanguard party, although under military control. If the formation of a single party is hardly a new occurrence in Africa, and not only among the socialist countries, the insistence that it should be a vanguard one has been a choice unique to the Marxist-Leninist states. So has the emphasis on setting up a party school for the systematic training of professional cadres and their indoctrination in the history, theory, and practice of Marxism-Leninism.

Conventionally enough, the Marxist-Leninist African states have also tried to combine the vanguard party, with its highly exclusive character, with broader national organizations and various local bodies allowing for mass participation of a kind. Women's and youth organizations, labor unions, neighborhood "action committees," village peasant associations, communes and cooperatives, worker production councils in enterprises, mass rallies and national campaigns of various types have all been used to promote a high degree of involvement by the general public in the political life of the country. Different countries have, however, stressed different institutions. Ethiopia has relied primarily on its peasant and urban neighborhood associations.

Mozambique has used extensively the dynamizing groups and informal local meetings as well as the communal village people's assemblies, while Angola tried to institutionalize participation through the *poder popular* action committees.

The issue of popular participation in the Marxist-Leninist countries is a complicated one. Political participation is virtually seen as a must for all citizens, and the system generally does not approve of the private individual content to mind his own business. As a result, there is certainly more emphasis on participation in these countries than elsewhere in Africa. Participation does not mean, however, interest group representation or the free expression of demands. Only a minority, party members, participate even indirectly in the debate on major policy issues of national importance. The decisions are finally taken by a handful of individuals at the top of the party hierarchy. For all the other citizens, participation is circumscribed by party decisions, regimented by party cadres, and mostly limited to attempts at solving local problems within the limits set by party directives—or, in Ethiopia, by the *Derg's* directives. When participation goes beyond these boundaries, as it has happened in Ethiopia quite regularly, in Angola with *poder popular,* and in Mozambique before Frelimo established a firmer hold on the urban areas, it has been suppressed as soon as possible. Despite all the restrictions placed upon the autonomy of committees, assemblies, and mass organizations, the population does have some real say about local problems and issues. Other forms of participation such as mass rallies and celebration parades, on the other hand, are simply tests of loyalty and support administered by the government to its citizens.

There are also similarities among the African Marxist-Leninist states in the economic realm stemming from their ideological outlook. Some are quite obvious, others less so. The nationalization of virtually all major enterprises, banks, and insurance companies falls into the first category, together with the establishment of state control over exports and imports. So, too, does the emphasis placed on the need for overall economic planning, even if in practice so far this has meant little more than drawing up general investment budgets and setting production goals. Less obvious is the common ambivalence toward private enterprise. On the theoretical level, the hostility is nearly total and unremitting, extending down to small businesses and individual entrepreneurs. Even successful family farms are regarded as breeding grounds for dangerous individualism and a petty bourgeois mentality from which a kulak class is likely to emerge. As a result, Angola and Mozambique have nationalized even small businesses, and only given back some when the pressure of managing large numbers of small concerns became unbearable. Ethiopia has allowed small private traders and craftsmen to pursue their activity, but has not encouraged them and has even executed some merchants for hoarding and profiteering. But the attitude toward large foreign private corporations has been very different from what the theory would suggest. The multinationals may be seen by radicals as the capitalist world's major tool for exploiting underdeveloped countries, but they offer the investment, skills, and technology all Third World countries so badly need. Furthermore, the logic of Marxism-Leninism can be used to provide a justification of sorts for dealing with large foreign corporations. Multinationals invest generally in large projects which can more easily be integrated into an economy aspiring to be planned than small businesses. Furthermore they promote industrialization or large-scale agriculture and thus the growth of a proletariat. And they have proven very amenable to working with state companies as minority partners. As a result, as we have already discussed, all three countries by 1980 were actively seeking deals with, and investments by, foreign corporations.

The choice of Marxism-Leninism has also created a series of dilemmas common to the three countries we are considering. Some of these stem from the considerable difference between the economic and social conditions of African countries and those posited as necessary by the ideology. Marxism-Leninism envisaged the building of socialism in societies that are both more conflict ridden and more industrialized than is the case in Africa. Class conflict is a very artificial concept in both Angola and Mozambique; only in Ethiopia does it possess a reality. This has deprived the revolution in the two former countries of much of the spontaneous social dynamics Marxism-Leninism presupposes and has forced the government to become the motor of change, substituting an artificially induced sense of class conflict for a real one. More important are the dilemmas created by the low level of industrialization. While it is true that no socialist revolution has taken place in highly industrial societies, they have not taken place either in countries as underdeveloped as these. The most often cited dilemma is how to establish a "dictatorship of the proletariat" in countries with a tiny working class. Furthermore, this group, far from being exploited and downtrodden is better off than most of the rest of the population by virtue of assured wages and urban living conditions. A less often discussed dilemma is that while Marxism-Leninism prescribes industrialization as the avenue to socialism and freedom from Western neocolonialism, the development of industry in Africa has actually led to increased dependency on the West for everything from raw material to spare parts and markets. Theoretically, the vicious circle of dependency can be broken by the development of heavy industry. In practice this is very difficult, because internal demand in most African countries can only support consumer industries that simply replace import of finished products with imports of machines and even raw materials.

While the conflict between the conditions posited by the ideology and those existing in the African countries does pose questions of adaptation and interpretation, it does not make the ideology completely ineffectual as a guideline for change. We said earlier that this problem arose in respect to African socialism, which based its vision on a traditional village model bearing no relation to contemporary conditions. The lack of "fit" between Kaunda's humanism and the reality of a copper-dominated country, for example, made the ideology completely ineffectual in Zambia. But Marxism-Leninism is quite different. Since Marx's original formulation did not fit the socioeconomic conditions of any of the now communist countries, the ideology was reelaborated continually, by Lenin, Mao, and innumerable forgotten ideologues, including those now squabbling over fine points in African universities. The result of all this work is that what goes under the name of Marxism-Leninism has now become a grab bag of theories in which something can be found to deal with most conditions. For example, Marxism in its ideological formulation as a theory of class struggle and dialectical change nicely fits Ethiopia, but does not really fit Mozambique and Angola. Marxism-Leninism as a theory of hierarchical organization and engineered change, however, can be applied to countries like Angola or Mozambique with a low degree of social conflict and class consciousness without much difficulty. The dictatorship of the proletariat may make little sense in any African country, but a vanguard party purportedly representing its interests is an admirable instrument of rule in new nation-states badly in need of a centralizing institution. In other words, there are various aspects of Marxism-Leninism which do fit African conditions.

The dilemmas arising from the imperfect fit between ideology and African conditions can be defined out of existence to some extent by a theoretical slight of hand. But those deriving from the inherent contradictory prescriptions of Marxism-Leninism are much less amenable to solution or compromise. The ideology contains a series of *de facto* mutually exclusive principles: a high level of participation which does not lead to pluralism, but to the confined debate of democratic centralism; democratic centralism which does not produce overcentralization, but remains democratic, a planned economy which does not result in stifling bureaucratism; separation of party and state without conflict between the two; dialectical change, but no independent centers of power to provide the antithesis. The theory provides a coherent justification for these prescriptions. In practice, no Marxist-Leninist country anywhere in the world has been able to reconcile these contradictory expectations, but all have quietly chosen one horn of the dilemma. The African countries have not made a clear choice yet, but the tensions are quite clear. In all of them, there has emerged one faction or tendency, generally referred to as "Trotskyite," whose exponents accuse the established government of having betrayed the revolution by choosing the authoritarian horn of all these dilemmas. More specifically, they charge than centralism has prevailed over democracy, bureaucracy over participation, and the state over the party, resulting in state capitalism rather than socialism. For their part, they favor a more participatory and less centralized model of socialism, in short some form of direct democracy. This tendency was embodied in the *poder popular* movement in Angola, the EPRP in Ethiopia, and in the faction arguing for communal villages in Mozambique. There is nothing unique or African about the emergence of this trend and conflict. It has appeared with great regularity in all Communist revolutions. It seems

Marxism-Leninism is bound to spawn a struggle between those who stress participatory democracy and those who favor the greater authoritarianism of a vanguard party. It also seems inevitable that the ruling group should prefer centralism and the opposition direct democracy, since the former already controls the central institutions, while the latter can more easily infiltrate local, decentralized committees using them as a springboard to power and eventually to the control of central institutions. The "Trotskyite" faction always represents the conflict as one between a dictatorial elite which has usurped power and betrayed the revolution and the real representatives of the revolutionary forces shut out of office. In fact, the conflict is a highly political one between the ins and the outs, each interpreting the ideology to suit its own needs.

While the conflict between the centralist, or statist, tendency and the participatory one is typical of all Marxist-Leninist systems, it takes on different manifestations and has different historical roots in each country. In Ethiopia, as we have argued, its antecedents were the splits in the student movement. The conflict was then embittered at the onset of the revolution through the exclusion of all civilian groups from the central decision-making body, the *Derg,* composed solely of military men. In Mozambique and Angola, the wars of national liberation gave rise to a powerful tradition of decentralized direct democracy, made necessary by the exigencies of the struggle. Direct participation, thus, was not only an abstract interpretation of what the ideology meant, but also a live historical tradition, the "revolutionary experience of the people" which was then supposed to be integrated with the universal principles of Marxism-Leninism. The attempt to merge the two only made sharper the dilemmas inherent in the conflicting dictates of the ideology.

Marxism-Leninism and African Socialism

There is nothing specifically Marxist-Leninist, or even new for that matter, in the choices and dilemmas we have described, some will argue. Marxist rhetoric has been heard before on the continent, and in any case rhetoric is just that and should not be taken seriously. Almost all African countries have single-party systems, state enterprises, and manifest conflicting centralizing and decentralizing tendencies. Conflicts between central authority and local groups are not related to ideology, but are inherent in all political systems with a short history as states, intense tribal conflicts, and generally weak and inefficient central administrative apparatus. At best, Ethiopia, Angola, and Mozambique are latter-day examples of African socialism. There is, in other words, nothing new under the African sun.

That the Marxist-Leninist states share certain problems inherent to the conditions of all the new African nations none would dispute. But certainly there are perceptibly different kinds of political and economic systems being established on the continent, some more capitalist and others more socialist in their orientation. It is easy, too, to find piecemeal examples to support the contention that the so-called Marxist-Leninist countries are basically no different from the African socialist ones. Mozambique has its *aldeais communais* and Tanzania its *ujamaa* villages. There is a strong statist trend in Angola, but the same has been true in Algeria since 1965: the cause, then, is oil and not ideology. Marxist Mozambique is putting large amounts of money into state farms; so are Tanzania and Guinea. Parallels can certainly be found. But it is our contention that if one looks at the overall systems and the rationale behind them, the differences between the African socialist and the Marxist-Leninist countries are more pronounced and significant than the similarities. And while it is undoubtedly true that ideological choices do not exempt any country from the problems common to the continent, they certainly do influence their thinking on how to solve them. There is no good reason, after all, to assume that geography is destiny.

There are a number of salient characteristics of the three Marxist-Leninist regimes setting them apart from the African socialist ones and justifying in our view the use of a separate label. The differences in ideologies and foreign policies we have already discussed in detail, and we shall not return to them here. Instead, we shall focus on the process of change and the character of institutions. By and large, the African Marxist-Leninist states started out with an overall vision of where they wanted to go and how to get there, of the institution needed to attain their goal and of the social groups which would support, and those which would oppose, the effort. In other words, they had a vision not only of the final goal but also of the dynamics of the process of change. Hence the pace of reform was much swifter more systematic and marked by fewer contradictions than was the case in the African socialist countries. There has been much less experimentation with different institutions and possible solutions to problems in the Marxist-Leninist states than in Tanzania, Guinea, or Zambia. One needs only to think of the variety of institutions littering the landscape of rural Zambia in its struggle to improve agricultural productivity, or of the array of committees, corps, or associations used by Guinea in an attempt to mobilize the population to realize the relative continuity that the ideology has imparted to the policies and institutions of the three Marxist-Leninist countries. To be sure, the swiftness of reform was facilitated in Angola and Mozambique by the vacuum created by the mass departure of the Portuguese and in Ethiopia by the inherently revolutionary situation. But the systematic character of the reforms cannot be explained by the vacuum of power; in Guinea and initially in Algeria similar circumstances only led to a chaotic process of adopting *ad hoc* solutions and creating *ad hoc* institutions.

The continuity of ideas and institutions has served to make the African Marxist-Leninist states less personal and dependent on a single individual. Guinean socialism could not possibly remain the same without Touré, because he has made himself virtually into the one and only stable institution in the country. Similarly, it is difficult to think of humanism perpetuating itself without Kaunda. Even in Tanzania, *ujamaa* as an ideology and a system still appears too vague to survive unchanged in the absence of Nyerere. In other words, there is a very strong element of personalism in the African socialist system. By contrast, Marxism-Leninism has already continued unchanged despite the death of President Neto, and there is no reason to believe that the demise of Samora Machel in Mozambique would alter the system. Machel was not the incarnation of Mozambican socialism, but a product of Frelimo. Ethiopia, for its part, has already undergone a series of upheavals in the leadership with very little change in ideology or policies. In other words, the element of personalism in the Marxist-Leninist states is far less pronounced.

The African Marxist-Leninist countries also distinguish themselves by their attitude toward the state and its role. As we have already pointed out, all African socialist countries evolved toward statism, no matter how contrary that was to their declared intentions. The reason for this development was the failure of voluntarism and of schemes relying upon spontaneous mobilization. The state took over by default. In the Marxist-Leninist countries, statism is openly accepted and theoretically justified as so vividly shown by the MPLA argument that "people's power" had to be understood as "state power" and by the space devoted in its and Frelimo party documents to explaining the importance of the state in the making of a socialist revolution. What is the difference, then, between acknowledged and theoretically justified statism and an unwanted drift in same direction? The answer is that a system that openly accepts statism is more coherent and can consciously use the institutions of the state to move the society toward socialism, promote a collective spirit, and develop it economically. Mozambique, for example, held that state farms were the highest form of economic organization in agriculture, put its money and efforts into organizing this sector, and succeeded in reviving production. Zambia, on the other hand, has been incapable of deciding what role the state should play in agriculture. It has divided its funds and energies among state farms, rural reconstruction centers, and an ineffectual extension service to help emerging farmers. As a result of the absence of any clear strategy, no scheme has worked. The issue here is not whether state farms are more productive than private ones, but simply that a coherent strategy has a greater chance of succeeding than a vacillating one. Another example is the use of state companies in Angola to stand up to, and forge a new relationship with, the Western multinationals. Guinea, on the other hand, failed to make use of state power to achieve the same results, allowing both Western private corporations and the Soviet Union to exploit its bauxite on terms highly disadvantageous to Guinea itself.

The one exception in the attitude toward the state among the African socialist countries has been Algeria. There, as we have seen, state power is acknowledged and indeed glorified as part of the resurrection of the Algerian nation. It is relied upon as the motor of economic development. Algeria has, in fact, taken over many of the techniques of Marxism-Leninism without accepting the ideology in its entirety. It has nationalized the major means of production, set up a complex of interlocking state companies, and relied on the state to provide services, loans, and marketing for the rural sector. It has finally gone further than any other country in Africa toward trying to integrate all economic activity through centralized, overall development plans. The Algerian experience suggests that the real relevance of the Marxism-Leninism to African countries may reside in the fact that it offers a package of techniques and solutions to the problems of organizing a society for radical change. It is true that Marxism-Leninism also offers a set of articles of faith, but the Algerian example clearly shows that the techniques can be used equally well by those of little faith. This point is particularly relevant in relation to contemporary African Marxist-Leninist states. One common objection to the use of the term is that there are so few true believers and ideologues in these countries that they cannot possibly be considered Marxist-Leninist. The answer to this objection as found in the Algerian case is that as long as the institution and techniques of Marxism-Leninism are adopted, the number of true believers may not matter all that much. After all, we don't really know how many members of the Chinese or Soviet Party Central Committee really have the faith. The one area where ideology as a faith rather than as a package of techniques and solutions may be very important is foreign policy. The African Marxist-Leninist states are, after all, more closely aligned to the Soviet bloc than Algeria.

In our overview of the African socialist countries, we concluded that they all have developed into very unbalanced systems giving rise to four distinct models. We argued specifically that Zambia had become an example of an "upper class welfare state," Tanzania one of "development without growth, Guinea an extreme case of "politics in command," and Algeria one of "economics in command." The question we are now ready to consider is whether the three Marxist-Leninist states are avoiding the pitfalls that led to such great imbalances in these four African socialist countries or whether the same distortions are emerging. To be sure, the very economic characteristics of some countries guarantee that certain extremes will not emerge. There is no way, for example, that Mozambique or Ethiopia can embark on an Algerian-style policy of heavy industrialization. But in all countries, very unbalanced systems could theoretically emerge. Our tentative conclusion, though, is that while some hints of the distortions plaguing the African socialist countries are beginning to appear in the Marxist-Leninist ones, by and large their systems appear, so far, to be more balanced. The one probable exception is Angola, which seems to be embarking on the same path Algeria took 15 years earlier.

At this point, none of the Marxist-Leninist countries are duplicating the Zambian model of an upper class welfare state and thus evolving away from socialism. This is not to say that there is no elite in these countries or that privilege no longer exists. There is much evidence that the gap between high and low salaries remains substantial, as we have shown in the case of Mozambique and Ethiopia. Even more pronounced is the gap between salaried workers and subsistence farmers in all three countries where the living standards of the vast majority of the population are so abysmally low. Thus, we would not hold that the existence of an income gap is in and of itself sufficient to justify talking about an upper-class welfare state. What made Zambia such was not only the income disparity but also the diversion of substantial resources from development to elite consumption—as in the case of government subsidized luxury housing and car loans—coupled with a reluctance to undertake reforms which would seriously affect the living standards of the urban elites. We do not see this same trend developing in the Marxist-Leninist countries—yet. On the contrary, at least in Ethiopia the wealthy urban elite has been made to give up much of what it previously enjoyed. In Angola and Mozambique, where no national bourgeoisie existed in the first place, measures have been taken to prevent one from forming, and there has so far been no evidence of a major diversion of scarce resources to elite consumption, not even through corruption.

Some traces of the Guinean model of "politics in command" are apparent in Ethiopia, although they are counterbalanced by a far greater awareness of the importance of economics to the revolution. The *Derg* has time and again surprised, and sometimes alarmed, all observers by its willingness to take economic risks in the name of the political imperatives of the revolution. The latest example was the 1979 decree on collectivization. Such a measure had the potential for greatly decreasing agricultural production but was taken anyway to satisfy an ideological requirement. The government was already working at that time, however, to spur production through its second *zemacha* and through an expanded agricultural extension service to the peasant associations. In fact, it succeeded in increasing production the very same year that collectivization was introduced. In other words, while politics in command in Guinea meant a total disregard for economics, in Ethiopia economic imperatives were not totally disregarded in the process of pursuing the implementation of political principles.

The Tanzanian model of "development without growth" could eventually be reproduced in Mozambique. We have seen how that country has devoted substantial sums to improving social services in order to rapidly uplift the standard of living of the rural population. The issue is whether this commitment to spread education and health care against a background of economic stagnation will not lead to the Tanzanian dilemma. Mozambique shares many characteristics with its neighbor to the north: scarcity of natural resources, a relative lack of social conflict making it difficult to mobilize the population for radical change, and a political commitment to discourage individual enrichment, which thwarts the growth of a kulak class but also of agricultural production. The base for economic growth is weak in both countries. There are some indications, however, that Mozambique is taking steps to avoid falling into the same trap as Tanzania. First of all, it has understood from the beginning the importance of the modern farm sector and social services the government could not otherwise have financed out of its own funds. Whether by design or inability to attract foreign assistance, invested large sums and much energy into reviving production on the abandoned Portuguese estates. Second, it has made a more systematic effort to mobilize the population for change and has a stronger and more dynamic party to do this. Third, Mozambique has not, so far, received the enormous amount of foreign aid that has so greatly contributed to the Tanzanian imbalance between growth and development by building up a system of Mozambique is much closer to living within its own means than Tanzania and thus probably less likely to develop the same degree of imbalance.

Only the Algerian example of "economics in command" seems well on its way to being duplicated among the Marxist-Leninist countries, specifically in Angola. Two major factors are encouraging this trend: as an oil producer, Angola has a sizable economic base to work from and as a country still afflicted by nationwide mobilization and far-reaching political reforms at the local level. MPLA control over part of the country remains partial, because the Ovimbundu in the south and Bakongo in the north have historically sided with UNITA and the FNLA. On the other hand, the government does totally control the oil sector, the major industries, and the state farms and can use these to begin fashioning a new economic system and to launch the country's development. The similarities between the Algerian and Angolan domestic experiences are striking: demobilization of the two populations following a civil war and a bad experience with participatory democracy run amok; government concentration on oil, industry, and state farms; an industrial and urban-oriented development strategy; and reliance on Western corporations, technology, and consulting firms to strengthen the state sector. Many MPLA leaders were thoroughly familiar with the Algerian model as a result of their long stays in Algiers during the liberation struggle and they later sought Algerian advice in mapping out an oil strategy; this strongly suggests that the similarities are not accidental and that Angola regards the Algerian model as a valid one. Whether the Angolan system would become as unbalanced as the Algerian one was difficult to predict with any degree of certainty at the time of this writing. There was at least one very important remaining difference between the two countries: whereas the FLN had never succeeded in displacing the army as the center of power in Algeria, the MPLA was very clearly emerging as the central decision-making institution of Angola. Furthermore, despite the initial devastating experience with the people's power movement, the MPLA was still committed to setting up its institutions and slowly began to do so in mid-1980. Thus, there was some reason to believe that a somewhat better balance might emerge between economics and politics, between the state and party, in Angola then had occurred in Algeria.

Marxism-Leninism, Revolutionary Democracies, and Revolutions Betrayed

We have not yet come directly to terms with the radical contention that the self-defined Marxist-Leninist countries of Africa are "revolutions betrayed" and thus not worthy of the name by which they have chosen to call themselves. This is an issue we are very tempted to beg because of the lack of agreement about the meaning of Marxism-Leninism. In a world where one man's orthodoxy is another man's deviationism, the answer to whether Angola, Mozambique, and Ethiopia are Marxist-Leninist becomes largely tautological. After all, the question is still being raised whether the Soviet Union is really socialist, let alone Marxist-Leninist.[3] Nevertheless, we shall try to address two questions of central concern to radical critics, namely "the question of state power: which class holds the power which decides everything," and that of direct popular participation and worker control in a revolution.[4] The radicals charge that the African Marxist-Leninist states have put power in the hands of the wrong class and prevented worker participation in the decision-making process. As a result, they are "petty bourgeois puppet regimes of Soviet imperialism committed to preparing the ground for the massive defeat of the working class and a reversal of its spontaneous revolutionary will."[5]

Concerning the issue of participation, we have already noted the dilemma built into an ideology which calls simultaneously for "centralism" and "democracy," and for "people's power" and the rule of a vanguard party. We have also discussed how this dilemma has given rise to two conflicting interpretations, one stressing participatory democracy and the other statism. We have in addition noted the tension between those upholding the two opposite views within Ethiopia, Angola, and Mozambique. Although the outcome of the struggle is not yet clear, the forces favoring centralism seem to be winning out. If Marxism-Leninism is defined only in terms of direct participatory democracy, then these three countries seem condemned to join the swollen ranks of revolutions betrayed. We would only point out here that by such a stringent definition there are no examples of successful revolutions anywhere in the world, for statism has become a dominant characteristic of all socialist systems. It is not our intention here to defend statism, centralization, and bureaucracy. What makes the radical argument untenable is not their rejection of such tendencies and their advocacy of participatory democracy and workers' control. Rather, it is the assumption that such democracy and control are reconcilable with the "dictatorship of the proletariat," the rule of a vanguard party, and centralized economic planning. In other words, the radicals are refusing to recognize the dilemmas built into Marxism-Leninism and to make a choice.

The second issue, determining which "class holds power," is one of those theoretical conundrums on which it is difficult to get a grip empirically. In nineteenth-century England where the franchise was limited by law to certain classes, the class nature of state power may have been quite evident. In a socialist country, it is far from clear whether power is based in a class or simply in institutions. In dealing with Africa, the Soviet Union certainly thinks in terms of institutions as seen by the fact that it concentrates its aid on organizing the party, training cadres, and strengthening the military and security apparatus. A further problem in dealing with African countries is that "classes" are embryonic with scarcely a national bourgeoisie and only a tiny proletariat. The African countries are well endowed only in peasants and a burgeoning urban petty bourgeoisie. It is the latter which inevitably plays the dominant role as both Fanon and Cabral pointed out long ago very convincingly. Even in the absence of a detailed sociological study, it is clear that petty bourgeois elements are predominant in the apparatus of the state and party as well as the upper echelons of the army. For given the conditions of Africa, skilled and literate individuals to fill these positions can only come from the petty bourgeoisie. The question then becomes whose interest does the ruling petty bourgeois group represent and defend. In our view, the policies pursued by the three countries are aimed at bettering the living conditions of the peasantry and workers and at redistributing the wealth in their favor. Certainly they are not encouraging the creation of a national bourgeoisie, nor are these countries becoming Zambia-style upper-class welfare states.

Revolutionary military regimes such as the one in Ethiopia pose an additional analytical problem as regards the class base of state power. Radical critics charge that so long as the country is run by the army rather than by a vanguard party it cannot possibly become a Marxist-Leninist regime, because power is not rooted in the working class. For all their weaknesses, Angola and Mozambique at least have a vanguard party. Ethiopia still does not, and the military leadership has time and again demonstrated that it will only set up a party on its own terms, that is, one it can control. It is our contention that the *Derg* at this point needs a party very badly in order to pull together the too autonomous institutions that have developed since the onset of the revolutions and to counterbalance the centrifugal forces of ethnic nationalisms. As a tool for the exercise of power, a unified, disciplined, well-integrated party of trained cadres would be very useful even to the most authoritarian military regime. To see in the *Derg's* reluctance to form a party the manifestation of incompatibility between its social base and that of a future party is to accept a view of the party as literally the vanguard of a social class or classes, rather than as the bureaucratic, tightly organized institution for the exercise of power it is in communist countries. From the point of view of the overwhelming majority of the population, the difference between a military regime and one led by a tightly organized vanguard party is probably very small. In neither case does the population at large have much to say about major decisions. One important difference between a military regime and a vanguard party system, however, resides in the relationship between the leadership of the country and the institution upon which its power is based. Because of the hierarchical nature of armies and their downward structure of command, there is no mechanism, other than insubordination—that is, a coup—by which the military could remove its top leaders. In a party system, a mechanism by which top leaders can be removed and new ones chosen does exist. In this limited sense, party regimes are indeed more democratic than military ones. It is worth remembering, though, that the party's power to remove a leader has historically been exercised only in mature, well-established systems and never to bring down the founding father. The Soviet Communist party had to wait until Khrushchev before exercising its prerogatives. The Chinese Communist party did not dream of ousting Mao, nor the Yugoslav one, Tito. In other words, there is no historical example of a party ousting in a democratic process its original leader. Thus, the difference between a regime led by a vanguard party and a military one in the initial phase appears in practice much less momentous than it is made out to be. The "dictatorship of the proletariat" is a myth in either case, if by that is meant its direct rule. If this term is taken in its historical reality as the rule of an apparatus claiming to represent the interest of the working classes, then there seems no inherent reason why a petty bourgeoisie in uniform could not do this as well, or as badly, as one in civilian togs.

In the final analysis, the self-defined African Marxist-Leninist regimes are certainly not socialist utopias, or likely to become so. Their shortcomings, however, are not unusual and some are found in all Communist systems. To be sure, they are newer and less well established than the Soviet system with its 60-odd years of consolidation or even Cuba with its 20. While they are certainly in their infancy, they do not appear at this point to belong to a different species. The Soviet insistence that they are "revolutionary democracies" and not "Marxist-Leninist" states seems based simply on prudence. Like people in some African societies where infant mortality is high, the Soviets seem to be waiting until the years of greatest vulnerability have passed before naming the baby.

Prospects for Afrocommunism

The presence of Marxist-Leninist countries in Africa conjures up in the United States the specter of communism spreading through the continent, a region of the world long considered to be rightfully within the Western orbit of influence. Communism in Africa conveys threatening images of Soviet satellites ready to do their master's bidding against American interests. But the leaders of these nations, as we have tried to show, do not see the situation in these terms. To them, Marxism-Leninism is a way not of enslaving their countries to yet another master but rather of achieving real independence by freeing them from their dependency on the West. It is a way of radically reordering their societies, a set of specific institutions, a rigorous approach to development through centralized planning and state control. In foreign policy, the choice of Marxism-Leninism is a decision to become part of the "world revolutionary process" and thus to try to change the established world order rather than to simply find a niche for their countries on its periphery. It is a commitment to furthering the cause of socialism but as free agents, as independent and equal partners with other socialist countries around the world. It is this vision of what Marxism-Leninism means that we call Afrocommunism.

We have chosen the term Afrocommunism deliberately for its analogy to the foreign policy component of Eurocommunism, because we think there is a valid parallel. In the highly industrialized nations of Western Europe, the idea has gained increasing acceptance among Communists that it is time to rethink not only the issue of how a Communist state might come into existence in such conditions and what policies it should pursue internally, but also that of how it should relate to the Soviet Union. One important aspect of Eurocommunism is the determination to maintain complete national autonomy from the Soviet Union and a rejection of the Brezhnev doctrine of "limited sovereignty." It is this same determination to maintain national autonomy and sovereignty vis-a-vis the Soviet Union that characterizes the posture of the African Marxist-Leninist countries and justifies in our opinion the use of the term Afrocommunism. The roots of the phenomenon, we believe are found in the great concerns of all African countries for protecting national independence and furthering economic growth. The Marxist-Leninists believe that there can be no real independence for countries whose economies remain mere appendages of the Western ones in the colonial pattern. Hence their intense preoccupation with refashioning their ties to the West. The Marxist-Leninist leaders are convinced that the socialist countries provide the best model for establishing control over their economies. But they realize there can be no economic growth without capital investment, modern technology, and the hard currency needed to buy it, all of which they have found to be far more available from the West than from the Soviet bloc. In other words, in order to attain their goals, the African Marxist-Leninist countries need both the East and the West. Their actions show quite clearly that this is not simply our conclusion but theirs as well.

The final issue we wish to address is what the prospects are for Afrocommunism to survive and consolidate itself on African soil. There are two parts to the answer: first the prospects for its survival as an internal political system, and second the possibility of its success as an international posture. We have pointed out that the African Marxist-Leninist regimes are young and immature, thereby implicitly acknowledging that they could collapse as a result of any number of happenings, including their failure to satisfy the economic and political needs of their countries. The ideological commitment, for one thing, is still that of a minority. Furthermore, many of the ideologues can be considered for a variety of reasons as in some sense outsiders to their societies. A disproportionate number of the Angolan and Mozambican Marxist intellectuals did, and still do to this day, belong to ethnic minorities. They tend to be *mesticos,* whites, and, in Mozambique, even Goans. This is perfectly understandable because as we have pointed out earlier, these were the groups that had more access to education, study, and travel abroad. In addition, a large proportion of the Portuguese whites who stayed on after independence did so out of ideological conviction. As logical and straightforward as the explanation may be, the association of the ideology with racial minorities creates a situation that can easily be exploited for political purposes. This indeed happened in Angola, as we have seen, when Alves tried to use the issue of black nationalism to overthrow Neto. That the issue was still alive became clear after the death of Neto: the succession struggle was decided in favor of dos Santos, a black of relatively modest political stature, while the two, far more prominent *mesticos* controlling the party and army, Lara and Carreira, lost out. In Ethiopia, the Marxist-Leninist ideologues were at a disadvantage as well, since, as civilians, they were by definition outsiders to the military; they simply acted as advisers and technocrats of the revolution but had no power base of their own. The *Derg* could and did dismiss them at will. In all three countries, then, the original true believers in Marxism-Leninism were especially vulnerable.

The demise of the ideologues, should this happen, does not automatically imply the demise of the ideology or of the system based on it. Whoever first introduced it, the ideology in Angola and Mozambique is now associated with an entire movement and, as we have shown, has its roots deep in the nationalist guerrilla struggle. Expunging the ideology from the movement would require much more than an ouster of a few individuals. The crucial question is not who believes and how many believe, but how well implanted the system has become in order to perpetuate itself regardless of the rise and fall of individuals. The longer the system is in place, the more people have a vested interest in it. Party cadres have an interest in the party continuing to rule. Peasant association leaders may not know or care about the Maoist vision of society that led to the creation of the institution, but nonetheless would doubtlessly oppose their abolition. The Ethiopian military leadership is now publicly committed to a certain system, whether out of ideological conviction or political opportunism. Thus, it is far more important to look at the state of institutions than at the fate of individuals. The African Marxist-Leninist states seem all too well aware of this, for they have been working hard, even in Ethiopia, to create structures capable of perpetuating the system. The Soviet Union, East Germany, and Cuba have given them full backing in this enterprise. While their institutions are still fragile and innumerable problems remain, it is already clear that the element of personalism so characteristic of most African regimes is already far less pronounced in the three Marxist-Leninist ones and the components of a coherent economic and political system are emerging. These regimes are not necessarily "better" than others in Africa, but they are more concerned with building a system capable of perpetuating itself beyond the political lifetime of an individual leader.

The success of Afrocommunism as an international posture depends not only on the policies of the African regimes but also upon the response these policies elicit from the great powers. We have stressed the strong strain of nationalism apparent in the foreign outlook of all three countries, but also their continuing dependence upon the Soviet bloc for military assistance to safeguard the very national sovereignty of which they are so jealous. While the existing threats to these states persist, this dependency cannot decrease:

so long as Eritrea and the Ogaden remain in a state of war, Ethiopia cannot do without the Soviet Union and Cuba; so long as South Africa continues supporting UNITA and attacking Angola, the MPLA needs the assistance of these two communist countries; and although the Rhodesian threat to Mozambique has ended, the danger of South African aggression has not, and Frelimo also may need substantial military aid in the future, particularly as the black nationalist struggle inside South Africa escalates. Basically, the international environment for all three countries is inherently a hostile one because of the underlying persistence of regional conflicts. The United States has within its power the capability of aggravating these conflicts by assisting directly or indirectly the enemies of the Marxist-Leninist regimes. But such a policy would only assure their continuing dependency on the Soviet bloc and serve to drive them closer to it, as happened earlier in the case of Cuba. The US government is more likely to adopt such a self-defeating policy if it insists upon looking at the alliances between the Marxist-Leninist states and the Soviet Union only in geopolitical terms while failing to recognize that regional enmities have led them to turn to the Soviet bloc for military and diplomatic assistance in the first place. From their point of view, the Friendship Treaties with the Soviet Union and East Germany are directed mainly against regional enemies and not the United States. To be sure, there are geopolitical implications to the military presence of a great power in an African country as elsewhere in the world, but overlooking the regional rationale for this presence risks exacerbating the problem rather than solving it.

Ethiopia, Angola, and Mozambique have already made it clear they are not interested in becoming other Cubas—countries completely dependent upon the Soviet Union for their survival. An antagonistic policy on the part of the United States pursued in the hope of forcing their collapse, however, could push them in that direction. Their dependence would probably never be quite as total because of alternative economic ties to Western Europe. Nonetheless, a closer relationship to the Soviet bloc than even the Marxist-Leninist regimes seek, or desire, would hardly serve American interests, not to mention their own. The United States can influence to some extent the closeness of their relationship with the Soviet bloc. By refusing to recognize the MPLA government, for example, the Carter administration did not make its demise any more likely but did increase its dependence upon the Soviet bloc and vulnerability to Soviet pressure. Conversely, that administration's policy of seeking a peaceful resolution of the Namibia conflict, if successful, would be certain to reduce the South African threat to Angola and thereby make it possible for the MPLA to dispense with Cuban troops. Similarly, while Washington cannot itself resolve the conflicts in the Ogaden and Eritrea, it could worsen them by offering arms to Somalia in order to obtain air and naval facilities there. By so doing, however, it would only help to perpetuate Ethiopia's reliance upon Soviet and Cuban military aid.

The question remains of what the United States can reasonably expect to gain by accepting the existence of the Afrocommunist states, establishing normal diplomatic ties, and even extending some aid to them. On the economic side, an answer has already been given by the American corporations that have shown an interest in investing there or in buying their minerals and agricultural produce. Politically, the answer is more complex, for there is little likelihood that these states will ever become close allies of the United States. Realistically, they can only evolve in their foreign policy in one of two directions: they could become more like Cuba or they could become more like Algeria. The Algerian outcome seems not only infinitely preferable but distinctly possible if the United States does not become obsessed by the fear of the spread of communism in Africa and implacably hostile to the Afrocommunist regimes. Algeria is a militant spokesman of Third World demands for a new economic order, but it is simultaneously an important trading partner for the United States and the West, as well as a country offering excellent opportunities for Western investment. It is not nonaligned in the sense of being neutral or equidistant from the East and West, but neither is it a close ally of the Soviet Union or does it allow the Soviets "access to facilities" on a regular basis. The United States has learned to live with, and has come to respect, Algeria as a representative of a militant but independent Third World position. The Afrocommunist states already share with Algeria its militant Third World outlook and its desire for economic relations with the West. They could well evolve toward a less aligned position on geopolitical issues once they feel they are not so threatened and their need for the Soviet military shield slackens. In other words, they could well become similar to Algeria in the degree of their independence in foreign policy from the Soviet bloc.

We have used Ethiopia, Angola, and Mozambique to illustrate what we believe is the emergence of a new phenomenon on the African continent, namely Afrocommunism. These three countries are not typical or representative in all respects of all the other self-professed Marxist-Leninist regimes in Africa. They are more radical in their domestic policies, often more orthodox in their ideological outlook, and more closely aligned with, and dependent upon, the Soviet Union. In other words, they are the purest examples of Afrocommunism. Other Marxist-Leninist governments nonetheless share the same general world outlook and are moving roughly along the same road in their domestic policies. The concept of Afrocommunism, then, has a broader relevance in the long run than for just the three countries we have examined in this study. Afrocommunism is still in its infancy, but some of its characteristics are already becoming clear enough to argue that it is something distinct from African socialism. Whether it is a desirable phenomenon can only be answered in light of the likely alternatives. The West doubtless would regard it as preferable if Africa remained within its sphere of influence as it has been since the nineteenth century. But it is already evident history is not moving in that direction. Marxism-Leninism is spreading on the continent and is likely to continue doing so given the failure of both socialist and nonsocialist countries to solve the two central problems of real national independence and economic growth. It is entirely possible that the Marxist-Leninist regimes will also fail to solve these problems, in which case Afrocommunism, like African socialism before it, will become a passing and self-containing phenomenon in the long run. For the time being, Afrocommunism still has its appeal within Africa, and the United States will have to learn to deal with its proponents. It is at least preferable to the multiplication of outright Soviet satellites on the African continent and less risky than embarking upon a policy of active destabilization of the Marxist-Leninist regimes, an activism which could so easily turn against American interests across the continent.

Notes

Chapter I

1. David D. Newsom, Under Secretary of State for Political Affairs, Remarks before the Subcommittee on African Affairs of the House Committee on Foreign Affairs, October 18, 1979.
2. Walter Laquer, "Communism and Nationalism in Tropical Africa," *Foreign Affairs*, 39, no. 4 (July 1961).
3. René Dumont, "Un Nécessaire Aggiornamento des Socialismes," in Réne Dumont et Marcel Mazoyer, *Dèvelopment et Socialismes* (Paris: Editions du Seuil, 1969), p. 97.
4. See, for example, William H. Friedland and Carl C. Rosberg, Jr., *African Socialism* (Stanford: Stanford University Press, 1964), pp. 1–11, and Kenneth Jowitt, "Scientific Socialist Regimes in Africa: Political Differentiation, Avoidance and Unawareness," in Carl G. Rosberg and Thomas M. Callagy, *Socialism in Sub-Saharan Africa* (Berkeley: Institute of International Studies, University of California, 1979), pp. 133–173.
5. Interview with President Julius Nyerere, January 5, 1979.
6. See "'Afrocommunism' Seen New Force in Mozambique," in the *Washington Post*, February 16, 1977.
7. See the *Washington Post*, December 15, 1978.

Chapter II

1. Julius Nyerere, *Ujamaa—Essays on Socialism* (Dar es Salaam: Oxford University Press, 1968), p. 11.
2. Ibid.
3. Lépold Senghor, *On African Socialism*, trans., Mercer Cook (New York: Frederick A. Praeger, 1964), p. 26.
4. Ibid., p. 94.
5. K. D. Kaunda, *Humanism in Zambia, Part I* (Lusaka: Zambia Information Services, 1976).
6. Ahmed Sékou Touré, *The Doctrine and Methods of the Democratic Party of Guinea, Part II* (Conakry: n.d.), p. 26.
7. Kwame Nkrumah, *Revolutionary Path* (New York: International Publishers, 1973), p. 205.
8. Nyerere, p. 77.
9. Nyerere, p. 78.
10. Touré, *Doctrine and Methods,* part II, p. 24.
11. Nkrumah, *Revolutionary Path,* p. 436.
12. Idrissa Diarra, "The Mass Party and Socialist Construction," in *Africa: National and Social Revolution* (Prague: Peace and Socialism Publishers, 1967), p. 120.

13. Lansana Diané, Interview with the *World Marxist Review* 19, no. 8 (August 1976): p. 110.

14. Afro-Shirazi Party Declaration to the 25th CPSU, Congress, *World Marxist Review* 19, no. 5, (May 1976): pp. 82–83.

15. Kaunda, p. 6.

16. Nyerere, p. 89.

17. Ibid.

18. Sékou Touré, part I, p. 160.

19. Kwame Nkrumah, *Consciencism* (New York: Monthly Review Press, 1964), p. 79.

20. Nkrumah, *Revolutionary Path,* p. 181 ff.

21. Nkrumah, " 'African Socialism' Revisited," *African Forum,* I, no. 3 (1966), in *Revolutionary Path,* p. 440.

22. Ibid.

23. Ibid.

24. Ibid., p. 442.

25. Ibid.

26. Ibid., p. 446.

27. Nkrumah, Extracts from *Class Struggle in Africa,* in *Revolutionary Path,* p. 489.

28. Ibid.

29. "Constitution of the Convention People's Party," in Nkrumah, *Revolutionary Path,* p. 59.

30. Nkrumah, *Revolutionary Path,* p. 163.

31. Ibid., p. 169.

32. Nkrumah, "The Myth of the 'Third World,' " in *Revolutionary Path,* p. 436.

33. Ibid., p. 438.

34. Ibid., p. 439.

35. Sékou Touré, *Le Pouvoir Populaire* (Conakry: Imprimerie Patrice Lumumba, 1968), vol. XVI, p. 161.

36. *Horoya—Special,* October 2, 1970.

37. *Horoya,* No. 2204, January 10, 1976.

38. Ibid.

39. Quoted by Lansana Diané, *World Marxist Review* 19, no. 8 (August 1976): p. 109.

40. "Message from President Sékou Touré," in *Resolutions and Selected Speeches from the Sixth Pan-Africanist Congress* (Dar es Salaam: Tanzania Publishing House, 1976), pp. 16–17.

41. Ibid.

42. Ibid.

43. See Front de Libération Nationale, *La Charte d'Alger* (Algiers: Imprimerie Nationale Algerienne, 1964).

44. Front de Libération Nationale, *Charte Nationale* (Algiers: Editions Populaires de l'Armee, 1976), pp. 26–7.

45. Ibid., p. 46.

46. Ibid., p. 27.

47. Ibid., p. 36.

48. Speech of November 1, 1965 in *Les Discours du Président Boumédiène* (Algiers: Ministry of Information, 1966), p. 91.

49. *Charte Nationale,* p. 108.

50. Ibid.
51. Ibid.
52. Ibid., p. 110.
53. Ibid., p. 114.
54. Ibid.
55. Unpublished interview with David Martin of the London *Observer,* August 11, 1977.
56. *The African Communist,* no. 74 (1978), p. 65.
57. *World Marxist Review* 19, no. 5 (May 1976), p. 71.
58. *Central Committee Report to the Third Congress of Frelimo* (London: Mozambique, Angola and Guinea Information Center, 1978), p. 23 ff.
59. Amilcar Cabral, *Revolution in Guinea: Selected Texts* (New York: Monthly Review, 1969), pp. 56–75.
60. *The African Communist,* no. 74 (1978), p. 33.
61. Cabral, p. 110.
62. Interview with Lucio Lara, *The African Communist,* no. 74, (1978), p. 33.
63. *Central Committee Report to the Third Congress of Frelimo,* p. 22.
64. Ibid., p. 64.
65. *The African Communist,* no. 74 (1978), p. 31.
66. Ibid., p. 30.
67. "Theses: What Are Their Objectives?", a document presented for discussion by Frelimo prior to the Third Congress, February 3–7, 1977, mimeo.
68. Ibid.
69. Speeches to the nation, November 13 and 14, 1977, quoted in Amnesty International, Swedish Medical Group, "Human Rights Violations in Ethiopia," 1977, p. 6.
70. "Fourth Anniversary of the Ethiopian Revolution," speech delivered by Lt. Col. Mengistu Haile-Mariam, September 12, 1978 (Addis Ababa: Ministry of Information).
71. Interview with President Didier Ratsiraka, *Afrique-Asie,* no. 151 (December 26, 1977).
72. "The Non-aligned Movement: A Decisive Force in the Anti-Imperialist Struggle," January 30, 1979, Agencia de Informaçao de Moçambique, mimeo.
73. Pyotor Manchkha, *Africa on the New Road* (Moscow: Novosti Press Agency Publishing House), p. 56.
74. Ibid., pp. 130 and 139.
75. Ibid., p. 149.
76. George Padmore, *Pan-Africanism or Communism* (New York: Doubleday & Company, Inc., 1972).

Chapter III

1. *The Daily Mail,* May 7, 1979.
2. See, for example, International Labor Office, *Narrowing the Gaps* (Addis Ababa: 1977); Alan Marter and David Honeybone, *The Economic Resources of Rural Households and the Distribution of Agricultural Development* (Lusaka: University of Zambia, Rural Development Studies Bureau, 1976); United States Agency for International Development, *Development Needs and Opportunities for Cooperation in Southern Africa, Annex A. Zambia* (Washington: 1979).

3. Richard Sklar, *Corporate Power in an African State* (Berkeley: University of California Press, 1975), p. 193.
4. *Narrowing the Gaps*, p. 212.
5. Ibid., p. 8.
6. Ibid., pp. 221-222.
7. Ibid., pp. 213-14.
8. Ibid., p. 34.
9. *Development Needs, Zambia*, p. 26.
10. *Industrial Zambia*, April 1979, p. 34.
11. Kenneth Kaunda, *Humanism in Zambia and a Guide to Its Implementation*, part I (Lusaka: Zambia Information Services, n.d.), p. 27.
12. Kenneth Kaunda, *Zambia's Economic Revolution* (Lusaka: Zambia Information Services, 1968), p. 14.
13. Personal communications with researchers on unemployment in the squatter compounds.
14. Doris Jansen Dodge, *Agricultural Policy and Performance in Zambia* (Berkeley: Institute of International Studies, University of California, 1977), p. 56.
15. Ibid., p. 68.
16. *Narrowing the Gaps*, p. 115.
17. Kenneth Kaunda, *Zambia's Guideline for the Next Decade* (Lusaka: Zambia Information Service, 1968), p. 32.
18. For a detailed discussion, see Patrick Ollawa, "Rural Development Strategy and Performance in Zambia: An Evaluation of Past Efforts," *The African Studies Review*, 21, no. 2 (September 1978): pp. 101-124.
19. Ibid., p. 116.
20. Jan Pettman, *Zambia: Security and Conflict* (London: Julian Friedmann, 1976), p. 139.
21. Personal communication. The Zambia Cooperative Federation claimed to have 300 affiliated unions with a total of 100,000 members. These figures seem doubtful in view of the fact that most of the cooperatives were not functioning. See the *Times of Zambia*, March 12, 1979.
22. Ollawa, p. 112.
23. Kenneth Kaunda, *The Watershed Speech* (Lusaka: Zambia Information Services, 1975), p. 4.
24. William Tordoff, ed., *Politics in Zambia* (Manchester: Manchester University Press, 1974), p. 385.
25. Kenneth Kaunda, speech of March 23, 1970 before the Lusaka Seminar on Rural Development. Author's notes.
26. *Watershed Speech*, p. 31.
27. The authors visited Mwenda Pole in January 1979. The information presented here is based on this visit and talks with village officials.
28. Unpublished World Bank report.
29. Dean E. McHenry Jr., *Tanzania's Ujamaa Villages* (Berkeley: Institute of International Studies, University of California, 1979), p. 45.
30. McHenry, p. 117.
31. Estimates of various Western embassies in Dar es Salaam.
32. Personal communication with officials in the office of the presidency, January 1979.
33. Julius Nyerere, *The Arusha Declaration Ten Years After* (Dar es Salaam: Government Printer, 1977), p. 1.
34. Ibid., p. 2.

35. Ibid., pp. 2–3.
36. Ibid., p. 27.
37. Ibid., p. 32.
38. Ibid.
39. United Nations Economic Commission for Africa, *Survey of Economic and Social Conditions in Africa, 1977–78,* part II, section B, p. 370.
40. Ibid., p. 372. The World Bank, in an unpublished report, estimated that there had been no growth rate at all in per capita production during the same period.
41. *Survey of Economic and Social Conditions,* p. 370.
42. Ibid.
43. Personal communication, January 1979.
44. Shankar N. Acharya, "Perspectives and Problems of Development in Low Income, Sub-Saharan Africa," in *Two Studies of Development in Sub-Saharan Africa,* World Bank Staff Working Paper No. 300, October 1978, p. 21.
45. Unpublished World Bank report.
46. *Arusha Ten Years After,* p. 34.
47. Ibid., p. 16.
48. Acharya, p. 22.
49. *Arusha Ten Years After,* p. 52.
50. Acharya, p. 52.
51. In 1975, a Swedish survey found that many pumps were inoperative even though in good mechanical order. J. E. Engstrom and J. F. Wann, *An Inventory of Rural Water Supply Projects in Tanzania,* Swedish Development Agency, 1975. More recent reports suggest that the situation has become markedly worse with a sharp increase in mechanical breakdowns.
52. *Arusha Ten Years After,* p. 15.
53. McHenry, particularly Chapter III.
54. Ibid., pp. 61–74.
55. Unpublished World Bank data.
56. Ibid.
57. W. Edmond Clark, *Socialist Development and Public Investment in Tanzania, 1964–73* (Toronto: University of Toronto Press, 1978), p. 195.
58. Unpublished World Bank data.
59. Quoted in Claude Rivière, *Mutations Sociales en Guinée* (Paris: Marcel Rivière et Cie., 1971), p. 394.
60. Julien Condé, "La Situation Démographique en République de Guinée," in *Revue Française d'Etudes Politiques Africaines,* no. 123 (March 1976), p. 122.
61. U.S. Department of State, "Foreign Economic Trends and Their Implications for the United States, Guinea," December 1978, p. 2.
62. Henri de Decker, *Nation et Développement Communautaire en Guinée et au Sénégal* (Paris: Mouton, 1967), p. 73.
63. Sekou Touré, *The Doctrine and Methods of the Democratic Party of Guinea, part II* (Conakry: n.d.), p. 48.
64. See *Africa Contemporary Record,* X (1977–78): p. B659.
65. Quoted in Thomas E. O'Toole, *Historical Dictionary of Guinea,* (Metuchen, NJ: Scarecrow Press, 1978), p. 55.
66. Ladipo Adamokekun, "The Socialist Experience in Guinea," in Carl Rosberg and Thomas Callaghy, eds., *Socialism in Sub-Saharan Africa* (Berkeley: Institute of International Studies, University of California, 1979), pp. 61–82. See also "Foreign Economic Trends, Guinea," p. 7.
67. Adamolekun, p. 69.

220   Notes

68. Personal communication with Ambassador William C. Harrop, December 1979.
69. *Horoya,* No. 2228, July 4–10, 1976.
70. *Area Handbook for Guinea* (Washington: U.S. Government Printing Office, 1975), p. 253.
71. U.S. State Department sources.
72. See *Area Handbook,* pp. 273–83; Claude Riviè, "L'Economie Guinéenne," in *Revue Française d'Etudes Politiques Africaines,* no. 114 (June 1975), pp. 48–49; and Alain Cournanel, "Le Capitalisme d'Etat en Afrique: le Cas Guinéen," in *Revue Francaise,* no. 123 (March 1976), pp. 42–51.
73. Ibid.
74. *Area Handbook,* p. 270.
75. International Monetary Fund report quoted in *Jeune Afrique,* no. 942 (Jan. 24, 1979), p. 28. Translation by authors.
76. For Algeria, see US State Department, "Foreign Economic Trends and Their Implications for the United States, Algeria," 1979, p. 1. For Tanzania, see US State Department, "Foreign Economic Trends and Their Implications for the United States, Tanzania," 1978, p. 1.
77. For more details, see the authors' book, *Algeria: The Politics of a Socialist Revolution* (Berkeley: University of California Press, 1971).
78. Proclamation of June 19, 1965, in *Les Discours du President Boumèdiène, 1965–66* (Algiers: Ministry of Information, 1966), p. 5.
79. *Révolution Africaine,* No. 279, June 24–30, 1968.
80. Paolo Santacroce, *Transizione o Nuova Dipendenza? l'Algeria degli Anni Settanta* (Torino: Rosenberg & Sellier, 1978), p. 27 and p. 74.
81. Ibid., p. 29.
82. "Foreign Economic Trends, Algeria," p. 4.
83. Boumédiène's speech to the National Assembly, March 31, 1977, quoted in *Afrique-Asie,* no. 178 (Jan. 8, 1979), p. 44.
84. Boumédiène's speech to special session of the United Nations on raw materials, April 10, 1974, ibid.
85. "Foreign Economic Trends, Algeria," p. 4.
86. IMF report quoted in *Jeune Afrique,* no. 942 (Jan. 24, 1979), p. 31.
87. Government figures for the amount of land, number of cooperatives and number of socialist villages established quoted in *Afrique-Asie,* no. 178, (Jan. 8, 1979), p. 26. Estimate of dropout rate from Peter Knauss, "Algeria's 'Agrarian Revolution:' Peasant Control or Control of Peasants?.," paper delivered to the annual meeting of the African Studies Association, Boston, November 1976, p. 18.
88. Front de Libération Nationale, *Charte Nationale* (Algiers: 1976), p. 46.
89. Ibid., p. 31.
90. Ibid., p. 91.
91. *Révolution Africaine,* May 16–22, 1979, p. 17.

Chapter IV

1. Samora Machel, *Le Processus de la Révolution Démocratique Populaire au Mozambique* (Paris: Editions l'Harmattan, 1977), p. 50. This volume collects all the main wartime Frelimo documents, in addition to the essay which provides the title

2. Ibid., p. 70.
3. Ibid., p. 70–71.
4. Ibid., p. 77.
5. Ibid., p. 81.
6. Anders Johansson, *Struggle in Mozambique* (New Delhi: Indian Council for Africa, n.d.). This pamphlet by a Swedish journalist is based on a visit to the liberated zones with Eduardo Mondlane in 1968.
7. Ibid.
8. *Central Committee Report to the Third Congress of Frelimo* (London: Mozambique, Angola, and Guinea Information Center, 1978), p. 14.
9. Machel, *Le Processus*, p. 67.
10. Ibid., p. 69.
11. United States Agency for International Development, "Development Needs and Opportunities for Cooperation in Southern Africa, Annex A, Mozambique," 1979, p. 35.
12. United Nations General Assembly, Report of the Economic and Social Council, "Assistance to Mozambique," October 1976, p. 10.
13. *Quarterly Economic Review of Angola and Mozambique*, Annual Supplement, 1977, p. 19. Other studies, including Portuguese statistics, put the figure of "modern" farms at 4,000, without specifying whether all modern farms were Portuguese. See Allen Isaacman, *A Luta Continua: Creating a New Society in Mozambique* (Binghampton, NY: Fernand Braudel Center for the Study of Economies, Historical Systems, and Civilizations, 1978), p. 123.
14. Western embassy sources provided the figures for the drop in production of cashews and cotton. For those concerning overall exports, see "Development Needs, Mozambique," p. 41.
15. Ibid., p. 8.
16. Department of State, "Annual Economic Trends Report, Mozambique," 1974.
17. *Central Committee Report*, p. 24.
18. Frelimo *Statutes*, art. 3.
19. "Extracts from the Report of the Standing Political Committee to the Fourth Session of the Central Committee of Frelimo, Presented by President Samora Machel," in Agencia de Informação de Mozambique, *Dossier*, 4th Session of the Central Committee of Frelimo Elected by the Third Congress, Maputo, August 7–16, p. 4.
20. Ibid., p. 6.
21. *Central Committee Report*, p. 21.
22. Thesis n. 2, in "Theses: What are They and What are Their Objectives?", mimeo, n.d.
23. Ibid.
24. Samora Machel, "Nôtre Tâche Pour 1979," Entrevue Accordée par le Président Samora Machel à La Presse Nationale à la Fin de l'Année 1978. Agencia de Informação de Mozambique, pp. 11–12.
25. Ibid., p. 22.
26. Thesis no. 4, in "Theses: What are They?"
27. "The New Man is a Process," speech by Sergio Vieria to the Second Conference of the Ministry of Education, December 1977, mimeo., p. 10.
28. Ibid., p. 15.
29. "La Libération de la Femme Est Une Necessité," in Machel, *Le Processus*, p. 164.
30. Frelimo *Statutes*, art. 1.
31. Ibid., art. 11.
32. Ibid., art. 13.

33. "Economic and Social Directives," in *People's Power in Mozambique, Angola, and Guinea-Bissau,* no. 7-8 (June 1977), p. 20.

34. Ibid.

35. Ibid.

36. Ibid., p. 27.

37. Oscar Monteiro, "L'Action du Parti dans l'Appareil de l'Etat," Ministry of Information Release, n.d., mimeo.

38. Frelimo *Statutes,* art. 9.

39. For more detail on the election, see Isaacman, ch. 2, and *People's Power,* no. 10 (October–December 1977), pp. 10-15.

40. *Central Committee Report,* p. 56.

41. Ibid.

42. For example, see *Tempo,* no. 468 (September 30, 1979), p. 39 ff.

43. Machel "Notre Tache Pour 1979," pp. 3-4.

44. Monteiro, p. 1.

45. "Résolution sur Les Villages Communautaires," 8 ème Session du Comité Central, Maputo, 11-27 February 1976 (Paris: Centre d'Information sur le Mozambique, n.d.), p. 3.

46. United States Agency for International Development, "Development Needs and Opportunities for Cooperation in Southern Africa, Annex B, Agriculture," March 1979, p. 3.

47. "Development Needs, Mozambique", p. 53.

48. Ibid., p. 50, and United Nations General Assembly, Report of the Economic and Social Council, "Assistance to Mozambique," June 1977, p. 28.

49. Agencia de Informação de Mozambique, Information Bulletin No. 26, August 1978, p. 8.

50. Personal communication.

51. *Tempo,* no. 466 (September 16, 1979), p. 6.

52. Personal communication with Job Chambal, Head, National Commission for the Communal Villages, June 1979.

53. These figures were given by the National Commission for Communal Villages in June 1979. The figure of 1,500 villages, which has appeared in some official speeches earlier, was apparently wrong.

54. *Tempo,* no. 419 (October 15, 1978), p. 28ff. Case studies of communal villages also appeared in nos. 418, 434, and 435.

55. Government figures published in early 1980 showed the following percentage increases without making it clear whether it was over the preceeding year or since independence: rice, 15 percent; maize, 50 percent; peanuts, 50 percent; cotton, 38 percent; citrus fruits, 40 percent. In addition, coal production was reported to have jumped from 118,000 tons to 210,000 tons; sugar from 179,300 to 214,000 and the shrimp catch from 1,800 tons to 2,500 tons. *Tempo,* Jan. 13, 1980. For the government estimate of food import needs, see United Nations General Assembly, Report of the Economic and Social Council, August 16, 1979, p. 9.

56. Decree-Law 18/77, trans., Department of State, Division of Language Services, LS no. 64325, mimeo, p. 2.

57. For a discussion of the law on the nationalization of land, see *Tempo,* no. 459 (July 29, 1979), and no. 468 (September 30, 1979).

58. *People's Power,* no. 10 (October–December 1977), p. 21.

59. See Carole Collins, "Dynamizing the People," *Issues* 8, no. 1 (Spring 1978), pp. 12-16, and *People's Power,* no. 10 (October–December 1977), p. 21 ff. For a very positive view of production councils' role in management at least one industrial enterprise, see Peter Sketchley, "Problems of the Transformation of Social Relations of Production in Post-Independence Mozambique," in *People Power,* no. 15 (Winter 1979).

60. See Isaacman, p. 121.
61. For discussion of villagers' grievances, see *Tempo,* no. 435 (February 4, 1979).
62. "Development Needs, Mozambique," p. 49.
63. From diplomatic sources.
64. United Nations, "Assistance to Mozambique," 1979, p. 7.
65. Ibid.
66. United Nations, "Assistance to Mozambique," 1976, p. 3.
67. "Development Needs, Mozambique," p. 47.
68. United Nations, "Assistance to Mozambique, 1979," p. 5.
69. Isaacman, p. 69.
70. "Development Needs," Mozambique," p. 67ff.
71. *People's Power,* no. 13 (Spring 1979), p. 32. The entire issue is dedicated to the health system of Mozambique and contains additional detail.
72. Ibid., p. 42.

Chapter V

1. Interview with Lucio Lara, *African Communist,* no. 75, fourth quarter (1978), p. 54.
2. Agostinho Neto, in *Afrique-Asie,* no. 198 (October 15, 1979).
3. Ibid.
4. Ibid.
5. Gerald Bender, *Angola under the Poruguese, The Myth and the Reality* (Berkeley: University of California, 1978), p. 158.
6. John A. Marcum, *The Angolan Revolution, vol. II, Exile Politics and Guerrilla Warfare* (Cambridge: The MIT Press, 1978), p. 53.
7. Basil Davidson, *In the Eye of the Storm* (New York: Doubleday, 1972), p. 211.
8. Agostinho Neto, in *Afrique-Asie,* no. 198 (October 15, 1979).
9. Mouvement Populaire de Libération de l'Angola, *Angola: Exploitation Esclavagiste, Résistance Nationale,* pp. 63–67.
10. Donald Barnett and Roy Harvey, *The Revolution in Angola* (Indianapolis: The Bobbs-Merrill Company, 1972), p. 259.
11. Ibid., pp. 20–21.
12. *Textos do M.P.L.A. Sobre a Revolução Angolana* (Lisbon: Ediçoes Maria da Fonte, 1974), p. 81.
13. Davidson, "Walking 300 Miles with Guerrillas," p. 8, quoted in Marcum, p. 229.
14. Ibid., p. 56.
15. Barnett and Harvey, p. 19.
16. Davidson, p. 286.
17. Ibid., p. 287.
18. Commander Spartacus Monimambu provides the only credible figure for the civilian population under MPLA control, but his estimate was given in 1968. Another commander, Setta Likambuila, claimed in mid-1970 that "over half a million" Angolans were living in semiliberated zones. This figure seems high given the fact that over one million Angolans in guerrilla areas were put in Portuguese resettlements, including 70 percent of the total population in the eastern provinces of Lunda and Moxico. Bender quotes the Governor of Moxico as saying that at one point 140,000 in his district were "under guerrilla control," but 80 percent had been subsequently resettled. See Barnett and Harvey, p. 284, and Bender, p. 171.

19. Davidson, p. 282.
20. Ole Gjerstad, *The People in Power* (Oakland: LSM Information Center, 1976), p. 2.
21. Barnett and Harvey, p. 24.
22. Ibid.
23. See, for example, the account of the trip by Barnett and Harvey through the MPLA semiliberated zones in eastern Angola during 1966, ibid., pp. 48–65.
24. Davidson, p. 282.
25. Barnett, pp. 18–19.
26. Ibid., p. 282.
27. Marcum, p. 202.
28. Daniel Chipenda, "MPLA: Nos Efforts en Faveur de l'Unité," Kinshasa, 1974, p. 10.
29. Ibid.
30. Amilcar Cabral was the assassinated first leader of the nationalist liberation movement in Guinea-Bissau. Hoji Ia Henda was the MPLA's top military commander in 1968, when he was killed while assaulting a Portuguese outpost near the Zambian border. The outside groups involved in setting up these committees included the Portuguese Communist Party, the Maoist Portuguese MRPP and independent Portuguese Marxists and Trotskyites. For more details on the work of these groups, see C. Gabriel, "Angola in the Whirlwind of Permanent Revolution," London, n.d.
31. Marcum p. 257. The number of militia members is the author's best estimate based on personal observation during the civil war.
32. Ibid., p. 259.
33. Agostinho Neto, speech delivered to the 15th Assembly of OAU Heads of State and Government, Khartoum, the Sudan, July 20, 1978, mimeo.
34. Marcum, p. 252.
35. MPLA First Congress, "Central Committee Report and Thesis on Education" (London: Mozambique, Angola and Guinea Information Center, 1979), p. 28, and United States Agency for International Development, "Development Needs and Opportunities for Cooperation in Southern Africa, Annex A, Angóla," 1979, p. 58.
36. "Development Needs, Angola," p. 2.
37. Ibid.
38. *Washington Post,* July 17, 1975.
39. *Quarterly Economic Review of Angola, Mozambique,* Annual Supplement 1977, p. 5.
40. Portuguese Ministry of Foreign Affairs, *Portuguese Africa, An Introduction* (Lisbon: 1973), p. 67.
41. *Quarterly Economic Review of Angola, Mozambique,* Annual Supplement, 1977, p. 9.
42. "Development Needs, Angola," p. 68.
43. Henrique Guerra, *Angola* Luanda: Ediçoes Maiaka, n.d.), p. 131.
44. "Development Needs, Angola," p. 36, and Guerra, p. 65.
45. Guerra, p. 55.
46. Ibid., p. 70.
47. Bender, p. 168.
48. Ibid., p. 228.
49. Ibid., p. 229.
50. Ibid., p. 195.

51. Ibid.

52. United Nations High Commission for Refugees estimates provided to the authors in Kinshasa. The UNHCR high commissioner in Luanda was quoted as estimating the number of displaced persons and refugees as "more than a million." See *Quarterly Economic Review of Angola, Mozambique,* 3rd Quarter (1977), p. 9.

53. See David M. Abshire and Michael A. Samuels, *Portuguese Africa* (New York: Praeger, 1969), p. 7, and Bender, p. 222.

54. "Development Needs, Angola," p. 11.

55. Angola's estimated GNP was $2.34 billion in 1974 and $1.83 billion in 1976, a drop of about $500 million, or roughly 20 percent. See "Development Needs, Angola," p. 20.

56. Ibid., p. 69 and p. 38.

57. Ibid., p. 74.

58. Ibid., p. 73.

59. Ibid., p. 86.

60. Ibid., p. 81.

61. Ibid., p. 39.

62. Ibid., p. 45.

63. Conselho da Revolução, "Lei do Poder Popular," no. 1/76, p. 5.

64. Ibid.

65. Ibid.

66. Ibid., p. 11.

67. Ibid., p. 15 and p. 26.

68. Ibid., p. 13.

69. "Documents," MPLA Central Committee, Plenary, 23–29 October 1976, (London: Mozambique, Angola, and Guinea Information Center, 1976), pp. 4–5.

70. Ibid., p. 8.

71. Ibid., p. 10.

72. Ibid., p. 11.

73. Ibid., pp. 11–12.

74. Ibid.

75. Ibid., p. 21.

76. Ibid., p. 26.

77. Ibid., p. 24.

78. Ibid.

79. Ibid., p. 22.

80. Ibid.

81. Foreign Broadcast Information Service, "Daily Report, Sub-Saharan Africa," May 23, 25, 26, 1977.

82. For a detailed account of the Cuban role in helping to crush the Alves coup attempt, see Wilfred Burchett, *Southern Africa Stands Up* (New York: Urizen Books, Inc., 1978), pp. 113–116.

83. Ibid., p. 111.

84. Foreign Broadcast Information Service, "Daily Report, Sub-Saharan Africa," June 10, 1977.

85. "MPLA First Congress," p. 11.

86. Ibid.

87. Ibid., pp. 12–13.

88. "The Constitution of MPLA into a Party of the Working Class," *People's Power* in Mozambique, Angola and Guinea-Bissau, no. 11 (January–March 1978), p. 49.
89. "MPLA First Congress," p. 16.
90. Ibid.
91. Ibid., p. 17.
92. *Washington Post,* May 7, 1976.
93. "Development Needs, Angola," p. 69.
94. "MPLA First Congress," p. 30.
95. *Afrique-Asie,* "Special Angola," June 26, 1978, p. XXV.
96. Ibid., p. XXXI.
97. "Documents, MPLA Central Committee," pp. 10–11.
98. "MPLA First Congress," p. 29.
99. "Development Needs, Angola," p. 45, and *Afrique-Asie,* June 26, 1978, p. XXIV.
100. "Development Needs, Angola," p. 45, and *Afrique-Asie,* June 26, 1978, p. XXXIII.
101. *Afrique-Asie,* June 26, 1978, p. XXXIII.
102. Ibid.
103. Ibid.
104. Ibid.
105. *People's Power,* no. 5 (November-December 1976), p. 6.
106. Ibid., p. 7.
107. "Development Needs, Angola," p. 39.
108. *Angola-1978,* Bulletin d'Information, 1978 (French translation).
109. "MPLA First Congress," p. 11.
110. *Boletim de Informação* I, no. 2 (April 1979), p. 4.
111. Ibid.
112. *Afrique-Asie,* June 26, 1978, p. XI.
113. Ibid., p. X.
114. *Jornal de Angola,* Dec. 11, 1978.
115. Ibid.
116. *People's Power,* no. 11 (January–March 1978), p. 30.
117. "MPLA First Congress," pp. 40–41.
118. Ibid.
119. The 1978 budget contains an entry labeled "education, health, sports, and culture" and another labeled "economic and social development." Thus, it is impossible to establish the precise share for education alone. The breakdown of the total budget of 41 billion kwanzas is as follows: economic and social development, 26 percent; education, health, sports and culture, 16.8 percent; defense and security, 24.8 percent; general charges, 30.7 percent; and public debt servicing, 1.6 percent. See *Angola-1978.* The official exchange rate then was 29 kwanzas for one dollar.
120. "MPLA First Congress," p. 22.

Chapter VI

1. "Ethiopia *Tikdem:* The Origins and Future Direction of the Movement," Addis Ababa, December 20, 1974, mimeo.

2. The World Bank, "World Development Report, 1979," p. 126. The same report classifies Ethiopia as the world's fifth poorest country and the poorest in Africa.

3. Authors' estimate. For more detail see David and Marina Ottaway, *Ethiopia: Empire in Revolution* (New York: Africana Publishers, 1978), p. 17 ff.

4. Ibid., p. 21 ff.

5. "Address by Comrade Lieutenant Colonel Mengistu Haile-Mariam, Chairman of the PMAC and the Council of Ministers and Commander in Chief of the Revolutionary Army, at the Launching of the National Revolutionary Development Campaign," February 3, 1979, mimeo, p. 3.

6. All the information on which this section is based is derived either from clandestine pamphlets we were able to obtain or from personal communications with a variety of individuals closely involved in the events. Neither type of source lends itself to being documented. For a detailed analysis of the ideological debate, see also Marina Ottaway, "Democracy and New Democracy: The Ideological Debate in the Ethiopian Revolution," *African Studies Review*, April 1978.

7. See the mock debate between *Democracia* and the *Voice of the Masses* in *Addis Zemen*, April 3, 1976.

8. Mengistu's National Democratic Revolution speech (*Ethiopian Herald*, April 21, 1976) stated that "the nationalities are guaranteed regional autonomy." The same position was expressed in the *Derg*'s "Nine-Point Policy" on Eritrea, issued on May 16, 1976 (*Ethiopian Herald*, May 18, 1976).

9. *Ethiopian Herald*, April 21, 1976.

10. Proclamation no. 31 of 1975. "A Proclamation to Provide for the Public Ownership of Rural Lands," March 4, 1975. *Negarit Gazeta*, April 29, 1975.

11. Proclamation no. 71 of 1975, "Peasant Association Organization and Consolidation Proclamation," *Negarit Gazeta*, December 14, 1975.

12. Proclamation of June 26, 1979, on the "Establishment of Producers' Cooperatives," *Addis Zemen*, June 26, 1979.

13. For more detail on the *zemacha*, see Marina Ottaway, "Land Reform and Peasant Associations in Ethiopia: A Preliminary Analysis," *Rural Africana*, Fall 1975.

14. See also Ottaways, p. 85 ff.

15. The Provisional Military Government of Socialist Ethiopia, "National Revolutionary Development Campaign and Central Planning Supreme Council: Its Aims and Objectives," Addis Ababa, November 1978, p. 9.

16. Ibid.

17. Ibid.

18. Unpublished study prepared for the World Employment Research Program, 1979.

19. Ibid.

20. Ibid. Other estimates give a much higher number of producers' cooperatives, but these figures are probably more reliable in light of the difficulties the government faced in its attempt to form the cooperatives.

21. Mengistu's Speech of September 12, 1978, in Provisional Military Administrative Council, "The National Revolutionary Economic and Cultural Campaign," Addis Ababa, October 29, 1978, p. 9.

22. Proclamation of June 26, 1979, art. 33.

23. See, for example, the *Ethiopian Herald*, June 28, 1979, and July 1, 1979.

24. Since there had been 40 such producers' cooperatives either formed or in the process of organization in 1978, this means that only about 50 new ones had been established since the June 1979 proclamation. The *Ethiopian Herald*, March 4, 1980.

25. "National Revolutionary Development Campaign, Aims and Objectives," p. 10.

26. Proclamation no. 151 of 1978, *Negarit Gazeta,* October 7, 1978.
27. World Bank sources, personal communication, April 1980.
28. Personal communication with EPID officials, March 1979.
29. Proclamation no. 156 of 1978, "A Proclamation to Provide for the Establishment of the National Revolutionary Development Campaign and Central Planning," in Provisional Military Administrative Council, "The National Revolutionary Economic and Cultural Campaign," Addis Ababa, October 29, 1978, p. 28 ff.
30. "National Revolutionary Development Campaign, Aims and Objectives," p. 10 f.
31. Ibid., p. 11 ff.
32. Ibid., p. 14 f.
33. See the *Ethiopian Herald,* February 5, 27, March 4, 1980, and *Quarterly Economic Review of Uganda, Ethiopia, Somalia and Djibouti,* Fourth Quarter (1979).
34. Personal communication with the Director of the Party School, March 1979.
35. For more detail concerning these organizations, see Ottaways, p. 187 ff.
36. This is indicated by a mimeographed communique issued in Addis Ababa in June 1978 under the title "A Joint Communique on the Transition to Merger and Transitional Period Program of Action." The document indicated that the Union of Ethiopian Marxist-Leninist Organizations at this time only comprised Revolutionary Flame, the Labor League, and the Marxist-Leninist Revolutionary Organization.
37. Mengistu's Speech announcing the formation of COPWE, the *Ethiopian Herald,* December 18, 1979.
38. Ibid.
39. Ibid.
40. Unpublished study prepared for World Employment Research Program, 1979.
41. Personal communication with some of the authors, March 1979.
42. The committees were created by the second land reform proclamation. See Proclamation no. 71 of 1975.
43. Mengistu's speech of September 12, 1978, in "The National Revolutionary Economic and Cultural Campaign," p. 16.
44. Proclamation no. 151 of 1978.
45. Mengistu's Speech of September 12, 1978, in "The National Revolutionary Economic and Cultural Development Campaign," p. 17.
46. Ibid.
47. Ibid., p. 16.
48. Proclamation no. 151 of 1978.
49. Mengistu's speech of February 4, the *Ethiopian Herald,* February 5, 1977.
50. Don Bonker and Paul Tsongas, *War in the Horn of Africa: A Firsthand Report on the Challenges for United States Policy* (Washington: US Government Printing Office, 1978), p. 12.
51. Amnesty International, "The Military Government's 'Red Terror' Campaign," AI Index AFR 25/04/78, March 31, 1978.
52. Ibid.
53. Amnesty International Swedish Medical Group and Swedish Action Group for the Political Prisoners in Ethiopia, "Human Rights Violations in Ethiopia," December 14, 1977.
54. *Times of Zambia,* February 12, 1979.

Chapter VII

1. David Newsom, statement in US Congress, House of Representatives, Hearings before the Sub-Committee on Africa of the Committee on Foreign Affairs, "US Interests in Africa," October and November 1979, p. 50.

2. Ibid.

3. B. Ponomarev, "Invincibility of the Liberation Movement," *Kommunist*, no. 1 January 1980, translated in *Foreign Broadcast Information Service-Soviet Union* (FBIS), vol. III, no. 024, supp. 029, annex 004, Feb. 4, 1980.

4. Ibid., p. 2.

5. Ibid., p. 6.

6. Ibid., p. 14.

7. Ibid.

8. Fidel Castro interview with *Afrique-Asie,* translated in FBIS, *Latin America,* May 9, 1977.

9. For a more detailed analysis of the Soviet view, see David E. Albright, ed., *Communism in Africa* (Bloomington: Indiana University Press, 1980), pp. 35–66. Also see, Marina Ottaway, "Soviet Marxism and African Socialism," *Journal of Modern African Studies,* September 1978, pp. 477–485.

10. Anatoli Gromyko, "Socialist Orientation in Africa," *International Affairs,* no. 9 (1979), pp. 95–104.

11. Ibid., p. 95.

12. Ibid., p. 97.

13. Ibid.

14. Ibid.

15. "A Communist Call to Africa," *The African Communist,* no. 75, Fourth Quarter (1978), p. 18.

16. Friedel Trappen and Ulrich Weishaupt, "Aktuelle Fragen des Kampfes Um Nationale und Soziale Befreiung Um Sub-Saharischen Afrika," *Deutsche Aussenpolitik* 24, no. 2 (February 1979), as quoted by Melvin Croan, "East Germany and Africa," in David Albright and Jiri Valenta, eds., *The Communist States and Africa* (Bloomington: Indiana University Press, forthcoming).

17. Fidel Castro interview with *Afrique-Asie,* translated in FBIS, *Latin America,* May 9, 1977.

18. Ibid.

19. United States Department of State, "Sub-Saharan Africa and the United States," discussion paper, March 1980, p. 31.

20. "US Interests in Africa," p. 61.

21. The authors found no good estimates of East German aid to Africa as the issue is only just beginning to be studied.

22. "A Communist Call to Africa," p. 14.

23. Albright, "Moscow's African Policy of the 1970s," in *Communism in Africa,* p. 42.

24. Ibid.

25. "U.S. Interests in Africa," pp. 94–95.

26. Ibid., pp. 92–93.
27. Ibid., pp. 94–95.
28. *Africa Contemporary Record,* vol. IX, 1976–77, C153.
29. "US Interests in Africa," p. 61 and p. 95.
30. "Sub-Saharan Africa and the United States," p. 31, and "Communist Aid to Less Developed Countries of the Free World," National Foreign Assessment Center, September 1979, p. 13.
31. "US Interests in Africa," p. 95.
32. International Monetary Fund, *Direction of Trade Yearbook,* 1979, p. 65.
33. *Sadex* I, no. 3 (November/December 1979), p. 30.
34. *Africa Confidential* 21, no. 9 (April 23, 1980).
35. *Sadex,* 1, no. 1 (June/July 1979), p. 21.
36. "US Interests in Africa," p. 94.
37. Ibid., p. 61.
38. "Sub-Saharan Africa and the United States," p. 31.
39. *Washington Post,* May 6, 1980.
40. See "US Interests in Africa," p. 94.
41. The figure of $160 million appears in "Communist Aid to the Less Developed Countries of the Free World," p. 23. A spokesman for the National Foreign Assessment Center admitted the figure was wrong in a personal communication.
42. For a text of this treaty, see *Africa Contemporary Record* X (1977–78), pp. C17–19.
43. Quoted in Croan, "East Germany and Africa."
44. "Sub-Saharan Africa and the United States," p. 31.
45. *Washington Post,* March 30, 1977.
46. Computed from figures published in the United Nations General Assembly, Report of the Economic and Social Council, "Assistance to Mozambique," August 16, 1979, pp. 24–25.
47. US Congress, Joint Economic Committee, "Soviet Economy in a Time of Change," II (Oct. 10, 1979), p. 652.
48. Sergius Yakobson, "The Soviet Union and Ethiopia: A Case of Traditional Behavior," in *The Review of Politics* 25, no. 3 (July 1963): 329.
49. Quoted in Yakobson, p. 330.
50. *The Current Digest of the Soviet Press* 31, no. 37 (October 10, 1979), p. 5.
51. *Africa Contemporary Record* X (1977–78), p. B245.
52. "Speech Delivered by Comrade Lt. Colonel Mengistu Haile-Mariam, Chairman of the Revolutionary Army, "Sept. 12, 1978, Addis Ababa, Ministry of Information and National Guidance, p. 29.
53. Croan, "East Germany and Africa."
54. Commission of the European Communities, Spokesman Group, "Lome Convention, State of Commitments and Disbursements at September 30, 1979," December 4, 1979.
55. "MPLA First Congress, Central Committee Report," Mozambique, Angola and Guinea Information Center, London, 1979, p. 25.
56. Ibid.
57. Ibid., p. 26.
58. "Extracts from the Report of the Standing Political Committee to the 4th Session of the Central Committee of Frelimo," Mozambique Information Agency, August 7–16, 1978, p. 17.
59. "Speech Delivered by Comrade Lt. Colonel Mengistu Haile-Mariam," September 12, 1978.

60. "Speech by Mengistu during Kosygin's visit to Ethiopia, *The Current Digest of the Soviet Press,* 31, no. 37 (October 10, 1979), p. 6.

61. *Afrique-Asie,* no. 196 (September 17,1979): p. 22–23.

62. "Extracts from the Report of the Standing Political Committee," August 7–16, 1978, p. 17.

63. "Speech Delivered by His Excellency President Agostinho Neto of the People's Republic of Angola at the 15th Assembly of OAU Heads of State and Government Held in Khartoum," July 20, 1978, mimeo.

64. "MPLA First Congress," p. 20.

65. "Speech delivered by Comrade Lt. Colonel Mengistu Haile-Mariam," September 12, 1978, pp. 13–14.

66. Ibid.

67. *Africa News* XIV, no. 3 (January 21, 1980), p. 3.

68. The *Los Angeles Times,* August 3, 1979.

69. United Nations Department of Public Information, Press Section, GA/6170, January 14, 1980.

70. "MPLA First Congress," p. 23.

71. "The Party Programme," Mozambique Information Agency, Bulletins No. 9 and 10 (Congress Special Issue), March 25, 1977, pp. 21–22.

72. "Extracts from the Report of the Standing Political Committee," August 7–16, 1978, p. 18.

73. Ibid.

74. The *Washington Post,* December 15, 1978.

75. "US Interests in Africa," p. 47.

76. Resolution A/32/212.

77. Resolution 33/31.

78. Resolutions 31/5 A–D; 32/4A–C; and 33/13B–F.

79. Resolution 32/76 Additional Protocol.

80. Resolution A/32/87.

81. Resolution 32/85.

82. Resolutions 31/174; 32/181 and 33/136.

83. Resolution 31/165.

84. Resolution 31/158.

Chapter VIII

1. Henry Kissinger's address to the annual meeting of the American Newspaper Editors Asociation, Washington, DC, April 10, 1980, authors' notes.

2. The *Washington Post,* May 6, 1980.

3. For a recent example, see Milovan Djilas, "L'Union Sovietique, Est-Elle un Pays Socialiste?," *Commentaire* III, no. 9 (Spring 1980).

4. Lenin, as quoted by Michael Chege, "The Revolution Betrayed: "Ethiopia, 1974–79," *Journal of Modern African Studies* 17, no. 3 (September 1979), p. 368.

5. Peter Sketchley, "Problems of the Transformation of Social Relations of Production in Post-Independence Mozambique," in *People's Power,* no. 15, Winter 1979, p. 28. Sketchley in his article tries to refute this argument in the case of Mozambique.

Index

AAPSO, *see* Afro-Asian People's Solidarity Organization
Ad hocism, 3–4
Adan, Mohamed, 32
Afghanistan, 157, 158, 161, 180, 194
African-American Institute, 173
African Development Bank, 170
African National Congress (ANC), 33
Afro-Asian People's Solidarity Organization (AAPSO), 33, 102
Afrocommunism, 11; case for, 193–214; concept of, 209, 213; origins of, 30–35; prospects for, 209–214; theory of, 25–35
Albright, David, 167
Algeria: economic growth, 37, 59–65; French communist party in, 31; ideology, 5; independence, 4, 75; inter-African solidarity and, 179; multinational corporations in, 118; nationalism, 163; socialism, 2, 3, 6, 23–25, 35, 36, 76; Soviet bloc assistance to, 167, 168; statism, 66, 202, 203–204; trade, 166, 213; *wilayism* in, 99
All Ethiopian Socialist Movement (MEISON), 134–136, 147, 150, 152–153
Allende, Salvador, 23
Alves, Nito, 107, 108, 109, 115–117, 119, 120, 123, 126, 211
Aman Michael Andom, 130
Amnesty International, 153
ANC, *see* African National Congress
Andrade, Mario de, 105
Angola: Civil War, 6, 106–109; Communist Party in, 100; ciris in, 115–117; Cuba and, 33, 34, 35; East Germany and, 163; economic policies, 117–121, 206; evolving economic relationship with Soviet bloc and the West, 168–170; ideology, 112–115; Marxism-Leninism and, 2, 6, 11, 99–127, 197–209; *mesticos* in, 31; nationalism, 181–184, 193, 195; political organization, 122–124; poder popular movement, 104, 106, 107, 108, 112, 113, 114–115, 117, 120, 195, 198, 200; Portuguese communist party and, 32; proletarian internationalism, 177–181; recognition of MPLA government in, 12; social services, 124–125; Soviet block assistance to, 168; Soviet Union and, 8, 9, 29, 183; statism, 203; struggle against imperialism, 161; at time of independence, 109–112; Treaty of Friendship and Cooperation with Soviet Union, 162; wartime heritage, 99–106
Arab Bank for Economic Development in Africa, 170
Assimilados, 69, 100, 101, 109
Atnafu Abate, 29, 130, 153

Ben Bella, Ahmed, 4, 5, 18, 20, 23, 60, 61, 120, 162, 163
Bender, Gerald, 111
Benin, 2, 6, 7, 8, 35, 181, 183
Bonker, Don, 153
Boumèdiène, Houari, 5, 23, 24, 61–65, 120
Brazil, 170
Brezhnev, Leonid, 21, 157, 210
Britain, 31, 173, 174
Bulgaria, 171, 172, 179
Burundi, 5
Business International, 173

Cabral, Amilcar, 26, 208
Cambodia, 158
Canada, 48
Cape Verde Islands, 2
Carreira, Henrique Tiles, 109, 126, 211
Carter, Jimmy, Africa and, 4, 212
Carvalho, Joaquim de, 87
Castro, Fidel, 4, 10, 23, 29, 53, 159, 161, 179, 180, 181, 182
CEMEA, *see* East European Council for Mutual Economic Assistance
Centralism, 200
Chedli, Benjedid, 64
China, Africa and, 34, 55, 105, 133, 155, 167, 170–171, 182, 183
Chipenda, Daniel, 102, 105, 106
Chou En-lai, 1
Class struggle, 20, 22, 78, 128, 173, 199
Colonialism, struggle against, 9, 20, 21, 25, 30, 99–106, 178, 181
Commission for Organizing the Party of the Working People of Ethiopia (COPWE), 148–149
Communalism, 13–14, 19, 20
Communism: appeal of, 1; spread of, 3–4. *See also* Afrocommunism
Confédération Générale du Travail, 18, 53
Congo, 2–5, 8, 12, 35, 180, 189

Conservative view of African Marxist-Leninist states, 194
Convention People's Party (CPP), 20, 21
COPWE, *see* Commission for Organizing the Party of the Working People of Ethiopia
Corporations, multinational, 118, 198–199
Coutinho, Rosa, 32
CPP, *see* Convention People's Party
Cuba, 1, 7, 8, 28, 33–34, 35, 157, 159, 161, 162–163, 180, 181, 182, 211; Angola and, 9, 101, 102, 103, 107, 108, 115, 125, 168–169, 179; Congo and, 2; Ethiopia and, 148, 154–155, 173, 175, 176, 184, 212; Mozambique and, 171, 172; Zimbabwe and, 183
Czechoslovakia, 175, 176, 179

Dahomey, *see* Benin
Davidson, Basil, 101, 103, 104
de Gaulle, Charles, 54
Dumont, René, 6
Dunem, Jose van, 115

East European Council for Mutual Economic Assistance (CEMEA), 169
East Germany, Africa and, 1, 7, 28, 35, 68, 161, 162–163, 171, 172, 174, 175, 176, 179, 211
Egalitarianism, 20, 65
Egypt, 5, 162, 163, 166, 167, 181
ELF, *see* Eritrean Liberation Front
ELF-Aquitaine, 170
Engels, F., 26, 177
England, *see* Britain
EPLF, *see* Eritrean People's Liberation Front
EPRP, *see* Ethiopian People's Revolutionary Party
Eritrea, 130, 131, 136, 137, 143, 152, 153, 155, 156, 174, 184, 212
Eritrean Liberation Front (ELF), 130, 136, 153
Eritrean People's Liberation Front (EPLF), 130, 136, 153
Ethiopia, 6, 26, 193, 211–212; economy, 138–146, 205; evolving economic relationship with the Soviet bloc and the West, 173–176; external influences, 154–155; French communist party and, 32; ideology, 133–137; Marxism-Leninism in, 2, 7, 8, 11, 35, 128–156, 195–209; nationalism, 181–184; political and administrative organization, 146–151; population, 132; proletarian internationalism, 177–181; "red terror," 28–29, 150, 152–154; social services, 151–152; Somalia and, 10, 34; Soviet bloc assistance to, 168; Soviet Union and, 9, 163; struggle against imperialism, 161; Treaty of Friendship and Cooperation with Soviet Union, 158, 162; U.S. and, 12 Ethiopian Oppressed Revolutionary Struggle, 147
Ethiopian People's Revolutionary Party (EPRP), 134, 200
Eurocommunism, 210
European Economic Community, 173, 176

Fanon, Franz, 26, 208
FAPLA, *see* Forcas Armadas Populares para Libertação de Angola
FLN, *see* Front de Libération Nationale
FNLA, *see* Frente nacional de libertação de Angola
Forcas Armadas Populares para Libertação de Angola (FAPLA), 107–108, 115, 124, 125
France, 31, 32, 54, 55, 61, 174
Frelimo, *see* Frente de Libertação de Moçambique
French Congo, 5
Frente de Libertação de Moçambique (Frelimo), 25, 26, 27, 28, 29, 30, 33, 34, 68–98, 171–172, 177, 178, 179, 181, 182, 183, 193, 196, 198, 203, 212
Frente Nacional de Libertação de Angola (FNLA), 34, 100, 101, 102, 105, 106, 107, 111, 117, 125, 126, 206
Front de Libération Nationale (FLN), 23, 35, 61, 64, 99, 146, 206

Ghana, 4, 6, 18–19, 166, 168
Gobeze, N., 32, 148
Great Britain, *see* Britain
Gromyko, Anatol, 160
Guevara, Ché, 101
Guinea, 2, 4, 5, 6, 9, 12, 14, 16, 17, 18, 21–23, 27, 36, 37, 52–59, 65, 66, 67, 75–76, 168, 179, 183, 202, 203, 204; politics in, 52–59
Guinea-Bissau, 2, 6, 7, 26, 32, 33, 34, 179, 181
Gulf Oil Company, 118, 170

Haile Fida, 32, 134, 147
Haile Selassie, Emperor, 6, 128–130, 132, 138, 145, 149, 151, 174
Hassan, King, 57
Honecker, Erich, 162, 174
Human rights, 56, 185, 188
Humanism, 14, 15, 17, 19, 36, 39–43, 66, 199, 202
Hungary, 171, 179

Ideology, 193–201, 211
Imperialism, struggle against, 9, 20, 21, 25, 30, 78, 159, 161, 174, 178, 180, 181, 182
Industrialization, 199
Inter-African Force, 180

Index   235

International Fund for Agricultural Development, 143
International Labor Office, study of socialism in Zambia, 39–39, 41
International League for Human Rights, 56
International Monetary Fund, 39, 59, 169, 170, 172, 173, 176
Internationale (song), 177
Internationalism, proletarian, 29, 30, 79, 175, 177–181, 182, 191, 194
Iran, 158
Ivory Coast, 184
Islam, 36, 54
Italy, 31, 32

Japan, 173
João, Jacob Caetano, 115
JRDA, *see* Revolutionary Democratic African Youth Movement

Kaunda, Kenneth, 14, 15, 17, 20, 36, 37–44, 65, 70, 199, 203
Kavandame, Lazaro, 72
Keita, Modibo, 4, 5, 18, 20, 146, 162, 163
Kenya, 46, 183, 184
Kerékou, Mathieu, 6
Khrushchev, Nikita, 209
Kissinger, Henry, 7, 194
Kosygin, Alexei, 174

Labor League (Ethiopia), 147
Laos, 161
Laqueur, Walter, 4, 7
Lara, Lucio, 25, 26, 27, 100, 103, 109, 123, 126, 211
Lenin, V. I., 1, 13, 136, 159, 177, 195, 200
Liberal view of African Marxist-Leninist states, 194
Libya, 2, 166, 167, 179, 180
Little, Arthur D., 118
Lome Convention, 170, 173, 176
Lumumba, Patrice, 4, 5

Machel, Samora, 9, 25, 30, 69, 72, 76–78, 81, 84, 85, 91, 172, 178, 180, 181, 196, 197
Madagascar, 2, 6, 7, 8, 30, 35, 180
Maghreb, 3
Malagasy Republic, 29
Mali, 4, 6, 146, 168
Mao Tse-tung, 200, 209
Marcum, John, 109
Marx, Karl, 1, 13, 26, 131, 177, 200
Marxism-Leninism, 1-12, 195–209; Angola and, 99–127, 195–209; appeal of, 1, 30, 101, 194; Ethiopia and, 128–156, 195–209; from African socialism to, 13–35; Mozambique and, 76–98, 195–209; spread of, 2, 6–8, 11, 30–35, 213

Marxist-Leninist Revolutionary Organization (Ethiopia), 147
Mauritius, 3
McHenry, Donald, 12
MEISON, *see* All Ethiopian Social Movement
Menelik, Emperor, 174
Mengistu Haile-Mariam, 9, 26, 28–29, 32, 130, 136–137, 141, 144, 148, 152, 153, 154, 155, 161, 174, 175, 176, 177, 178, 179, 180, 184, 197
Mestiços, 31, 69, 100, 101, 109, 115, 126, 210
MMM, *see* Movement Militant Mauritien
Mobutu, Désiré, 5
Mobutu Sese Seko, 3, 34, 108, 180, 184
Mondlane, Eduardo, 69, 71, 72
Monimambu, Spartacus, 102, 104, 105
Monteiro, Oscar, 69
Moose, Richard, 12
Morocco, 2, 166, 168
Movement Militant Mauritien (MMM), 3
Movimento Popular de Libertação de Angola, see Popular Movement for the Liberation of Angola
Mozambique: China and, 34; communal villages, 71, 80, 86–90, 97, 193; communism and, 177; conditions at independence, 73; East Germany and, 163; economic policies, 90–95; evolving economic relationship with the Soviet bloc and the West, 170–173; ideology, 211; Marxism-Leninism in, 2, 6, 7, 11, 25–27, 193, 195–209; *mestiços* in, 31; nationalism, 181–184; political organization, 81–85; Portuguese communist party and, 32; proletarian internationalism, 177–181; social services, 95–96; socialism, 9; Soviet Union and, 14; state farms, 202; statism, 195; struggle against imperialism, 161; Treaty of Friendship and Cooperation with Soviet Union, 29, 162; U.S. and, 12; war legacy, 68–73
MPLA, *see* Popular Movement for the Liberation of Angola
Mugabe, Robert, 2, 34, 180, 183, 196
Multinational corporations, 118, 198–199

Nascimento, Lopo do, 109, 126
Namibia, 2, 11, 33, 179, 183
Nasser, Gamal Abdel, 5
NASSO, *see* National African Socialist Students' Organization
National African Socialist Students' Organization (NASSO), 21
National Front for the Liberation of the Congo, 179
Nationalism, 7, 9–10, 12, 31, 177, 181–184, 191, 193, 194, 195, 211; interlinking with Marxism-Leninism, 34

NATO, *see* North Atlantic Treaty Organization
Négritude, 14, 15, 22
Neo-colonialism, struggle against, 9, 21, 25, 30, 178, 181
Neto, Agostinho, 9, 32, 99, 101, 105, 107, 109, 115–116, 119, 121, 122, 124, 125, 126, 127, 177, 179, 182, 184, 193, 196, 211
Newsom, David, 3, 157, 183
Nicaragua, 158
Nigeria, 30, 166, 179
Nimeri, Jaafar, 5
Nkomo, Joshua, 33, 35, 183
Nkrumah, Kwamé, 4, 5, 14, 15, 18–21, 29, 162, 163
Nonalignment, 15, 21, 24, 29, 30, 178–181, 182
North Atlantic Treaty Organization (NATO), 7
Nyerere, Julius, 9, 14, 15, 17, 19, 20, 28, 36, 45–51, 65, 67, 70, 71, 105, 195

ODP, *see* People's Defense Organization
OMM, *see* Organization of Mozambican Women
Organization of Mozambican Women (OMM), 82

Padmore, George, 18, 21, 31
PAIGC, *see* Partido Africano de Independència da Guinée Cabo Verde
Pan-Africanism, 9, 15, 18, 19, 21, 22, 29, 31, 189
Pan-Africanism or Communism (Padmore), 31
Parti Déocratique de Guinée (PDG), 16, 22, 53, 55, 57
Participation, popular, 198, 207
Partido Africano de Independència da Guinée Cabo Verde (PAIGC), 33, 34
People's Defense Organization (ODP), 122
Personality, African, 15
Petrobras, 170
Poder popular movement, *see* Angola, *poder popular* movement
Podgorny, Nikolai, 171
Poland, 179
Polisario movement, 3
POMOA, *see* Provisional Office for Mass Organizational Affairs
Ponomarev, B., 158–159
Popular Movement for the Liberation of Angola (MPLA), 7, 8, 9, 12, 25, 26, 27, 28, 32, 33, 34, 99–109, 111, 112–120, 122–127, 168, 170, 177, 179, 181, 184, 203, 206, 212
Population, African, 2
Portugal, 6, 31, 32, 73, 99–106, 109–110, 120, 173, 174

Pouvoir Révolutionaire Local (PRL), 56–57, 65, 67
Pragmatism, 196–197
Principe, 2
PRL, *see Pouvoir Révolutionaire Local*
Proletarian internationalism, *see* Internationalism, proletarian
Provisional Office for Mass Organizational Affairs (POMOA), 137, 147

Radical view of African Marxist-Leninist states, 194–195
Radicalism, 1–12
Ratsiraka, Didier, 6, 29, 30
Rebelo, Jorge, 69, 85
Revolutionary Democratic African Youth Movement (JRDA), 55
Revolutionary Flame party (Ethiopia), 147
Rhodesia, *see* Zimbabwe
Roberto, Holden, 100
Rocha, Carlos, 109, 119, 126
Rumania, 169, 179
Russia, *see* Soviet Union

Sadat, Anwar, 5, 166
Santos, Jose Eduardo dos, 109, 126, 211
Santos, Marcelino dos, 69, 72, 85
Sáo Tomé, 2
Savimbi, Jonas, 105, 125
Senegal, 9, 30
Senghor, Leopold, 9, 14, 15, 18, 19, 20, 22
Seychelles Islands, 2
Siad Barre, Mohamed, 5, 25–26, 32, 164
Simango, Uria, 72
Socialism, African, 1, 2, 3, 6, 7, 8–9, 12, 36–67, 201–206; in Algeria, 59–65; in Guinea, 52–59; lessons from, 65–67; in Tanzania, 44–52; transition to Marxism-Leninism, 13–35; in Zambia, 37–44
Solidarity, Third World, 177, 179, 184–191
Somalia, 2, 5, 10, 25–26, 32, 34, 35, 131, 155, 156, 162, 165, 168, 175, 176, 181, 182, 183, 191, 212
Sonangol, 118, 170
South Africa, 2, 33, 93–94, 125, 173, 179, 212
Southwest African People's Organization (SWAPO), 2, 33, 34, 35, 125, 179, 180
Soviet Union, Africa and, 1, 2, 4–11, 21, 28, 29, 30–31, 33, 34, 35, 55, 58, 68, 102, 103, 105, 107, 108, 115, 133, 134, 148, 154–155, 157–192, 211–212
Spanish Sahara, 2, 3
Statism, 65–67, 114, 127, 203
Sudan, 5, 162, 163, 168
SWAPO, *see* Southwest African People's Organization
Sweden, 172
Swedish International Development Agency, 143

Tanzania, 2, 9, 14, 17, 36, 37, 44–52, 65, 66–67, 202, 203, 204, 205–206; development without growth in, 44–52
Tchombe, Moise, 5
Teferi Bante, 130, 153, 155
Texaco, 118, 170
Tito, Marshal, 30, 209
Tribal society, 13
Touré, Sékou, 4, 5, 9, 14, 15, 17, 18, 21–23, 28, 36, 52–59, 65, 67, 162, 202
Trade, 165–167, 170, 173, 191
Tsongas, Paul, 153

Uganda, 46, 51
Ujamaa, 14, 45–52, 65, 66, 71, 195, 203
União Nacional dos Trabalhardores de Angola (UNTA), 119, 120, 121, 122, 125
Union Nacional para a Independència Total de Angola (UNITA), 105, 106, 107, 108, 112, 117, 206, 212
Union of Ethiopian Marxist-Leninist Organizations, 147
UNIP, *see* United National Independence Party
United National Independence Party (UNIP), 42–43
UNITA, *see* Union Nacional para a Independencia Total de Angola
United Kingdom, *see* Britain
United Nations, 170; African bloc in, 15, 180, 184–189
United States: African policy, 1, 3, 12, 212; Ethiopia and, 155, 174, 176; fear of communism, 4, 157, 213; Mozambique and, 172, 173; trade with Angola, 170; views of African Marxist-Leninist states, 194–195
UNTA, *see União Nacional dos Trabalhardores de Angola*
Upper Volta, 146
Utopianism, 194–195

Vieira, Sergio, 69
Vietnam, 158, 161
Voluntarism, 16–17, 203

West Germany, 173
Western Somalia Liberation Front, 131
World Bank, 48, 50, 143, 168, 169, 172, 173, 176

Xiconhoca, 78–79

Yemen, 179
Young, Andrew, 4, 10, 12, 194
Yugoslavia, 30, 179

Zaire, 2, 3, 4, 34, 125, 179. 184
Zambia, 2, 12, 17, 36, 65, 66, 102, 200, 202, 203, 204, 205; as upper class welfare state, 37–44
Zanzibar, 16
ZANU, *see* Zimbabwe African National Union
ZAPU, *see* Zimbabwe African People's Union
Zimbabwe, 2, 4, 33, 183
Zimbabwe African National Union (ZANU), 34, 180, 183
Zimbabwe African People's Union (ZAPU), 33, 34, 35, 183

LIBRARY OF DAVIDSON COLLEGE

may be checked out for **two weeks**